global

UPPER INTERMEDIATE
coursebook

Lindsay Clandfield

Rebecca Robb Benne

with additional material by Amanda Jeffries

MACMILLAN

About Global

Lindsay Clandfield is a teacher, teacher educator and lead author of Global. He was born in England, grew up in Canada, taught at a university in Mexico, lives in Spain and has trained teachers from around the world. He is also the creator of the popular blog **Six Things** (www.sixthings.net), a collection of lists about ELT.

Rebecca Robb Benne is a freelance teacher and materials writer based in Denmark. She has taught English, French and German in the UK, Germany and Denmark.

Six quotes that inspired global

True education means fostering the ability to be interested in something.
Sumio Iijima, Japanese physicist

It is books that are the key to the wide world; if you can't do anything else, read all that you can.
Jane Hamilton, American author

The English language is nobody's special property. It is the property of the imagination ...
Derek Walcott, Caribbean poet

The important thing is not to stop questioning.
Albert Einstein, German-American physicist

The mind is not a vessel to be filled, but a fire to be kindled.
Plutarch, Greek historian

If you are going to write another coursebook for the English language, please try to do something a bit different.
An English teacher who wishes to remain anonymous

Global Upper Intermediate by numbers:

10 units **160** pages **14** extracts from literature & non-fiction **41** vocabulary sections **29** explanations of English grammar **10** functiona English lessons **24** accents from around the world in Global Voices **143** audio clips **30** video clips **150** interactive activities **100s** of curious and interesting facts

Content highlights

Contents

Speaking

1 Look at the two opinions below. Which one do you agree with more? Think of two or three reasons or examples to support your position.

'You can only feel alive if you live in a big city.'

'You can only feel alive if you live away from a big city.'

2 Discuss with a partner. Explain your reasons.

Reading

1 🔊 1.01–1.03 Read and listen to three people describing how their city makes them feel alive. Match the people to the correct headings.

a   A collective meeting point
b   An unusual climate
c   Human contact

2 Read the texts again. Underline phrases or sentences in the texts that refer to these aspects in a city.

1   transport
2   sounds
3   people
4   weather
5   city landmarks

3 Do the writers find the things in exercise 2 positive or negative? Discuss with a partner and support your ideas with references to the texts.

4 Answer the questions about verbs in the texts. Use the context to help you.

1   If you *hustle* onto a bus, are you moving slowly or quickly?
2   If a skyscraper *sparkles*, does it look bright or dull?
3   If music *blares*, is it quiet or loud?
4   If you *feel at one with* a city, do you feel at ease or not at ease there?
5   If something *stimulates* you, does it make you feel sleepy or awake?

5 Have you ever fallen in love with a city you have visited? Which one and why? Tell a partner.

Grammar

1 Look at the examples and complete the rules below with an auxiliary verb.

> *How **does** your city make you feel alive?*
> *You **don't** find a moment's peace.*
> *Cars **are** beeping loudly.*
> *It **has** invariably found its way back*

- use the auxiliary verb _____ with perfect tenses (present perfect, past perfect)
- use the auxiliary verb _____ with continuous tenses (present and past continuous) and to make the passive voice
- use the auxiliary verb _____ only with questions and negatives in the simple tenses (simple past and simple present)

2 Complete the questions with the missing auxiliary verb.

Where you born? You born in a big city?

Where were you born? Were you born in a big city?

1 You live in the capital of your country?
2 You ever been to a big city in a foreign country?
3 More people moving to the cities in your country now? Why?
4 Your parents live in the country or in the city when they were young? How it different?
5 How many different places you lived in?
6 Where you live when you were a child? Your family still live there now?

3 Choose three questions to ask and answer with a partner.

G **Grammar focus** – explanation & more practice of auxiliary verbs on page 134

Pronunciation and Speaking

1 🔊 1.04 Read and listen to the following sentence. How is it different from the 'rules' in grammar exercise 1?

Living in the city is often stressful, but it does make you feel alive.

> **Language note:** to add emphasis to or to correct a statement, we can put stress on the auxiliary. If it is in the simple present or past, we add the auxiliary *do* or *did*.

2 Find another example of emphatic 'do' in the text about San Francisco.

3 Work in pairs. Say one of the sentences below. Your partner corrects you by saying the opposite and using emphatic stress. Swap over.

A: You're not listening.

B: I am listening.

1 You haven't lived in a city.
2 You weren't born here.
3 You didn't study English here last year.
4 You don't understand me.

Anna lives in San Francisco, US

Stepping out into the cool wet fog on a summer morning, I am reminded that this is July in San Francisco. People leave their houses for work, hustling onto buses, boarding street cars, evading the fog as it snatches at any bare skin. The fog does disappear … usually … by late morning when the skyscrapers downtown are sparkling against the sun again. But by late afternoon, it has invariably found its way back fingering its way through the Golden Gate Bridge, hovering over the bay near Alcatraz, ready to wrap around us again as we return home.

Sandhya lives in Delhi, India

In Delhi, you don't find a moment's peace: cars are beeping loudly, people on bikes are ringing their bells, market traders are selling their products and proclaiming this loudly, and music is blaring out of windows. Pleasant smells and not so pleasant smells surround you. Overcrowded streets and buses will force you to be in close touch with other bodies and you will always find something to talk about to that stranger near you. Here in this city, you feel at one with the world around you, here you understand that you are just a small part of it and here you feel alive.

Stuart comes from Sydney, Australia

Sydney is waterborne. Life is intricately entwined in the crevices and crags of its harbour. It is public art, transport hub and leisure centre rolled into one. The salt spray and sea breeze stimulate the senses, and take the sting out of the ever-lingering summer heat. We Sydneysiders are drawn to the harbour – its waterside parks, renovated wharves, beach bars and cliff walks. It can be glimpsed from any viewpoint – from the forecourt of the majestic opera house or from the tops of the skyscrapers. It is the unifying essence, the civic adhesive that binds two million lives together.

> **Glossary**
>
> **evade** (*verb*) – to avoid being caught by something or someone
>
> **hover** (*verb*) – to remain in the same place in the air
>
> **crevice** (*noun*) – a narrow opening in a rock or a wall
>
> **crag** (*noun*) – a steep part of a cliff or a rock face
>
> **adhesive** (*noun*) – a substance used to make things stick together, glue

4 Make the verb phrases in bold more emphatic.

1 Well, **I've lived** in the capital, and I think that …
2 I **love** the city, mainly because …
3 I think the city **makes** you feel more dangerous. That's because …
4 You only feel alive when **you've left** the city, because …

5 Work in pairs. Read the sentences and try to keep talking for a minute longer.

Alive & Well

Part 2

Vocabulary

1 Match the adjective to the definition.

1	alive	a	not awake
2	awake	b	similar
3	asleep	c	not dead
4	ill	d	frightened
5	alone	e	not sleeping
6	afraid	f	not with other people
7	glad	g	not healthy
8	aware	h	happy and pleased
9	alike	i	knowing about a situation or fact

2 Read the sentences below. Which sounds better? The adjective before the noun (a) or the adjective after the verb (b)?

1 a My alive grandfather lives in Germany.
  b My grandfather is alive and lives in Germany.

2 a In this photo the children are asleep on the sofa.
  b In this photo the asleep children are lying on the sofa.

3 Work in pairs. Think of a person in your family. Describe them, using as many adjectives as you can. Include at least one of the adjectives from exercise 1.

Listening

1 Read the definition and statements. Do you agree?

'The English word genealogy comes from two Greek words: *genea* for generation and *logos* for knowledge. It refers to the study of families and their history. More and more people are now researching their own genealogy. The desire to find out who we are and where we come from exists in all cultures. It is about keeping our family history alive.'

2 🔊 1.05 You are going to hear a talk on how to find out about your family tree. Listen to the first part of the talk and answer the questions.

1 What is the problem according to the speaker?
2 What does she suggest?

3 🔊 1.06 Work in pairs. Think of two ways you can start research into your family history. Tell a partner. Then listen to the next part of the talk. Did you think of the same ways?

4 Listen again to the second part of the talk. What do the words in bold refer to?

... Some of the stories **they** tell though can be a bit painful, so don't push **them** too hard ...

... records of people who arrived in **these countries** by boat in the 19th and 20th centuries ...

This information is held at **their** national archive sites ...

Grammar

1 Look at the examples below. Underline the main verbs. Identify the tense: present simple, present continuous or present perfect.

> Interest **has grown** around the world. More than 24 million people **have used** websites to research their family history. Countries **are putting** information online. These days we **live** very busy lives. He **works** on his family tree website twice a week.

2 Match the uses to the example sentences in exercise 1.

1 facts or things that are true
2 a changing situation
3 habits and routines
4 actions happening now
5 something that started in the past but continues now

3 Identify which tense from exercise 1 often goes with each group of time expressions below. Then choose three time expressions and make a true sentence about your family for each one.

1 for generations
  since I was very little
  yet
  already

2 at this moment
  these days
  right now
  currently

3 every year
  once a week
  regularly
  every other day

4 Complete the text with the verb in brackets using one of the three present tenses.

My family origins (1) _____ (be) mixed. My ancestors (2) _____ (come) from Poland and England but we (3) _____ (be) in the United States for forty years. My parents (4) _____ (live) in Vermont, and I (5) _____ (be) in New York. I (6) _____ (live) in New York since last year. My wife (7) _____ (have) a three-year contract with a company here so we (8) _____ (stay) here until it finishes. I have a brother. Currently he (9) _____ (study) European history at the University of Warsaw. He (10) _____ (love) it, and he (11) _____ (already discover) lots about our family roots.

G **Grammar focus** – explanation & more practice of present tenses on page 134

Speaking

1 Choose **four** of these questions about your family that you would be comfortable answering. Mark them with an X.

Ten questions about ... your family

- Where does your family come from?
- How long have you lived in the home you live in now? Has your family moved around a lot?
- Do you have family reunions? How often? What is the largest family reunion you've been to?
- Is anyone in your family currently living in a different country? Who? Where?
- Are you interested in your family's history? Have you ever made a family tree?
- Do you take lots of photos of your family? Who is the 'family photographer'?
- Are your grandparents still alive? How old are they?
- How big is your family? Do you think it's better to come from a big family or a small family?
- Think of three members of your family. What are they doing right now?
- Are you and your mother alike? Or are you more similar to your father?

2 Work in pairs and show your questions. Ask and answer your partner's questions.

Speaking

Work in pairs. Read the fact box below and discuss the information.

According to the box, are most people optimists or pessimists?

Would you describe yourself as an optimist or a pessimist? Give examples.

All's well that ends well

Studies have shown that most human beings have a natural bias towards optimism: they tend to expect things will go well in the future, and that their future will be better than that of their fellow humans even when there is no evidence to support this. For example, 80% of motorists are convinced that they won't have an accident and almost all newlyweds expect that they will remain married forever.

Reading

1 Work in pairs. You are going to read answers to the question *What are you optimistic about?*

A: read Joichi Ito's answer below. B: turn to page 128 and read another answer.

Tell your partner what the writer is optimistic about and say if you share this optimism.

2 What idea do both answers have in common?

Listening

1 🔊 1.07–1.11 Listen to five people answering the question *What are you optimistic about?* Tick (✔) the correct speaker or speakers for each question.

Speaker	1	2	3	4	5
sounds quite pessimistic					
is optimistic about their personal future					
is optimistic about a global issue					

2 Listen again. Are the statements true (*T*) or false (*F*)?

1 Speaker 1 is going to retire next year.
2 Speaker 2 hopes that things won't get worse.
3 Speaker 3 is confident that blogs will further influence political affairs.
4 Speaker 4 thinks we will see a green future in her lifetime.
5 Speaker 5 is moving to a new company.

3 Are you optimistic about any of the things that the speakers mention? Discuss in pairs.

What are you optimistic about?

Joichi Ito, internet entrepreneur

I am optimistic that open networks will continue to grow and become available to more and more people. I am optimistic that computers will continue to become cheaper and more available. I am optimistic that the hardware and software will become more open, transparent and free. I am optimistic that the ability for people to create, share and remix their works will provide a voice for the vast majority of people.

I believe that the internet, open source and a global culture of discourse and sharing will become the pillar of democracy for the 21st Century. [...] I am optimistic that the internet will enable the collective voice of the people and that voice will be a voice of reason and goodwill.

Glossary

open source (*noun*) – the practice of writing computer programs that are based on a code that is available for anyone to use

Grammar

1 Look at the examples from the listening. Complete the rules with the form in brackets.

> *I'm* certainly **going to make** the most of this time. *(going to)*
> *I'll give* you an honest answer. *(will)*
> *With the state of the economy, it's* **going to be** *difficult to find a new job. (going to)*
> *I've just been promoted and my new job* **starts** *next month. (present simple)*
> *I'm* **having** *a job interview tomorrow. (present continuous)*
> *I have serious doubts that this* **will be** *in my lifetime. (will)*

- use _____ to talk about schedules or timetables
- use _____ to talk about fixed arrangements in the future
- use _____ to talk about plans and intentions
- use _____ to express spontaneous decisions
- use _____ for future predictions; we usually use _____ when a prediction is based on strong evidence

2 Complete the dialogues with a future form.

1. A: Have you decided what you _____ (*do*) in order to try to save the business?
   B: Yes, we _____ (*increase*) our online advertising. I think that _____ (*do*) the trick.
2. A: Ok, I've got the tickets. We _____ (*leave*) at 8.15 and the train _____ (*get*) in at 12.32.
   B: But the plane _____ (*depart*) at 13.45. We _____ (*not make*) it.
3. A: It looks as if talks with the unions _____ (*break down*).
   B: Yes, I don't think we _____ (*get*) what we want this time.
4. A: I _____ (*get*) some lunch. Are you nearly finished?
   B: Yes, _____ (*be*) there in a minute.

3 What are the speakers in exercise 2 talking about in each dialogue? Do you think speaker B is optimistic or pessimistic?

G **Grammar focus** – explanation & more practice of future forms on page 134

Vocabulary and Writing

1 Look at the examples from the listening. Which time phrase means 'soon'? Which means 'in the distant future'?

> The days of unlimited renewable energy, for example, are **light years away**.
>
> The days when blogs will determine elections are **just around the corner**.

2 Put the time phrases in bold into two lists: 'soon' or 'in the distant future'. Use a dictionary if necessary.

> It'll happen **any day now**.
> It'll happen **in the near future**.
> It won't happen **in my lifetime**.
> It's **a long way off**.
> It'll happen **before long**.
> Right now it's **just wishful thinking**.

3 Answer the question 'What are you optimistic about?' Choose a topic.

- your life (your career, your family, projects you are involved in)
- your city or local area (sports and leisure, transport, child care, crime)
- the world (the environment, medicine, the economy, technology, conflict)

4 Write a paragraph. Explain why you are optimistic about this topic and state any reservations you might have. Finish your paragraph with one of the time phrases from exercise 1.

Alive & Well

Vocabulary

1 Read the headline. What do you think the key word is and why?

Millions of people are dying from preventable diseases

2 Work in pairs. Match the adjectives with -*able* to a word in the box which the adjective can describe. Explain the meaning of the adjective. Swap over.

changeable   intolerable   respectable
drinkable   reliable   ~~suitable~~
incurable   renewable

| disease | energy | organisation | ~~present~~ |
| situation | water | weather | witness |

a suitable present

Reading

1 Look at the headings in *Winning the battle against disease* on page 13 and discuss your ideas in pairs.

What sort of text is it? Where might it come from?

What do you know about the three diseases described in the text?

2 Now read the text. Check your ideas in exercise 1 and find out which disease (or diseases) …

1 has more or less disappeared.
2 is not caused by a virus.
3 is still present in Europe.
4 relies on people to help each other in a community to stop it spreading.
5 can kill.
6 can lead to people not being able to support their families.

3 Find words in the text with these meanings:

1 can spread from one person to another (Introduction)
2 get rid of something completely (Introduction)
3 a substance that protects against a disease (Polio)
4 polluted with infection (Guinea worm disease)
5 get better after an illness (Measles)
6 weakness or illness because of lack of food or the right foods (Measles)

4 Work in pairs. Choose one of the statements. Pick the option you agree with and explain your reasons.

1 Keeping a dangerous virus alive for research purposes is *sensible / irresponsible*.
2 Eradicating disease is a question of *spending money / educating people*.

Extend your vocabulary – metaphors: illness

Dealing with illness is like fighting a war.
The virus **attacks** the nervous system.
He **fought** bravely against the disease.
Yesterday she **lost the battle** against cancer.
Her **defences** are very low.
More and more people are **falling victim to** AIDS.

Are there similar metaphors in your language?

Winning the battle against disease

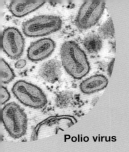
Polio virus

Smallpox is the only infectious disease which has been eradicated: in 1980 it was announced that the virus had been globally eliminated. Today it only exists as a research specimen in two locked vaults in Russia and the US. After the success of the smallpox eradication programme, the World Health Organisation and its partner organisations started programmes to eradicate other preventable diseases. Hopes are high that the following three diseases will have disappeared by 2020 at the latest.

Polio

Description: A virus that attacks the nervous system and can cause paralysis and even death. It mainly attacks children under five years old.

Where: In 1988 polio was found in 125 countries. At the time of writing, it is only found in four countries (Pakistan, Afghanistan, India and Nigeria). By the time you read this, it's possible that polio will have disappeared.

Cure and prevention: Polio is incurable but it can be prevented by vaccine. From now on health workers will be targeting the four remaining countries and vaccinating all children under five. Any cases of polio re-imported from other countries will be monitored.

Guinea worm disease

Description: A parasitic infection caused by drinking contaminated water. Water larvae grow into worms in the body. The disease doesn't kill but the worms can cause intolerable pain. Sufferers are often unable to work in the fields and therefore can't provide food for their families.

Where: In the 1980s 3.5 million people were infected in Africa and Asia. To date only four African countries are still reporting cases.

Cure and prevention: The disease can be prevented by installing new clean water supplies and filtering water. A programme of volunteers means that in future villagers will be checking their fellow villagers for disease to stop re-infection.

Measles

Description: A viral disease which mainly affects children. It spreads through coughing and sneezing. The main symptoms are fever and a bad rash.

Where: Measles is a leading cause of death among young children in developing countries. Because of some children not being vaccinated, measles has also been reintroduced in certain European countries.

Cure and prevention: There is no specific treatment and healthy children usually recover in 2-3 weeks. However, measles can have serious consequences for children or people with low natural defences – for example, because of malnutrition. Health workers will be implementing mass vaccination programmes in the next few years.

Measles virus

Grammar

1 Look at the examples in the grammar box. Which sentence talks about …

1 an action in progress at a certain time in the future? (future continuous)
2 an action completed by a certain time in the future? (future perfect)

2 Now complete the rules.

> *Hopes are high that the diseases **will have disappeared** by 2020 at the latest. From now on health workers **will be targeting** the four remaining countries …*

- Future continuous: _____ + _____ + verb + -ing
- Future perfect: *will* + _____ + _____

3 Read the five *VISION 2020* goals. Write what they will be doing over the next few years and what they will have achieved by 2020.

By 2020 they will …
Between 2010 and 2020 they will …

G **Grammar focus** – explanation & more practice of future continuous & future perfect on page 134

Speaking

1 Complete these sentences about your own personal goals (your health, your job, your family).

- By the end of the year …
- By this time next year …
- In five years' time …
- In ten years' time …

2 Explain your sentences to a partner.

VISION 2020

By 2020
- ◉ prevent the projected doubling of avoidable blindness
- ◉ eliminate the main causes of avoidable blindness

Between 2010 and 2020
- ◉ integrate an eye-care system into every national health system
- ◉ increase awareness of the problem
- ◉ secure the resources to increase prevention and treatment activities

Function globally generalising and making exceptions

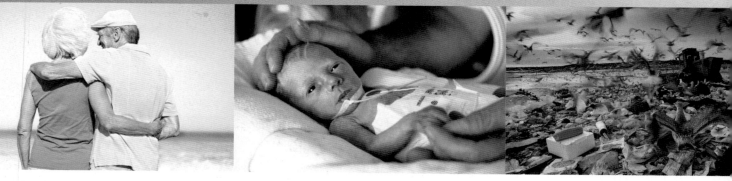

Warm up

1 Complete the sentence below in any way you choose, and think of three examples you could use to support it.

> ### Modern life is ... than in the past.

2 Now think of one exception to what you've just written. Tell a partner your sentence, examples and exception.

Listening

1 🔊 1.12–1.14 Listen to three people completing the sentence in the Warm up. Does anybody complete the sentence in the same way as you or mention the things you talked about?

2 Listen again and decide if the statements are true (*T*), false (*F*) or the listening doesn't say (*DS*).

Speaker 1:
uses a mobile phone at work
has to do many things more quickly
has more time to think

Speaker 2's parents:
lived through a war
went to visit family in America and Asia
are still alive today

Speaker 3:
smokes
thinks food is healthier
thinks people are living longer

Language focus: making generalisations

1 Look at the following sentences from the listening. Underline the words which are used to talk about making generalisations.

1 It typically took longer to get to places.
2 In my parents' time things were mostly better quality.
3 Modern life is, generally, healthier than it was in the past.
4 But people, ordinarily, are living longer and better than two or three generations ago.

2 Insert the missing word in each sentence. Choose from the words in the box.

in	and	as	most

1 general, modern life is more stressful than it was in the past.
2 but a rule I would say the stress caused is a more overwhelming factor.
3 but by large, things have just become a lot easier and better.
4 food is also better, more varied, fresher and, in cases, healthier.

3 Look at this list of phrases. Which two phrases **can't** be used to voice an exception?

Not counting …	Apart from	Except for
An exception is …	Personally …	Especially, …
This doesn't include …		

Speaking

Work in pairs. Choose **one** of the tasks below.

A Look at the sentences in Language focus exercise 1. Discuss how much you agree with them. Try to bring in other general examples to support your point. Your partner should think of exceptions.

B Look at the photos at the top of the page. Using your own ideas, make generalisations about each of these things. Then listen to your partner's ideas and think of one exception.

Global English

Languages **alive** and **dead**
by David Crystal

We often talk about languages as if they were alive. We say that English is a 'living language' and Latin is a 'dead language'. But this is slightly misleading. Languages don't have a life of their own. It's people who live and die.

A language is alive and well if it has people who speak it daily. And it dies when the last person to speak it dies – though some say that a language dies when the *second-last* person who speaks it dies, for then the last speaker has nobody to talk to.

Of the 6,000 or so languages in the world, about half are now so seriously endangered that they are likely to die out this century. Globalisation has made it difficult for minority languages to survive. People see the internationally used languages as a route to a better quality of life, and they allow their ancestral languages to decline as a consequence. It doesn't have to be that way. Millions around the world have developed a healthy bilingualism, maintaining their old language alongside the new.

Speaking is not the only criterion, of course. Languages can exist in a written form too. So if people continue to read and write a language, we might say that it is alive and well, even if it is never spoken. On that basis, Latin is certainly alive, for many people regularly read and enjoy the works of Latin writers, and the language continues to live on as an official language of the Roman Catholic Church. But to be 'fully alive', a language needs to be spoken as well as written, and to be used in everyday settings, not just in church.

Languages have always died out, throughout history, as the cultures and communities who spoke them disappeared. No language has ever lasted longer than a few thousand years. So, if history is a guide, English won't be with us forever. But, *is* history a guide? In a world where communication has been revolutionised by the internet, and where huge electronic databases store so much of what we say and write, the future of languages may be different from everything we have seen in the past.

Warm up

In your own words, explain what you think is the difference between 'a living language' and 'a dead language'. Can you name examples of each?

Reading

1 Read *Languages alive and dead*. Put the following points the author makes in order.

a ＿＿ English may die in a few thousand years.

b ＿＿ Languages don't die, people do.

c ＿＿ Latin is not really dead, but it is not completely alive.

d ＿＿ People don't have to lose their own language when they learn an international language.

e ＿＿ Technology might keep English alive.

2 Read the text again. How does the author answer these questions about language?

1 What makes a language truly alive?

2 When does a language die?

3 Why are so many languages in danger of dying out now?

4 Is it inevitable for minority languages to die? Why not?

5 Is Latin a dead language? Give one reason why it is and one reason why it isn't.

6 Will English survive another thousand years? Give one reason why it will and one reason why it won't.

3 Find words and phrases in the text with the following meanings.

1 not really correct (2 words, paragraph 1)

2 next to (1 word, paragraph 3)

3 belonging to your relatives in the past (1 word, paragraph 3)

4 something that helps you to make a judgement about something (1 word, paragraph 4)

Speaking

1 How much do you agree with the following statements? Mark them from 1 (agree completely) to 4 (disagree completely). Think of reasons why you agree or disagree.

- The life and death of a language is normal, we should not interfere. 1 2 3 4
- Learning English is a route to a better life. 1 2 3 4
- English should not be allowed to threaten other languages in my country. 1 2 3 4
- Children should learn more than two languages at school. 1 2 3 4
- Technology cannot keep all languages alive. 1 2 3 4

2 Work in pairs. Compare your statements. Which ones do you agree on? Discuss your reasons.

Writing a report (1)

Reading

1 Read Jiwon's report on changes in family life in South Korea. Which of the following topics does she mention?

> **arranged marriages**   **future trends**
> **cohabitation**   **polygamy**
> **divorce**   **single-parent families**
> **the extended family**   **wedding customs**
> **family size**   **work patterns**

a As a result of globalisation, there has been a huge amount of cultural exchange between different societies. In post-war Korea in particular, we have been influenced by western thought and have accepted it into many areas of our lives. This is especially true in our concept of the family.

b One of the most noticeable changes has been in our marriage customs. A hundred years ago, marriages were arranged by a match-maker and a couple's parents, and often the first meeting between a bride and groom took place on their wedding day. Moreover, it was not uncommon for a man to have more than one wife, if he had enough money. Today, however, 'love marriages' have become much more common, and polygamy is no longer practised.

c Divorce is viewed very differently nowadays. In the past, divorce and remarriage were very rare, and even if a couple divorced, the woman was usually blamed, even by her own parents. By contrast, divorce is no longer considered taboo by most people. The divorce rate is increasing, and more and more people are remarrying in later life.

d To conclude, family life is continuing to evolve in South Korea. Although our society is still quite conservative, it is possible that we will see new types of marriage and families in the near future. However, I am optimistic that the family will continue to exist as a strong institution in our country.

2 Complete the chart with facts from Jiwon's report.

	In the past	Nowadays
Choosing a partner		
Polygamy		
Attitudes to divorce		
Divorce and remarriage		

3 Are any of the changes that Jiwon mentions true of your society?

Writing skills: paragraphs

A Paragraphs

> Before you start writing, make a plan and organise your ideas in **paragraphs**. A paragraph can be defined as a group of sentences about a single idea or topic.

Choose the best topic for each of the paragraphs (a–d) in Jiwon's report.

a globalisation / changing cultural attitudes / western thought
b arranged marriages / polygamy / marriage customs
c the divorce rate / attitudes to divorce / remarriage
d ongoing changes in family life / new types of family / conservative attitudes

B Topic sentences

> Writers often state the main idea of the paragraph in the first sentence. This is known as the **topic sentence** and it helps the reader follow the structure of the writing.

1 Underline the topic sentences in Jiwon's report. How well do they summarise the idea of the paragraphs?

2 Now choose the best topic sentence for this paragraph.

> Finally, _____. Until recently, couples wanted to have several children because this meant prosperity for the family. For example, my father had six siblings, whereas I have only one brother. Currently, the average family size in my country is fewer than two children per couple.

1 my father's family was very different from mine.
2 the size of the average family in South Korea has decreased considerably.
3 siblings used to be much more important in the past.

3 Where would you place the paragraph in exercise 2 in the report? Why?

C Supporting sentences

The sentences after the topic sentence are called **supporting sentences**. They provide details, examples, a definition or an explanation of the topic sentence, and should follow a logical order.

Put the sentences below in a logical order to form a paragraph.

____ a This means a family that is composed of a parent or parents, and their child or children.

____ b In the past, parents and children used to live with their grandparents and great-grandparents.

____ c Nowadays, however, most people live in a nuclear family.

____ d Another area of change is in the extended family.

____ e For example, when my mother was young, she used to live with her grandparents and aunts.

Preparing to write

Choose **three** or **four** of the topics in Reading exercise 1, and discuss with a partner how these have changed in your society.

Writing a report

- There have been *huge / noticeable* changes in …
- The birth rate has *increased / decreased considerably / slightly*
- In the past, … / A hundred years ago, … / Until recently, …
- Nowadays, however, … / Today, by contrast, …
- One of the most important changes has been in … / Another significant change has been in …

Writing

Write a report on family life in your country based on your discussion with your partner. Write four or five paragraphs, including an introduction and conclusion. Include topic sentences and arrange your supporting sentences in a logical order.

Exploring your dictionary

1 Which of these types of English dictionary do you use? How and when do you use them? What are the advantages and disadvantages?

- a bilingual dictionary
- a monolingual learner's dictionary
- a dictionary of collocations
- a specialist dictionary (e.g. law)
- an electronic / online dictionary
- a thesaurus

Discuss your answers with a partner.

2 Study the dictionary extracts from the *Macmillan English Dictionary*.

hopeful [1] /ˈhəʊpfl/ *adj* *
1 believing that something will happen the way you want it to: *We resumed negotiations but we're not very hopeful.*
♦ **+ that** *In spite of our differences, we remain hopeful that a solution can be found* ♦ **+ of**
The board is quite hopeful of securing further investment.
2 expressing the feeling that something you wish for will happen or be true = OPTIMISTIC: *She gave us a bright-eyed, hopeful look.*
- hopefulness noun [U]

hopefully /ˈhəʊpfl/ *adv* **
1 *mainly spoken* used for saying that you hope something will happen: *Hopefully, we'll get more news next week.*
2 feeling or showing hope: *He looked at her hopefully.*

Find information about the following:

- grammatical usage
- frequency
- meaning
- pronunciation
- related words
- style

3 With a partner, look though a learner's dictionary. What other learning features or sections are included?

- ★ If you do not already have a monolingual learner's dictionary, plan to buy one.
- ★ If you have one, study the introduction.
- ★ Use your dictionary to extend and deepen your vocabulary.

Right & Wrong

Reading

1 Match the scientific theories to the definitions. Have you heard of them? Which ones do you think were most revolutionary?

1 Big Bang   3 Gravity
2 Evolution   4 Heliocentrism

a Animals and plants change gradually over a long period of time through a process of natural selection.
b The planets move around the sun, not the other way around.
c An explosion of heat that occurred 15 billion years ago and from which the Universe originated.
d The force which makes two objects move towards each other, most commonly when an object falls to the ground.

2 The text on page 19, *E pur si muove!* tells the story of a trial which concerned one of these theories. Which one? Read and put the paragraphs in order.

3 Read again and answer the questions. *Heresy*
1 Why was Galileo put on trial? *Heresy*
2 What is a geocentric theory of the universe? *Everything revolves around Earth*
3 What does *E pur si muove* mean in English? *And yet it turns*
4 Did Galileo really say it? *Probably not*
5 What does the phrase represent nowadays? *What authorities deny may still be true*

4 Find the words or phrases in bold in the text with these meanings:

controversial NOT BOLD

1 to completely oppose something that most people believe or accept
2 to talk in a low voice that is difficult to hear, especially because you are annoyed
3 which many people disagree with
4 an action or belief that opposes the official principles of religion and is considered wrong
5 to say something that you said was not true
6 well-known for being bad

5 Work in pairs. Including the words in exercise 4, retell the story of Galileo's trial in your own words.

Vocabulary and Speaking

1 Put the words into two groups.

Certain	Uncertain

convinced   definitely   doubtful
doubtless   positive   sure   unsure
unconvinced   to have reservations
without question

2 Rewrite the sentences using the correct form of the word in bold so that they mean the same. Choose from the words in the box.

Galileo is certainly a symbol for intellectual freedom.

QUESTION

Galileo is <u>without question</u> a symbol for intellectual freedom.

1 Historians are unconvinced that Galileo said that famous phrase.

SURE

2 It was doubtless one of the most important events in the history of science.

DEFINITE

3 As an astronomer, there was no doubt in his mind that he was right.

CONVINCE

4 I am doubtful about this theory.

RESERVE

3 🔊 1.15 Complete the expressions with the words in the box to make ways of talking about things which are true. Then listen and check your answers.

actual	~~denying~~	doubt	fact	~~matter~~
promise	ways	~~word~~		

Take my <u>word</u> for it …
There's no <u>denying</u> that …
The truth of the <u>matter</u> is …
1 The <u>fact</u> remains that …
2 In <u>actual</u> fact …
3 No <u>doubt</u> about it …
4 There are no two <u>ways</u> about it …
5 I <u>promise</u> you …

E pur si muove!

⑥ Galileo died in 1642, twelve years later. His work survived him, and his discoveries were eventually proved right by other scientists. In 1992 the Catholic Church officially recognised Galileo's views and, eight years later, issued an apology for 'mistakes' made in the past. Mistakes which many observers were sure included the **infamous** trial. Galileo was proved right in the end, and is today considered a symbol of intellectual freedom.

② Some twenty years earlier, Galileo had published a little book of scientific discoveries he had made thanks in part to the invention of the telescope. Many of these discoveries and claims **flew in the face of** current beliefs about the universe, beliefs that had been held since ancient times in the West.

① It is doubtless one of the defining moments in the history of science. In 1633 Galileo Galilei, the Italian physicist, mathematician, philosopher and astronomer, was ordered to Rome to face the Church on charges of **heresy**.

④ Galileo was brought before the Inquisition and found guilty of heresy, of holding the opinion that Earth turned around the sun and not the other way around. He was forced to **recant** his views on the matter. His work was banned and he was placed under house arrest for the rest of his life.

⑤ It was then, apparently, at the end of his trial, that Galileo **muttered** the following famous phrase: *E pur si muove!* (And yet, it turns!). Many historians now believe he did not actually say anything like this at all at the trial, but the phrase entered into legend. It is still sometimes used now to show that even though someone in a public position of power denies something it does not mean it is not true.

③ Most important among these controversial new ideas was that of heliocentrism. Heliocentrism is the astronomical theory that the sun is the centre of the universe and that other planets revolve around it. This is in contrast to geocentric theory, which claims the Earth is the centre of the universe and that other objects revolve around it.

Speaking

1 Work in groups. You are going to play a speaking game. One person is the 'speaker'. Read the rules.

1 The group chooses a topic. Use the examples in the box to help you, or choose your own topic.
2 The speaker starts giving their opinion about the subject. He / she must try to include some of the expressions in Vocabulary & Speaking exercise 3.
3 After thirty seconds, another person in the group calls out 'Change your mind!'
4 The speaker must continue his / her talk, but now saying the opposite of what he / she was saying before.

Cycling in the city
Being a vegetarian
Cheap air travel
24-hour shopping
Making English obligatory at school

2 Change speakers and continue.

Right & Wrong

Vocabulary

1 Look at the sentences with the word *right* in them. Tick (✔) the sentences in which *right* means **correct**.

1 That's **right**. Well done. ✔
2 Hold on, we'll be **right** with you!
3 I was just lucky to be in the **right** place at the **right** time. ✔
4 You have every **right** to complain in a situation like this.
5 It took them three times, but finally they got it **right**. ✔
6 Look out, he's **right** behind you.
7 Professor Shephard's office? Third door on your **right**.
8 She's **right** in saying that the house is too expensive. ✔
9 They arrived **right** after the party began.
10 Women have been struggling for equal **rights** in this company for years.

2 Match the other sentences to the different meanings of *right*.

a on one side of the body 7
b something you are allowed to do or have 4,10
c exactly, immediately or completely 2,6,9

3  **1.16–1.17** Listen to two examples of teachers talking. Match the best explanation of their use of the word *right* to what you hear.

1 to make someone pay attention 2
2 to show that you are moving on from one subject to another 1

Reading and Listening

1 Work in pairs. Read the *Right Answer Quiz* below and think of your answers. When you are ready, discuss each question with your partner. Do you have the same answers?

2 💿 **1.18** Now listen to the explanation of the correct answers to the *Right Answer quiz*. Do any of the answers surprise you?

3 Listen again and answer the questions.

1 What is the technical definition of a desert?
2 Where are the Dry Valleys?
3 Where does space start?
4 How far away from the Earth is the moon?
5 Where does the word *centipede* come from?
6 How long have centipedes been studied?
7 How do Canary birds get their name?
8 What was the Latin name for the largest of the Canary Islands?
9 Whose brain is 6 per cent of its total body weight?
10 How long have ants been around?
11 How long is the average blue whale?
12 What parts of the body do these words refer to: an elephant, a family car, a ton of food?

The Right Answer Quiz

Everything you thought you knew was *right* ...

1 **Where is the driest place on earth?**
  a The Sahara Desert **b** Antarctica **c** The United Kingdom

2 **Which man-made objects can be seen from the moon?**
  a Las Vegas casinos **b** The Great Wall of China **c** Nothing

3 **How many legs does a centipede have?**
  a 30-380 **b** 100 **c** 1000

4 **What animal are the Canary Islands of Spain named after?**
  a a small yellow bird **b** a dog **c** a pig

5 **Who has the largest brain in comparison to its size?**
  a an elephant **b** a human being **c** an ant

6 **What is the biggest thing a blue whale can swallow?**
  a a large mushroom **b** a grapefruit **c** a small family car

Grammar

1 Look at the examples above from the quiz and Reading and Listening exercise 3. Then answer the questions.

Find …

1 a question with *Who* as the subject. What do you notice about this kind of question?

2 a question about possession. What is the question word that goes with possession?

3 three questions that combine *How* with other words. What are these other words? Can you think of different ones?

4 a question with a preposition at the end. What preposition is it?

2 Work in pairs. You are going to make some more questions. A: turn to page 126. B: turn to page 133.

G **Grammar focus** – explanation & more practice of questions on page 136

Speaking

1 Look at *The Information Age* statements. For each statement, decide how much you agree from 1 (disagree) to 5 (completely agree).

2 Think of examples to support your opinions.

3 Work in pairs. Read your statements and explain how much you agree or disagree with them and why.

The Information Age

It is easy to find information today.	1 2 3 4 5
If you want to find some information the best place to go is the internet.	1 2 3 4 5
There is too much information out there.	1 2 3 4 5
It is difficult to know what is wrong or right with all the information we have.	1 2 3 4 5
A lot of the information available on the internet may be wrong.	1 2 3 4 5

Right & Wrong

Vocabulary and Speaking

1 🔊 **1.19–1.24** Listen to six short utterances or dialogues. Match them to the correct word in the box.

mishear	mispronounce	misquote
misspell	misunderstand	misuse

2 Complete the sentence below.

The prefix *mis-* is added to verbs to show that something is _____.

3 🔊 **1.25** Listen to the words in exercise 1. Is the stress on the prefix or on the verb? Listen again and repeat.

4 Choose two of the questions and discuss in pairs.

- Which words do people commonly misspell or mispronounce in your language? Why?
- Are there any words in English (or another foreign language) that you regularly misspell or mispronounce?
- Have you ever had a confusing or embarrassing experience when you misheard or misunderstood something?
- Older people often complain that younger speakers misuse language. Is this true in your country? Explain how.

Listening

1 🔊 **1.26** Listen to two ways in which people can get words wrong: Malapropisms and Spoonerisms. Tick (✔) the correct boxes for each type of mistake 1-5.

		malapropism	spoonerism
1	word sounds similar to another word		
2	sounds of the words are mixed up		
3	real words		
4	words that don't exist		
5	can be funny		

2 Listen again. What mistakes did people make?

to the best of my ability ➜ *to the best of my mobility*

1 civil servant ➜
2 nuclear power plants ➜
3 a pack of lies ➜

3 Work in pairs. Look at these sentences where the speakers said the wrong words. What did they want to say?

	Wrong ✘	Right ✔
1	We're late, have you shaken a tower yet?	
2	He can't hear you. He's death.	
3	I walked through the mental detector at the airport.	
4	I'll have a muffin and a coff of cupee.	
5	Can you give me a pacific example?	
6	The car won't start, it must be a bat flattery again.	

4 🔊 **1.27** Listen and check your answers.

Grammar

*Sometimes instead of **the word that they wanted to say** …*
*… a speaker uses a similar-sounding word. In some cases **the** word just sounds strange. Malapropisms occur in everyday conversations, on **the radio**, in speeches and presentations. Sports commentators and politicians seem to produce **the** funniest malapropisms.*

1 Look at the examples from Listening exercise 1. Explain why the definite article is used in the examples in bold. Explain why there is no definite article with the underlined examples.

2 Match each example to a category.

1 I live in **Africa**, in **Kenya**. f
2 I play **the piano**. c
3 What did people do before **the fridge** was invented? g
4 **The rich** should pay more tax. i
5 **The sky** was a beautiful clear blue. h
6 I did it for **love**. j
7 I was born on **the tenth of June**. d
8 It's an island in **the Pacific**. e
9 I love **spring**. b
10 What are we having for **dinner**? a

a meals
b seasons
c musical instruments ✓
d dates and decades ✓
e seas and rivers, deserts and groups of mountains ✓
f streets, towns, most countries and continents
g singular nouns which stand for a general type ✓
h something which is unique ✓
i adjectives used as plural nouns
j abstract nouns

3 Tick (✔) the categories that usually take a definite article.

4 🔊 1.28 Put in the articles where necessary. Then listen and check.

whole meaning of a song can change if you mishear   lyrics. Every day around   world, people sing   wrong words to all sorts of   songs. An English speaker, for example, might hear 'the ants are my friends' instead of 'the answer my friend'. With songs in   foreign languages, a strange thing happens if you don't speak   language: brain tries to understand it in your first language. An Arabic speaker in   Jordan, for example, might hear an English song on   radio and understand something completely different in Arabic. There are many examples of   songs with lyrics like this on   internet.

G **Grammar focus** – explanation & more practice of the definite article on page 136

Pronunciation

1 🔊 1.29 Listen to these four examples again from Grammar exercise 3. How is *the* pronounced in each one? Why is the pronunciation different?

the answer   the internet   the lyrics
the radio

2 🔊 1.30 Listen to the sentence below said in different ways. Match each way to the best meaning. How does *the* sound when it is emphasised?

This is the way to say it.

a Not the way to write it, but to say it.
b There is only one way, and this is it.
c Not the other ways, this way.

3 Practise saying the sentence in exercise 2 in different ways.

Part 4

Reading & Speaking
No longer at ease

Grammar
Narrative tenses

Extend your vocabulary
Metaphors: honesty & dishonesty

Writing
A moral dilemma

Reading and Speaking

1 Look at the book cover for *No longer at ease* and the background information about the novel on page 25. Why do you think Obi Okonkwo might feel 'no longer at ease'? Discuss with the class.

2 Now read the text and answer the questions.
1 What is Obi's job?
2 Who is Obi's visitor?
3 What happens?

3 Work in pairs and find information about Obi and his visitor in the text. Write a short description of each man. Refer to the lines in the text that give you, or suggest, this information.

Useful language

- honest / dishonest
- uncertain / confident
- have a clear / guilty conscience

4 Do you sympathise with either of the characters in the text? Why or why not? Discuss in pairs.

5 Work in pairs. Read more information about the context of the extract on page 128. Does it change your answer to the question in exercise 4?

6 Obi is found with the money by the Nigerian police and goes on trial. How do you think he reacts? Check your answer in the text about Obi's trial in Grammar exercise 2.

Glossary

listlessness (*noun*) – lack of interest and energy

treacherous (*adjective*) – disloyal, unfaithful

Grammar

1 Look at the examples from the text. Then complete the rules for narrative tenses with the words *continuous*, *simple* or *perfect*.

> *The man knocked on Obi's door ...*
> *He was just settling down to work ...*
> *The wad of notes lay where he had placed it*

- narrative tenses are used to tell a story
- past _____ is used to talk about actions in the past which are complete or happened at a specific time; we usually use this tense to tell the most important events in a story
- past _____ is used to talk about actions in progress in the past; we often use this tense to describe background events
- past _____ is used to talk about actions that took place before the main events in a story

2 Read about Obi's trial and choose the correct option.

Every available space in the courtroom was taken up. Almost as many people (1) *stood / were standing* as (2) *sat / were sitting*. The case (3) *was / had been* the talk of Lagos for a number of weeks.

Obi's listlessness did not show any signs of decreasing even when the judge (4) *had begun / began* to sum up. It was only when he (5) *said / was saying* 'I cannot comprehend how a young man of your education and brilliant promise could have done this', that a sudden and marked change (6) *was occurring / occurred*. Treacherous tears (7) *were coming / came* into Obi's eyes.

All that stuff about education and promise and betrayal had not taken him unawares. He (8) *had expected / expected* it and (9) *rehearsed / had rehearsed* this very scene a hundred times. But now when the supreme moment (10) *had come / came* he was betrayed by treacherous tears.

G **Grammar focus** – explanation & more practice of narrative tenses on page xxx

It is the 1950s and Nigeria is coming to the end of colonial rule. The villagers in Obi Okonkwo's village collect money so that Obi can study at university in England. After experiencing a very different way of life for four years in England, Obi returns to Nigeria.

Extend your Vocabulary – metaphors: honesty and dishonesty

Being honest and moral is like being in a **high** position. Being dishonest and being immoral is like being **low down**.

She has very **high** standards.
She's an **upstanding** member of the community.
Nobody believed she'd **stoop** to that.
She played an **underhand** trick on him.
Her **fall** from grace was swift.

Match the above sentences with these situations.

1 She lost her job in the government suddenly after a financial scandal.
2 She secretly deceived her husband with another man.
3 She's never been known to do anything wrong.
4 She expects everybody to share her values and expectations.
5 She stole money from her family to pay her gambling debts.

Writing

1 🔊 **1.31** Listen to a moral dilemma developed by American psychologists Joan Miller and David Bersoff. Make notes. Work in pairs and check your notes. Look at the audioscript on page 151 if necessary.

2 Write the end of the story. What did Ben do? Did he take the ticket and go to his friend's wedding? Or did he not take the ticket and ruin his best friend's wedding? Write what Ben did, what he was thinking when he did it and what influenced his decision.

3 Work in groups of three or four. Read out your ending and discuss what you have written.

No longer at ease

It was again the season for scholarships. There was so much work now that Obi had to take some files home every day. He was just settling down to work when a new model Chevrolet pulled up outside. Who could it be? It looked like one of those prosperous Lagos businessmen.

The man knocked on Obi's door and Obi jumped up to open it for him.

'Good afternoon,' he said.

'Good afternoon. Are you Mr Okonkwo?'

Obi said yes. The man came in and introduced himself. He wore a very expensive *agbada*.

'Please have a seat.'

'Thank you.' He brought out a little towel from somewhere in the folds of his flowing gown and mopped his face. 'I don't want to waste your time,' he said. 'My son is going to England in September. I want him to get a scholarship. If you can do it for me, here is fifty pounds.' He brought out a wad of notes from the front pocket of his *agbada*.

Obi told him it was not possible. 'In the first place I don't give scholarships. All I do is go through the applications and recommend those who satisfy the requirements to the Scholarship Board.'

'That's all I want,' said the man. 'Just recommend him.'

'But the board may not select him.'

'Don't worry about that. Just do your own …'

Obi was silent. He remembered the boy's name. He was already on the short list. 'Why don't you pay for him? You have money. The scholarship is for poor people.'

The man laughed, 'No man has money in this world.' He rose to his feet, placed the wad of notes on the occasional table before Obi. 'We will make good friends. Don't forget the name. Bye bye.'

The wad of notes lay where he had placed it for the rest of the day and all night. Obi placed a newspaper over it and secured the door. 'This is terrible!' he muttered. 'Terrible!' he said aloud.

Glossary

scholarship (*noun*) – money from an organisation to study at a school or university

agbada (*noun*) – a flowing robe worn in Nigeria by important men

Chinua Achebe

is a Nigerian novelist who writes in English. His books explore the impact of European life on African culture and society. *No longer at Ease* was published in 1960.

Function globally correcting and restating

a b c d

Warm up

Work in pairs. Choose one of the situations above and imagine the following situation. One of the people in the situation has been misunderstood by the other and wants to correct himself/herself. Create a short dialogue to illustrate this situation.

Listening

1 🔊 **1.32–1.34** Listen to three conversations in which this happens. Match the conversations to three of the photos. What is the problem in each one?

2 Listen again and answer the questions.

Conversation 1:

1 What is the problem with vegetarians, according to the woman?
2 Which vegetarian does the man mention?

Conversation 2:

3 Why are there no buses to the airport from the station?
4 What does the man have to do?

Conversation 3:

5 What is the woman's position?
6 Why does the woman say she is 'taking a break'?

Language focus: correcting

1 Look at how speakers can correct themselves or the other person. Try to complete the other phrases below from memory.

Well, let me put it another way …

If I said that then I didn't mean to …

1 Oh no, that's not _____ I said _____ all.
2 What I _____ was …
3 You _____ have misunderstood …
4 What I've been _____ all _____ …
5 I'm _____ saying …

2 🔊 **1.35** Listen to the phrases to check your answers. Practise saying them as naturally as you can.

Speaking

1 Work in pairs, A and B.

A: choose one of the following statements and tell it to B.

B: question A's statement.

A: restate your position using one of the phrases you have learnt. You can change your position if you like.

B: respond to A now giving your own opinion.

> I would never live in the capital of my country, not even if you paid me.
>
> I can't stand teachers, they're so lazy.
>
> I never use bad words or slang.
>
> Students these days are lazy and ignorant.
>
> Young people are terrible drivers.

Global voices

Warm up

Read about two different ways people get things wrong in English. What do you think? Are there any typical mistakes or errors that you make?

Errors and mistakes in language learning
Errors and mistakes are both used to describe when a language learner has got something wrong. However, some linguists make a distinction between the two words. A mistake is a slip of the tongue that the learner can usually correct by themselves. Learners make mistakes because they aren't paying attention or are speaking too quickly or are tired or careless.
An error is a mistake the learner makes consistently. Learners make errors because they have not learnt something yet, or they have learnt it in an incorrect way.

Listening

1 1.36–1.43 Listen to people answer the question: What mistakes do you make in English? Listen and decide what kind of mistake each speaker makes.

a vocabulary mistakes (differences between words, wrong words)
b grammar mistakes (tenses, word order)
c pronunciation mistakes (pronouncing letters or words wrongly)

Hao, China   ————
Eldar, Bosnia   ————
Frank, Germany   ————
Antonia, France   ————
Patricia, Brazil   ————
Erica, Italy   ————
Maria, Spain   ————
Faisal, Saudi Arabia   ————

2 Listen again. Which speaker or speakers ...

1 mixes up words with similar meanings?
2 does not pronounce the letter 'h' in her own language?
3 mixes future forms?
4 pronounces acronyms incorrectly?
5 confuses *his* and *her*?
6 makes mistakes with prepositions?

Language focus: typical errors

1 Identify the error in each of the following sentences.

1 Well, I 'ope you'll be very 'appy in the new 'ouse.
2 Don't mention football. He's been very sensible about it since his team lost.
3 Next week I will have a party at my house. Would you like to come?
4 My wife loves books. This is his favourite one.
5 It's a movie about the history of the CIA (pronounced, 'see-ah')

2 What kinds of errors are these? Match them to a category from Listening exercise 2.

Speaking

1 Think of your English. Make a list of ...

• three things you often get wrong
• three things you almost always get right
• one kind of mistake you want to stop making
• something you used to find difficult but now you think is easy
• one piece of advice about speaking English correctly

2 Work with a partner. Explain your lists.

Hao, China   Eldar, Bosnia   Frank, Germany   Antonia, France

Patricia, Brazil   Erica, Italy   Maria, Spain   Faisal, Saudi Arabia

Reading

1 Read Noriko's essay on the statement 'Nowadays women have achieved equality with men'. Does she:

a agree?   b disagree?   c have mixed views?

2 Tick (✔) the arguments that Noriko presents in her essay.

1 Women nowadays have greater equality than in the past.
2 Laws against gender discrimination have helped women.
3 More laws are needed to improve conditions for women.
4 There are invisible barriers that stop women obtaining top jobs.
5 Attitudes towards women have not essentially changed.
6 Most women are still housewives.

3 Do you agree with Noriko's arguments?

It is often said that nowadays women have achieved equality with men, and it is certainly the case that, in the last few decades, conditions for women have greatly improved in many parts of the world. However, in my view, there are still inequalities between men and women, particularly as far as attitudes are concerned.

The first major improvement for women is that, in almost all countries in the world, they have gained the right to vote and even to enter parliament. Second, as regards education, there is no longer any discrimination against girls in most countries. In contrast with the situation in the 19ᵗʰ century, when only a handful of girls could go to school, nowadays girls have the right to the same education as boys. Third, women can now do any kind of work they want. In Japan, a law passed in the 1980s allows women to choose any job they like. Before this law, it was very difficult for women to obtain a job in a company except in a subordinate position to men, or to keep it after marriage.

Despite these positive developments, I believe that a bias against women is deeply rooted in most societies. While legislation has certainly increased opportunities for women, the essential problem has not changed. In Japan, it is very rare to find women in management positions in companies, and there are very few women presidents in universities or even in academic positions. This suggests that a so-called 'glass ceiling' is preventing them from advancing in their career.

In conclusion, even though women have achieved equal opportunities with men, I do not believe that substantial equality has been achieved yet. In order to break through the glass ceiling, it is necessary to improve women's career paths. In particular, we need better childcare provision, and better role models for the younger generation. Most of all, we need to challenge prejudices in a society which still, unfortunately, tends to regard women as essentially housewives.

Writing skills: presenting an argument

A Structuring an essay

An essay developing an argument normally consists of three parts: the **introduction**, the **main body** and the **conclusion**. Each part may contain some of or all of these ideas:

Introduction (normally one paragraph)
Facts about the topic
Common opinions
A personal opinion

Main body (one or more paragraphs)
Arguments in favour of a statement or topic
Arguments against a statement or topic

Conclusion (normally one paragraph)
A summary of the arguments
A personal opinion
A recommendation, question, warning or prediction

In the main body, you can write about only the arguments in favour, only the arguments against, or both.

1 Divide Noriko's essay into three parts.

2 Tick (✔) the ideas that she has included in each part.

B Introducing topics

> To introduce a topic we can use:
> *as regards* + NOUN
> *with regard to* + NOUN
> *as far as* + NOUN *is / are concerned.*

*There are still inequalities between men and women, particularly **as far as attitudes are concerned**.*
***As regards education**, there is no longer any discrimination against girls in most countries.*

Complete the sentences with a suitable word.

1 As regards _____, it is not normally difficult for women to find a suitable job.

2 As far as _____ is concerned, it is usually women who stay at home to look after the children.

3 With regard to _____, men still earn more than women on average.

Preparing to write

1 Work in pairs. Choose **one** or **two** of these statements.

> It is wrong to tell a lie
> Everyone in the world should have the right to a house and a job
> Everyone should have the right to freedom of expression

2 Decide if you agree, disagree or have mixed views.

3 Discuss arguments in favour of the statement, against the statement, or in favour and against. Make notes.

Stating an opinion

- It is *often said / commonly believed / widely argued* that …
- It is certainly *the case / true* that … / It is not *true / the case* that …
- In my view, … / I believe that … / I do not believe that …
- It is *important / necessary / vital* to …

Writing

Use your notes to write an essay on the topic you have chosen.

Moving beyond the plateau

1 Read the statements about learning English. Tick (✔) the ones that are true for you.

- My progress seems slower than before.
- Learning English used to be more fun.
- I seem to keep making the same errors.
- I understand a lot more than I can say.
- I often feel frustrated with my lack of progress.
- I seem to use the same basic words and structures when I speak.
- I feel I should be making more progress.
- I have less motivation to learn than before.

If you have ticked some of these statements, you have probably reached the language-learning plateau. This is very common at upper intermediate level.

> When people start learning a language, they learn very rapidly and it is easy to see progress. Later, progress naturally slows down and it is easy to become discouraged. At this stage, the tasks of language learning are to **consolidate**, **activate**, **deepen** and **extend** what you already know.

2 Read the suggestions for moving beyond the plateau. Which seem helpful to you? Discuss your ideas with a partner.

> ★ Write a language-learning diary about your progress and difficulties.
>
> ★ Talk to your teacher and other students about your experience.
>
> ★ Set realistic short-term and long-term goals for improving your English.
>
> ★ From time to time, check how far you have achieved your goals.
>
> ★ Remind yourself why you are learning English.
>
> ★ Concentrate on things you enjoy doing in English.
>
> ★ Experiment with new language-learning activities.

3 Make two plans for moving forward.

> I am going to …
> a _____ _____.
> b _____ _____.

Land & Sea

Speaking

1 Look at the 19ᵗʰ century Cree Indian quotation below. How do you think it finishes? Work in pairs and brainstorm two different endings.

2 Compare your answers with another pair. Which do you think is the more interesting answer? Now check the original completed quotation on page 131.

ONLY WHEN THE LAST TREE HAS A DIED & THE LAST RIVER HAS BEEN POISONED & THE LAST FISH HAS BEEN A CAUGHT A WILL WE A REALISE A THAT WE ...

19TH-CENTURY CREE INDIAN PROVERB

Reading

1 You are going to read an extract from *The Sacred Balance*. Which of the arguments below do you think the author is making?

1 We have become disconnected from nature.
2 We are more connected with nature now than before.
3 It is impossible for humans to be connected to nature.

2 Read the extract to check your answer. Find at least three reasons that the author gives to support his argument.

3 Find the parts in the text where the author expresses the following ideas and discuss how he uses language to emphasise his opinions. Do you think this kind of language makes his argument more or less effective?

1 We believe we can control our surroundings and that nature can't control us.
2 Our food is not natural and we don't know where it comes from.
3 We don't know where our water comes from.
4 We are not prepared to change our way of life.
5 In the future, policy decisions will increasingly have little connection with reality.
6 We are very responsive to phones and computers.

4 Work in pairs. Discuss the questions.
- This book was written in 1997. Do you think the author's argument is more or less valid now?
- Do you feel that people are disconnected from the land? Do you feel like that?

Extend your vocabulary – *land* and *country*

Country is the usual word for talking about a large area of land with recognised political borders.
Brazil is a big country.
Land can mean the same as *country*, but it is often a literary word. People call a place a *land* when they want to be mysterious or to sound emotional or old-fashioned.
In a land far, far away …
Complete the sentences with *land* or *country*.
1 I'm quite proud of my _____; I think we have done many good things.
2 The old sailors say that there is a _____ across the sea where strange and wonderful things happen.
3 The _____ in the far north of Canada is largely uninhabited.
4 Malta, with its mixture of cultures, is a very interesting _____ to visit.

The sacred balance

In a human-made environment, surrounded by animals and plants of our choice, we feel ourselves to have escaped the limits of nature. Weather and climate impinge on our lives with far less immediacy. Food is often highly processed and comes in packages, revealing little of its origins in the soil. (…) We forget the source of our water and energy, the destination of our garbage and our sewage. We forget that as biological beings we are as dependent on clean air and water, uncontaminated soil and biodiversity as any other creature. Cut off from the sources of our food and water and the consequences of our way of life, we imagine a world under our control and will risk or sacrifice almost anything to make sure our way of life continues.

As cities continue to increase around the world, policy decisions will more and more reflect the illusory bubble we have come to believe as reality.

As we distance ourselves further from the natural world, we are increasingly surrounded by and dependent on our own inventions. We become enslaved by the constant demands of technology created to serve us. Consider our response to the insistence of a ringing telephone or our behavioural conformity to the commands of computers. Divorced from the sources of our own existence, from the skills of survival and from the realities of those who still live in rural areas, we have become dulled, impervious, slow.

Through our loss of a worldview, our devotion to consumerism and our move into the cities and away from nature, we have lost our connection to the rest of the living planet. (…) We must find a new story, a narrative that includes us in the continuum of Earth's time and space, reminding us of the destiny we share with all the planet's life, restoring purpose and meaning to human existence.

The Sacred Balance was written by David Suzuki, Japanese-Canadian academic, science broadcaster and environmental activist

Vocabulary and Speaking

1 Match the words in the outer circle with the words in the inner circle to describe features of the natural world.

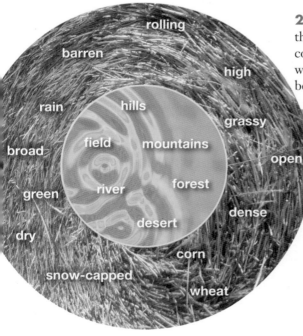

rolling
barren
high
rain
hills
grassy
broad
field mountains
open
green
river forest
dense
dry
desert
corn
snow-capped
wheat

2 Prepare a short talk describing the natural features of your country, or a country you know well. Use some of the words from exercise 1 and the expressions below to help you.

Useful phrases

- In the north / south / east / west of the country there are …
- The capital is in the … part of the country, and it's surrounded by …
- There's a famous …
- People love to go and see the …

THE
SACRED BALANCE
REDISCOVERING
OUR PLACE IN NATURE

DAVID
with AMANDA MCCONNELL & ADRIENNE MASON

SUZUKI

UPDATED & EXPANDED

'A celebration of wonder, a scientific journey of insight and wisdom'

Land & Sea

Speaking and Writing

1 Work in pairs. Read the questions. Then think of two more questions you could ask a partner.

- Do you read a newspaper? Which one?
- Do you ever get news from the internet? Which site?
- How often do you get the news? Every week? Every day? More than once a day?
- Do you know anyone who works in the news? What do they do?
- Do you think there is too much bad news these days?
- What is the latest interesting news story you remember?

2 Work in pairs. Choose four questions to ask and answer. Include your own questions.

3 You are going to write a short news story. Look at the words in the box. Follow the rules below.

- the news story must contain all these words
- you can add any other words you like
- you can change the form of the words
- the words can appear in any order
- you can repeat the same word

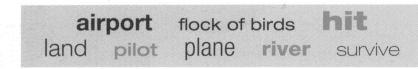

airport   flock of birds   **hit**
land   pilot   plane   river   survive

4 Work in small groups. Read and compare your news stories. Then choose the most interesting one to read to the class.

Listening

1 🔊 1.44 You are going to hear a true news story which contains all the words from Speaking and Writing exercise 3. Listen to the story. How similar is the story to yours?

2 Listen again. Put the words from Speaking and Writing exercise 3 in the correct order.

3 Work with a partner. Retell the story that you just heard, using the words from exercise 2 to help you.

4 Discuss the following questions:

- Had you heard this story before?
- How would you describe the pilot?
- This is an example of what news broadcasters call a 'feelgood story'. Why do you think that is?
- Can you think of any other feelgood stories in the news recently?

5 Look at some examples of the characteristics of news stories. Then turn to the audioscript on page 151 and find other examples.

1 An example of direct speech: *'filled with big, brown birds'*
2 Very specific details about the event or characters: *... flew into a flock of birds at 1,000 metres*
3 Adjective phrases to give more detail: *a split-second decision*
4 Time phrases: *At the moment of impact ...*

Pronunciation

1 Read the sentence from the pilot's transcript:

'We're gonna be in the Hudson.'

What does 'gonna' mean?

2 What do you think these reduced forms mean?

didja	doncha	dunno	gimmie
gotta	kinda		

3 🔊 1.45 Listen to the sentences and write what you hear. Then check your answers to exercise 2 above.

> **Language note:** these forms are characteristic of spoken English. They are considered very informal and incorrect in formal writing. 'Doncha' /dəntʃə/ and 'didja' /dɪdʒə/ are very rarely written even in informal English.

Vocabulary

1 Look at the summary of the dictionary entry for the different meanings of the verb *land*. Match each meaning to a sentence a to e.

> **land** /lænd/ (*verb*) ***

1 arrive / bring
2 come down to ground
3 get something you wanted
4 be in a bad situation
5 catch fish

a At the age of 19 she **landed** a small part in a musical play.
b … they managed to **land** quite a good catch of tuna despite the weather conditions.
c Thousands of letters **land** on her desk every morning.
d I think my plane **lands** a little after midnight.
e She **landed** up in hospital with a broken leg.

2 Choose two categories from the *Happy Landings!* questionnaire. Complete with your ideas. Then compare with a partner.

HAPPY LANDINGS!

Think of three …

❗ things that, if they landed on your desk, would make you very happy.

❗ things that could land you in serious trouble with the police, especially in your country.

❗ places you might have landed up if your life had been different.

❗ people who, if they landed on your doorstep, you wouldn't be happy to see.

❗ jobs you would love to land, if you had the chance.

Land & Sea

Vocabulary and Speaking

1 🔊 1.46 Close your books. Listen to the sounds on the recording and write all the words that they make you think of. Compare with a partner.

2 Put the words below into different groups and give each group a heading. Use a dictionary to help you. Were any of these words on your list from exercise 1?

current	dive	jellyfish	sand	seagull
seashells	seaweed	shellfish	ship	
snorkel	tanker	tide	waterskiing	
wave	yacht			

3 Work in pairs. A: draw a picture of one of the words but don't say what it is. B: say the word. Swap roles and repeat.

Reading

1 Read *Amazing Ocean Facts* on page 35. What do you think? Give each fact a rank from 1 to 3.

1 = yes, this is an amazing fact
2 = this is interesting, but not amazing
3 = this is not really an amazing fact

2 Look at the sentences below. Find them in the text. What words has the author written / changed to make the sentences sound more 'amazing'?

▶ Although deaths from shark attacks get a lot of attention, more people are killed each year by elephants, bees, crocodiles, lightning or many other natural dangers.

▶ Up to 80% of all life on earth is found under the ocean surface.

▶ This wave occurred in the Gulf of Alaska in 1899.

▶ If all the world's ice melted, scientists estimate that the oceans would rise by 66 metres, causing great damage to human life.

▶ Even in this day of modern technology, the seas are still used for a lot of human activity.

▶ Life on land has existed for 400 million years, which is just a short time, geologically speaking.

3 Work in pairs. Choose three questions from the list below and discuss.

• How far do you live from the sea? Would you like to live closer?
• What role does the sea play in your country's economy?
• Would you ever live on a boat if you had the chance? Why or why not?
• Do you know any other interesting facts about the sea?
• Are there any sea expressions or proverbs in your language? What are they in English?

Amazing Ocean Facts

1 Each year there are 50–75 shark attacks resulting in 3–10 human fatalities, according to the International Shark Attack File. The number of reported shark attacks has been rising, but this is perhaps because of an increase in media coverage. Although deaths from shark attacks get a lot of attention, far more people are killed each year by elephants, bees, crocodiles, lightning or many other natural dangers.   1 2 3

2 On the other hand, there are anywhere between 20 to 100 million shark deaths each year resulting from human fishing activity.   1 2 3

3 Over half of all life forms on the planet, and perhaps even up to a staggering 80% of all life on earth is found under the ocean surface. Around 99% of the living space on the planet is under the sea. Human beings have explored less than ten per cent of the oceans, especially the dark, cold environment called the deep sea.   1 2 3

4 Although volcanoes are thought of as something happening on land, around 80% of volcanic activity occurs in the oceans. Undersea earthquakes and volcanoes can cause *tsunamis*. *Tsunami* is a Japanese word which means 'harbour wave'. The height of the largest recorded *tsunami* caused by an earthquake was 60 metres. This gigantic wave occurred in the Gulf of Alaska in 1899.   1 2 3

5 The seas have been rising steadily. Over the past 100 years sea levels across the world have risen between 10 and 25 centimetres; scientists expect this rate to increase. The rise in sea level is usually attributed to climate change, and sea levels will continue rising even if the climate has stabilised, because the ocean reacts slowly to changes.   1 2 3

6 If all the world's ice melted, scientists estimate that the oceans would rise by 66 metres, causing catastrophic damage to all human life everywhere.   1 2 3

7 Even in this day of modern technology, the seas are still used for vast amounts of human activity. More than 50% of communications between nations is transported by underwater cables.   1 2 3

8 Life in the oceans has existed for over 3 billion years. Life on land has existed a mere 400 million years, which is just a short time, geologically speaking.   1 2 3

9 At the deepest point in the ocean, the pressure is 11,000 tons per square metre. This is the equivalent of one person trying to support 50 jumbo jets.   1 2 3

Grammar

*Shark attacks **have been rising**, …*
*Human beings **have explored** less than ten per cent of the oceans, …*

- use the present perfect simple and the present perfect continuous in very similar ways
- use the continuous form when we emphasise the duration of the action
- use the simple form when we emphasise the result of the action, about single completed actions or with state verbs
- use past simple to talk about finished actions in the past and when we specify the time of an action

1 Look at the examples above from the text of the present perfect and the present perfect continuous. Now find other examples of the tenses in the text.

2 Read the rules on when to use present perfect simple and continuous. Decide why the author chose each tense in the examples you found in the text.

3 Look at the words in the box. Which are usually used with present perfect (simple or continuous) and which words are used with past simple? Which can be used with both?

a few years ago	already	for years	in
last year	never	since I was a child	
yesterday	yet		

4 Complete the sentences with the present perfect or present perfect continuous. If both are possible, use the continuous form.

1 Sea levels _____ (*rise*) over the past 100 years.
2 The sea level _____ (*rise*) by 2 centimetres in this part of the world.
3 _____ you ever _____ (*live*) on the coast?
4 How long _____ you _____ (*live*) on the coast?
5 I _____ (*be*) afraid of water since I was a child.
6 I _____ (*take*) diving lessons over the past three weeks.

5 Make as many true sentences about yourself and the sea as you can. Use the time words above and the phrases below or other ideas. Discuss your experiences with a partner.

be on a boat	be afraid of water
go fishing at sea	go to the beach
live on the coast	sleep on the beach
swim in the sea	

G **Grammar focus** – explanation & more practice of present perfect simple & continuous on page 138

Land & Sea

Speaking

1 Work in pairs. Choose three of the questions below and ask and answer.

- Do you like maps?
- Are you good at reading maps?
- Do you have a map in your home? What is it? Where is it?
- Have you ever used a 'satnav' (a satellite navigation system)? Do you prefer using it to a map?
- Could you draw a reasonably accurate map of your country?

2 Look at the *Carta Marina* map below. What does it show? How old do you think it is?

Listening

1 🔊 1.47 Turn to page 132 and listen to a description of a section of the *Carta Marina*. Point to the items in the order that you hear them.

2 Listen again and answer the questions.

1 When and where was the *Carta Marina* drawn? How big is it?
2 What weren't ancient mariners worried about, according to the speaker?
3 What is interesting about the monster?
4 What is a Leviathan?

3 Here are descriptions of common sea monsters that appear in legends of many different cultures. Do you recognise any of them? Do you know of any other ones?

- An enormous squid or octopus that pulls boats down to the bottom of the sea.
- A giant white shark that eats people and terrorises beaches.
- A huge sea serpent that lives in very deep lakes.
- A creature with the head and body of a woman, and the tail of a fish.
- A giant sea monster with several heads.

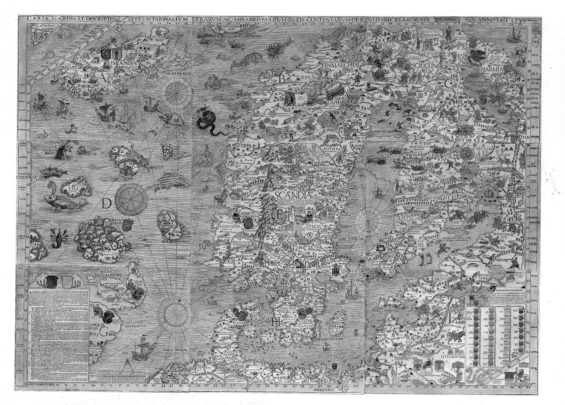

Grammar

1 Look at the examples and complete the rules with the words in the box.

after	before	colour	size

> *a **fantastic ancient** map*
> *a **strange giant** serpent*
> *a **wonderful old** story*

- put adjectives of description _____
  adjectives of opinion

> *an **old Swedish** priest*
> *a **huge green** head*
> ***large wooden** blocks*

- with adjectives of description we use this order: _size_ / age / _colour_ / origin / material. All other adjectives of description come immediately _before_ the noun

2 Try to rearrange the words into the correct order. Check your answers with the audioscript on page 152. Were you correct?

1 detail   small   painstaking
2 modern   belief   popular
3 colourful   monsters   sea   fantastic
4 intricate   tiny   details
5 right   corner   upper
6 sailing   English   an   ship
7 head   large   green
8 moon   a   small   crescent

3 Look at the map again. Think of as many adjectives as you can to describe it, or parts of it. Take turns making sentences to build up a description of the map.

In the top left corner, you can see a huge brown bird.

 Grammar focus – explanation & more practice of adjective order on page 138

Pronunciation

1 Find six pairs of words with the same sound in the box. Then match each pair to the sounds below.

break	clear	cloud	down	dream
sky	steer	whale	wheel	white

/iː/   /aʊ/   /aɪ/   /eɪ/   /ɪə/

2 🔊 1.48 Listen and check your answers. What are the common spellings for these sounds? Can you think of other words or spellings for these sounds?

3 🔊 1.49 Read and listen to a famous poem about the sea. Then work in pairs. Read each line one at a time. Pay attention to the sounds in exercise 1.

John Masefield (1878–1967) was an English novelist and poet famous for the novels and poems he wrote for children. He was poet laureate for Great Britain for over thirty years.

Sea Fever

I must go down to the seas again, to the lonely sea and the sky,
And all I ask is a tall ship and a star to steer her by,
And the wheel's kick and the wind's song and the white sail's shaking,
And a grey mist on the sea's face, and a grey dawn breaking.

I must go down to the seas again, for the call of the running tide
Is a wild call and a clear call that may not be denied;
And all I ask is a windy day with the white clouds flying,
And the flung spray and the blown spume, and the sea-gulls crying.

I must go down to the seas again, to the vagrant gypsy life,
To the gull's way and the whale's way, where the wind's like a whetted knife;
And all I ask is a merry yarn from a laughing fellow-rover,
And quiet sleep and a sweet dream when the long trick's over.

Sea Fever comes from a collection of poems called *Salt Water Ballads*, published in 1902.

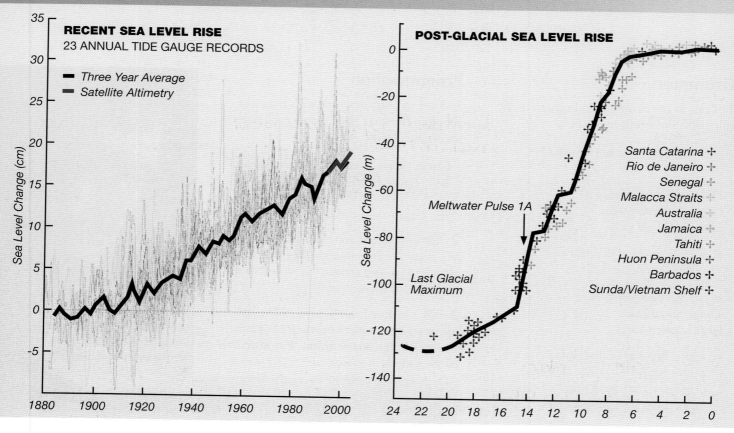

RECENT SEA LEVEL RISE
23 ANNUAL TIDE GAUGE RECORDS

— Three Year Average
— Satellite Altimetry

Sea Level Change (cm)

POST-GLACIAL SEA LEVEL RISE

Sea Level Change (m)

Meltwater Pulse 1A

Last Glacial Maximum

Santa Catarina ✛
Rio de Janeiro ✛
Senegal ✛
Malacca Straits ✛
Australia ✛
Jamaica ✛
Tahiti ✛
Huon Peninsula ✛
Barbados ✛
Sunda/Vietnam Shelf ✛

Warm up

Work in pairs. Look at the two graphs and take turns comparing and contrasting the data shown.

Listening

1 🔘 **1.50** Listen to someone describing the two graphs above. What is his conclusion?

2 Listen again. What do the following numbers refer to?

120	1.8	3	6,000

Language focus: interpreting data

1 Put the elements in order to make sentences.

1 for thousands of years / sea levels / in effect / have been rising
2 a case of / this / is / global warming
3 this points to / human activity / a recent increase in
4 the seas / the data / are rising / suggests / more rapidly
5 that / this / could indicate / a normal phenomenon / it is
6 to worry about / there is / could mean / nothing / this

2 🔘 **1.51** Listen to check your answers. Then underline the phrases which are used to interpret data.

Speaking

1 Look at the graph below and make some notes about how you could describe it – include your own interpretation, using the phrases you have learned.

2 Work in pairs. Describe the graph and your interpretation.

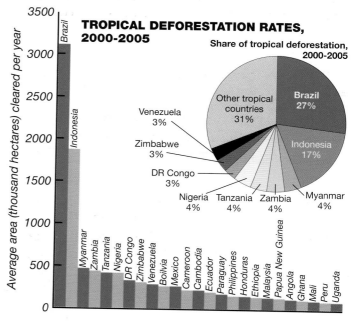

TROPICAL DEFORESTATION RATES, 2000-2005

Average area (thousand hectares) cleared per year

Brazil, Indonesia, Myanmar, Zambia, Tanzania, Nigeria, DR Congo, Zimbabwe, Venezuela, Bolivia, Mexico, Cameroon, Cambodia, Ecuador, Paraguay, Philippines, Honduras, Ethiopia, Malaysia, Papua New Guinea, Angola, Ghana, Mali, Peru, Uganda

Share of tropical deforestation, 2000-2005

Other tropical countries 31%
Brazil 27%
Indonesia 17%
Venezuela 3%
Zimbabwe 3%
DR Congo 3%
Nigeria 4%
Tanzania 4%
Zambia 4%
Myanmar 4%

Global English

Trade language
by David Crystal

How long does it take for a new global variety of English to evolve? Not very long at all.

In 1607, after a long and eventful sea voyage from England, Captain John Smith arrived in America, and soon after became president of the council of Jamestown in Virginia. A highly controversial figure, he explored the new territory at length, and wrote about his encounters with the native American tribes. He became well-known because of the story that he was saved from execution by Pocohontas, the daughter of an Indian chief – though whether this actually happened in the way he described has been greatly debated.

Smith sent his account of the new colony back to Britain, where it was published. English people would never have seen such place names as *Rappahannock* and *Nandtanghtacund* before. The fauna and flora of the new country introduced them to *racoons* and *skunks*. Other accounts talked of *moccasins*, *wigwams*, and *squaws*. These words were being read in Britain within a few years of the colonists' arrival – the first signs of a future American English.

We see the same kind of process happening all over the world, as English has travelled to new shores. Within a very short time of settlers arriving, we find them using a local vocabulary and writing home about it. After only a few years, these new words can number several hundred. The manner of speech alters too, so that a distinctive accent is one of the earliest signs of a new variety of English.

Probably the most dramatic linguistic result of world exploration is the invention of a *pidgin* or *trade* language. What happens when sailors and the local people meet and have no language in common? They do their best to communicate. Everyone instinctively talks in a simpler way, making sentences shorter, repeating words, and avoiding difficult sounds and grammar. After a while, a pidgin language can become quite sophisticated, and be used as an everyday means of communication. It can even end up as a national language, as has happened to *Tok Pisin* in Papua New Guinea – one of most impressive linguistic consequences of sea travel ever.

✶ WHERE CAN WE PARK ⊕ OUR SPACESHIP? ✶∨/✗

Glossary

controversial (*adjective*) – likely to lead to public disagreement

Warm up

1 Read the following phrases out loud. What do you think they mean?

Gutbai.   *Plis, Tenkyu.*   *Wan, tu, tri ...*   *Mi sori.*

2 These are all examples of Tok Pisin, a national language in Papua New Guinea. Tok Pisin started out as a trade language, or pidgin. How do you think it was invented?

Reading

1 Read *Trade language* and check your answer to Warm up exercise 2.

2 Read the text again and choose the correct answer.

1 The English Captain John Smith was saved from execution by Pocohontas.
  a   This is probably true.
  b   This is probably untrue.
  c   People are not sure if this is true or not.
2 The beginnings of American English came from ...
  a   the names of local animals and plants.
  b   Captain John Smith's Virginia accent.
  c   the books and history of American tribes.

3 Pidgins and trade languages ...
  a   start with a more simple structure.
  b   can be quite sophisticated.
  c   both a and b.

3 Complete the sentences with the correct form of the word in bold. All the words are in the text.

1 We had an _____ journey to the airport and almost missed our plane.   **EVENT**
2 This island was occupied by English _____ for two hundred years.   **COLONY**
3 Oh, you can't miss her. She wears very _____ clothes.   **DISTINCT**
4 It was rather a boring film, but it had a very _____ ending.   **DRAMA**
5 When I saw the ball coming towards me I _____ covered my head.   **INSTINCT**

Speaking

Work in pairs. Read the situation below and discuss the question.

> Some people argue that what the world needs is a simplified form of English.

Do you think a trade language for English is a good idea? List the possible advantages and disadvantages of such a system.

Writing an email to a friend

Reading

1 Read Daniel's email to Emily and answer the questions.

1 Where has he been recently? *National Centre for Traditional Arts in Yi-Lan*

2 What recommendations does he make? *have to go, need more than 1 day*

Hi Emily,

How are you? It's ages since we had that brilliant meal at your house (I'm attaching some photos!). What have you been doing? How was your holiday? Did you get a chance to go to the seaside in the end? Or did you have too much work?

Please forgive me for not emailing you for so long. A lot of things have happened actually, which have stopped me from contacting you …

I'm now back at work and I've been really busy, catching up with emails and other things.

Remember you told me about the National Centre for Traditional Arts in *Yi-Lan*, that you've been dreaming of visiting? Well, I went there with some friends last weekend! We had an amazing time!! It's a huge place, and you really need more than one day to see it properly. There are loads of old buildings, restaurants and shops where you can buy traditional handicrafts like ceramics, toys and clothes and calligraphy. We also watched some fascinating performances of traditional dance, as well as demonstrations of traditional crafts. And we ate loads of delicious Taiwanese snacks!

For me the most interesting part was a beautiful old town inside the centre which is basically a reconstruction of a traditional Taiwanese town. The whole town is built and decorated in an authentic style, so that when you go inside you feel as if you're walking into Taiwan of the 19th century. It has a really peaceful, nostalgic atmosphere. I took loads of pictures – I can't wait to show you them! Anyway, you really have to go and check it out for yourself – as you said, seeing is believing, isn't it?!

All for now – keep in touch, and email me soon to let me know how you're getting on.

Best wishes

Daniel

2 What do you learn about the following?

1 The last time Daniel saw Emily. *brilliant meal at (...)*

2 Emily's summer plans. *seaside*

3 Daniel's recent activities. *back at work catching up with (...)*

4 Things to buy at the Centre.

5 What Daniel saw and did at the Centre.

6 The most interesting part of the Centre.

7 The appearance of the town.

8 The atmosphere of the town.

Writing skills: an email to a friend

A General advice

1 Read the advice on writing an email or a letter to a friend.

1 Use informal salutations
e.g. Hello Gina, Hi Jon.

2 Use informal punctuation
e.g. ! ( ) – …

3 Use contractions *e.g. I've, it's, hasn't.*

4 Ask questions about your friend.

5 Mention things that you both know about.

6 Use informal endings
e.g. Cheers, Take care, All for now, Love, All the best, Best wishes.

2 Underline examples of the advice in exercise 1 in Daniel's email.

B Informal language

Use informal language in an email or letter to a friend.

Complete the sentences below from the email.

Informal words and expressions:

1 It's ages since we had that _brilliant_ meal at your house.
2 We had an _amazing_ time!!
3 We took _loads of_ pictures.
4 You really have to go and _check_ it _out_ for yourself.

Informal discourse markers:

5 A lot of things have happened _actually_
6 _Well_, I went there with some friends last weekend!
7 _Anyway_, you really have to go.

Starting sentences with a conjunction (*and, but, so, or*):

8 _Or_ did you have too much work?
9 _And_ we ate loads of delicious Taiwanese snacks!

Preparing to write

Think of an interesting place you have visited recently. Ask and answer questions with a partner.

- Where and when did you go?
- What was it like?
- What did you see and do?
- What was the most interesting part?
- Is it worth visiting? Why / Why not?

Email expressions

- Thanks for the *mail / email*
- Hope *you're OK / all is well with you*
- *Please forgive me / Sorry* for not *emailing / getting in touch* for so long
- I'm *glad / sorry* to hear that …
- *Keep in touch / Email me soon* and let me know how you're getting on
- Hope to hear from you soon

Writing

Write an email to a friend describing your visit. Use informal language and follow the advice in Writing skills.

Communication strategies

1 Do the quiz and then compare your answers in pairs.

What do you do in these situations?

1 You can't think of a word or expression when you are speaking.
   a Do you pause and feel embarrassed?
   b Do you avoid the topic?
   c Do you find another way to express your ideas?
2 You don't understand something that another person says.
   a Do you smile and pretend to understand?
   b Do you finish the conversation?
   c Do you ask for clarification?
3 You think that someone doesn't understand you.
   a Do you just carry on speaking?
   b Do you give up and change the topic?
   c Do you ask what isn't clear or rephrase your ideas?

If you answered c to all the questions, you have good communication strategies. If you answered a or b, consider using some of the strategies below.

2 Match the strategies (1–9) to the examples (a–i).

1 Ask for clarification.
2 Check that other people understand.
3 Give yourself time to think.
4 Ask for help.
5 Use a general word.
6 Explain or define the word.
7 Use translation.
8 Invent a word in English.
9 Use mime or gesture or facial expression.

a Are you with me?
b If you ride a motorcycle, you have to wear a hat.
c It went like this (hands demonstrate explode).
d We eat, how do you call it, those plants that grow under the sea.
e Sorry, I'm not clear what you mean. Could you repeat that please?
f For my birthday she made me a *gateau*.
g Just a minute, let me think how to say this.
h What's the word in English?
i He is very 'compromised' with his political party – can you say that in English?

⋆ Learn some of the phrases from exercise 2.
⋆ Plan to try out a new strategy every week.

Magic & Mystery

Listening and Speaking

1 Look at the image below. Make a note of three interesting things in the painting. Compare your notes with a partner.

2 🔊 1.52 Listen to a talk about this painting. Does the speaker mention the same things as you did in exercise 1?

3 Listen again and complete the notes.

This painting in particular shows how people are deceived and tricked by illusion.

1 The magician is at a …, in a town in Europe in …
2 Is holding up …
3 The spectator is leaning forward but does not see …
4 The assistant is taking …
5 We know the magician is intelligent because of the artist's use of …
6 The woman next to the assistant is …
7 This painting represents the tension between …

4 Work in pairs. Choose two of the questions below and ask each other the questions.

- Have you ever seen a magic show?
- Can you do a magic trick?
- Do you think the events in this painting still happen now at street magic shows?
- Do you know of any famous magicians?

Extend your vocabulary – metaphors

In English, deceiving someone is like taking them on a journey in the wrong direction.

Complete the examples with a word from the box.

taken	garden	on	wild	giving

1 It had all been a _____–goose chase.
2 Do you think he's just leading her _____?
3 I found out I'd been _____ for a ride.
4 Ann was furious when she discovered she'd been led up the _____ path.
5 I think they've been _____ us the runaround.

The Conjurer is a Hieronymus Bosch painting from the 1500s.
It is currently in the Musée Municipal in St-Germain-en-Laye, in France.

Grammar

> He **may understand** *what is really happening.*
> *The fair* **could have been** *in any town in Europe.*
>
> - use *could, may, might, must* and *can't* to speculate about events or situations
> - in the present use modal verb + infinitive
> - in the past use modal verb + *have* + past participle

1 Rewrite the sentences with the modal verbs in brackets to add speculation. The tense should stay the same as in the first sentence.

The man is the magician's assistant. (*must*)
The man must be the magician's assistant.
The artist thought magicians were dishonest. (*may*)
The artist may have thought magicians were dishonest.

1 The scene is at a fair or market of some kind. (*could*)
2 The artist didn't have a good opinion of magicians. (*can't*)
3 The object in the magician's hand is a pearl. (*could*)
4 The dog under the table represents something. (*might*)
5 The spectator didn't see the assistant. (*can't*)

2 Look at these sentences from people at a different magic show. Complete with *can't, must* or *might.*

1 He _____ have known the card I was thinking of. I don't think so, anyway.
2 He _____ have used a fake deck of cards. I'm positive.
3 He _____ have seen the card I chose. That wasn't possible.
4 He _____ have an assistant in the audience. I'm not sure.
5 He _____ have had a lot of practice, he's so good.

3 What magic show were the people watching in exercise 2? Choose the correct picture on the right. Then write similar sentences for one of the other pictures.

G **Grammar focus** – explanation & more practice of modals of speculation on page 138

Vocabulary

1 Look at the words in the box and identify the suffixes.

magician   assistant   spectator   painter

2 What are the words for the people who do this work? Use the suffixes above to help you. Can you think of other examples for each one?

What do you call someone who ...
1 labours (works) in a field?
2 attends to people during a flight?
3 translates things?
4 works in politics?
5 supervises other people?
6 works in the civil service (for government)?
7 directs?
8 makes bread?
9 works with maths?

3 🔊 1.53 Listen and check your answers. Repeat the words, paying attention to the word stress.

4 Read the popular counting rhyme in English. What are the jobs mentioned? Which jobs are not very common now?

> Tinker, tailor,
> Soldier, sailor,
> Rich man, poor man,
> Beggar man, thief!

5 Create your own version of the counting rhyme in exercise 4 with new job words. Then read it to your partner.

a

b

c

Magic & Mystery

Reading

1 Do you know any places that could be called 'magical'? Think of famous buildings, monuments or natural places that people say have magical powers. Tell a partner.

2 Look at the pictures of the different magical places on page 45. Do you know anything about them? What do you think makes them magical?

3 Read *Magical places* quickly and check your answers with a partner.

4 Work in pairs. Close your books. Take turns telling each other what you remember about the places. Try to remember the answers to these question cues.
- Where?
- What?
- Magical properties?

Grammar

1 What is another way of saying the following sentences? Find the answers in the text. Then answer the questions.
1 There is a rumour that bathing in the waters of this lake will help women to become pregnant.
2 People say that if you throw a coin into the fountain then you will return to Rome one day.
3 People report that if you toss three coins into the fountain with your right hand over your left shoulder then this brings good luck.

What tense is being used? What is the subject of these sentences?

It is said that if you throw a coin into the fountain then you will return to Rome one day.
It is rumoured that bathing in the waters of this lake will help women to become pregnant.

- this use of *it* is more common in written and academic English
- the passive voice is used

2 Change the sentences so they mean the same thing. Begin each sentence with *It* ...
1 People say that if you kiss someone in this place you will have eternal love.
2 They claim that if visitors touch one of the statues on this bridge they will return to the city.
3 There is a rumour that if you touch the head of this statue you will make lots of money.
4 People report that if you walk backwards under this bridge you will have good luck.
5 They say that if you put your hand in its mouth you will be healthy.
6 People believe that if you stand here at midnight then you will be lucky for a year.

G **Grammar focus** – explanation & more practice of impersonal passive on page 138

Writing

1 Look at the sentences in Grammar exercise 2.
Are there any places in your country with a similar legend?

2 You have been asked by a tourism agency to write a short text in English about a place with magical powers or a legend that you know. Use the texts on page 45 to help you. (If you can't think of a real place, then invent one.)

3 Read your partner's text. Which place would you like to visit?

Magical places

Tasik Dayang Bunting, Malaysia

According to one local tourist website, Malaysia is a country with many mysterious and magical attractions. One of the most interesting of these must be the freshwater lake of Tasik Dayang Bunting on the island of Dayang Bunting in Malaysia. The legend says that the waters used to be the favourite bathing place of a celestial princess. Sadly, her first child died from a mysterious illness at the age of seven days. She left the child's body in the lake and returned to her home in the sky.

It is rumoured that bathing in the waters of this lake will help women to become pregnant. In fact, the translation of the name is the Lake of the Pregnant Maiden, and many women come to bathe in its waters every year.

The Fountain of Trevi, Italy

One of the most popular tourist attractions in Rome, the Trevi fountain dates back to the mid 1700s. It is an iconic site and was made popular in films such as *Three Coins in the Fountain* and *La Dolce Vita*.

It is said that if you throw a coin into the fountain then you will return to Rome one day. A newer interpretation says that if you throw two coins into the fountain you will find romance, but three coins mean you will get divorced. It is also reported that if you toss three coins into the fountain with your right hand over your left shoulder then this brings good luck. Visitors to the site leave an average of 3,000 euros in the fountain every day.

The Blarney Stone, Ireland

Located in the battlements of Blarney Castle near the city of Cork in Ireland, the Blarney Stone is one of the area's biggest tourist attractions. According to legend, whoever kisses the Blarney Stone is given 'the gift of the gab' (being able to talk a lot without feeling shy, especially to get out of difficult situations). To actually kiss the stone is quite difficult as you need to lie down and lean backwards over the castle wall. It is claimed that many world politicians, literary figures and film stars have made the journey to the famous piece of rock and gained from its powers.

Glossary

celestial (*adjective*) – in or relating to the sky, heaven, or space

rumour (*noun*) – unofficial information that may or may not be true

iconic (*adjective*) – very famous and well-known, and believed to represent a particular idea

interpretation (*noun*) – an explanation of the meaning or importance of something

battlements (*noun*) – a wall around the top of a castle, with spaces through which weapons could be fired

Magic & Mystery

Vocabulary

1 Read the sentences below and identify the names of people.

> 'We don't want Joe Bloggs mending a huge truck in front of his house but we're not going to discourage someone working from home on their PC,' said the spokesman …

> 'There is no sign of foul play,' said the police chief spokesman, who identified the dead man only as John Doe until more is known about him …

> The incident involved a confrontation between a family, let us call them the Joneses, and a number of young people …

> In this country, awards may be earned by any Tom, Dick and Harry …

2 Complete the explanation of placeholder names with the names from above.

> In English there are several names used for people whose name we don't know. These are sometimes called placeholder names. Here are some examples:
>
> 1 _____ is used to talk about an average person.
> 2 _____ are names for a group of unspecified people. Even though they are male names this could include females.
> 3 _____ is the name for a typical, average family.
> 4 A _____ is the name for an unidentified dead person, injured person or a suspect in a court case.

3 Do you have any similar names in your language?

Reading and Listening

1 🔊 **1.54** Read and listen to an extract from a famous English story. Which of the names in Vocabulary exercise 1 might be appropriate for the man in the story?

2 Read again and decide if the statements are true (*T*), false (*F*) or the text doesn't say (*DS*).

1 Mrs Hall could not see his whole face.
2 The man had hurt his head.
3 She had not been expecting to see the bandages.
4 The man had been waiting for her.
5 The man did not want her to take the hat.
6 The man's appearance shocked Mrs Hall.
7 Mrs Hall had never seen an injured man before.

3 Work in pairs. Discuss the questions.

- What might have happened to the man?
- Do you know this book? Do you know any other books by H.G. Wells?

Turn to page 128 to check your answers.

Grammar

> It **had been snowing** heavily and the visitor **was** very wet.
> In the kitchen she **realised** she **had forgotten** the mustard.
>
> - use the past perfect when talking about the past and want to talk about an earlier time in the past
> - use the past perfect continuous to talk about actions that were in progress at an earlier time in the past
> - use the past simple for finished actions

1 What is the difference in meaning between the pairs of sentences?

1a She noticed he put his coat on the chair when she entered the room.
b She noticed he had put his coat on the chair when she entered the room.
2a She had been eating dinner when he arrived at the inn.
b She had eaten dinner when he arrived at the inn.

The Invisible Man

One winter's day, Mrs Hall, the owner of the Coach and Horses Inn, received a mysterious visitor. It had been snowing heavily and the visitor was very wet and cold. Mrs Hall made him dinner, but in the kitchen she realised she had forgotten the mustard. She went back to his room.

She put down the mustard pot on the table, and then she noticed the overcoat and hat had been taken off and put over a chair in front of the fire, and a pair of wet boots lay on the floor. She went to these things resolutely. 'I suppose I may have them to dry now,' she said.

'Leave the hat,' said her visitor, in a muffled voice, and turning she saw he had raised his head and was sitting and looking at her.

For a moment she stood gaping at him, too surprised to speak.

He held a white cloth – it was a serviette he had brought with him – over the lower part of his face, so that his mouth and jaws were completely hidden, and that was the reason of his muffled voice. But it was not that which startled Mrs Hall. It was the fact that all his forehead above his blue glasses was covered by a white bandage, and that another covered his ears, leaving not a scrap of his face exposed excepting only his pink, peaked nose. It was bright, pink, and shiny just as it had been earlier. He wore a dark-brown velvet jacket with a high, black collar turned up about his neck. The thick black hair, escaping as it could below and between the cross bandages, projected in curious tails and horns, giving him the strangest appearance conceivable. This muffled and bandaged head was so unlike what she had anticipated, that for a moment she was rigid.

■ ■ ■

Her nerves began to recover from the shock they had received. She placed the hat on the chair again by the fire. 'I didn't know, sir,' she began, 'that …' and she stopped, embarrassed.

'Thank you,' he said drily, glancing from her to the door and then at her again.

'I'll have them nicely dried, sir, at once,' she said, and carried his clothes out of the room.

Glossary

muffled (*adjective*) – not easy to hear because it's blocked by something

mustard (*noun*) – a yellow substance with a hot taste

rigid (*adjective*) – stiff, not easy to bend

---

2 Circle the correct answers.

1 She *didn't know / hadn't known* who the man was, because he *had not told her / did not tell her* his name.

2 Nobody in the village *knew / had known* how he *had arrived / had been arriving*.

3 It *had snowed / had been snowing* for hours and it *had been / was* very dark.

4 He *had covered / covered* his face, and Mrs Hall couldn't see him when she *came / had been coming* into the room.

3 Why was the man covered in bandages? Make sentences with the past perfect or past perfect continuous form of the verbs in brackets. Then add an idea of your own.

1 He _____ (*fall*) and hurt himself.

2 He _____ (*conduct*) experiments and one _____ (*go*) wrong.

3 He _____ (*have*) a terrible accident.

4 He _____ (*work*) in a laboratory and there _____ (*be*) an explosion.

5 He _____ (*commit*) a terrible crime and _____ (*disguise*) himself.

ⓖ **Grammar focus** – explanation & more practice of past perfect simple & continuous on page 138

Pronunciation and Speaking

1 🔊 1.55 Listen to how the words in italics are pronounced in these sentences. Repeat the sentences.

1 The *man had* raised his head and was looking at her.

2 The *man had* hurt his head.

3 *She had not been* expecting to see the bandages.

4 *She had* never seen an injured man before and was startled.

2 Choose two of the sentences below and complete with true information about yourself.

- I had been living in … for … years when I met …
- Why did I choose to study English? It must have been because …
- I had been studying … for … when I decided I wanted to …
- I had never understood … until I …
- I could have been a … but I decided in the end to …

3 Read your sentences with a partner. Give more background information about these events.

H.G. Wells (1886–1946) was an English writer. His work spanned many genres, from fiction to politics and social commentary, but he became best-known for his science fiction works. Together with the French author Jules Verne, Wells has been referred to as the father of Science Fiction.

Magic & Mystery

Speaking

Work in pairs. Read the quotation below and discuss the questions.

> **❝ If my books had been any worse, I should not have been invited to Hollywood, and if they had been any better, I should not have come. ❞**
>
> **Raymond Chandler, American writer of mystery and detective fiction**

1 Can you explain this quotation in your own words?
2 What does this quotation tell us about his opinion of Hollywood?
3 What does it say about his opinion of his mystery stories?

Listening

1 Work in pairs.

Can you think of any thriller films that feature ...
- secret papers? ✓
- a suitcase?
- a locked room? ✓
- a top secret weapon? ✓
- a necklace? ✓
- a country mansion? ✓
- a policeman who is about to retire?
- a disguise?
- a rich businessperson?

2 🔘 1.56 Listen to a lecture about the plot devices used in the cinema. Answer the questions.
1 What is a plot device? *object/ character that maes the p[lot]*
2 Which words from exercise 1 are *forward* mentioned? *see ticks above*
3 What are the other plot devices that are mentioned? *locked room plot voucher deus ex machina*

3 Work in groups of three, A, B and C. Listen again. Each person take notes about different parts of the listening.

A: Take notes on the **first** plot device mentioned.
B: Take notes on the **second** plot device mentioned.
C: Take notes on the **third** and **fourth** plot device mentioned.

4 Compare your notes with other people in the group.

5 Read the following comments about mystery films. Which plot devices are they talking about?

1

> I never quite understood what the briefcase was all about.

McGuffin

~cked
~om

2

> I never guessed who the murderer was, it could have been any of them on the boat!

3

> I thought the ending was completely unrealistic. You know, when the alien just mysteriously died from a virus.

deus ex machina

plot voucher

4

> It was so obvious, especially the bit where the main character suddenly 'found' a card that helped him open the door.

6 Can you think of any films or books that use these plot devices?

Vocabulary and Speaking

1 Read the sentences below. What could the highlighted words refer to?

1 Do you think the hotel has a whatchamacallit? You know, so I can recharge my phone? *charger*

2 Computer technology is developing all the time, and there may be a great new gizmo just around the corner. *technical device*

3 What's all this stuff on my desk? *unwanted things*

4 I need one of those things that you put in a book to save your place. *bookmark*

2 Work in pairs. You are going to describe different objects using vague language.
A: turn to page 126.
B: turn to page 133.

3 🔊 1.57 Vague language is very common in spoken English. Read the following dialogue. Then listen and insert the extra words you hear.

A: What did you think of the film?
B: I though it was ~kind of~ predictable.
A: Predictable?
B: Yeah. ~All that stuff~ At the end … Anyway, I don't like those old mystery movies.
A: Oh, I do. I love those films. I love suspense. ~and that sort of thing~
B: I don't hate them but they don't surprise me. If I see a suspense movie I ~kind of~ want to feel tense. I want to feel nervous. ~and stuff~
A: You're being ~a bit kind of~ difficult.

4 Read the dialogue together.

Writing

Work in pairs and choose **one** of the tasks below.

A 1 Look at the list of words in Listening exercise 1. Choose three and think of an idea for a film containing all three.
2 Write the beginning of your film in no more than 50 words.

B 1 Write about a film you know that includes one or more of the plot devices.
2 Exchange paragraphs with your partner.

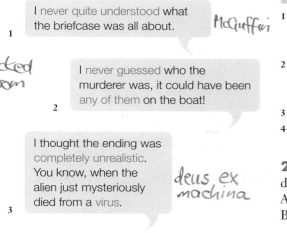

Function globally expressing doubt

Fountain of Youth, St Augustine, Florida, US
In 1513 the Spanish explorer Juan Ponce de León sailed along the Atlantic coast in search of the legendary Fountain of Youth and came ashore in the vicinity of St Augustine. Drinking from the waters of the spring grants the drinker eternal youth and everlasting vitality.

Statue of Daikokuten, Hasedera Temple, Kamakura, Japan
Daikokuten is one of the Seven Japanese Gods of Fortune. He is considered the god of wealth (or more specifically, the harvest).
Daikokuten's statue should be rubbed on its head and shoulders for good fortune and wealth.

Warm up

1 Read the extracts from two guide books. What positive effects do they suggest these places can have on visitors?

2 What do you think of these claims?

Listening

1 🔊 1.58–1.59 Listen to two conversations. What are the attitudes of the speakers towards the two places?

2 Listen again. Tick (✔) the arguments that the speakers express.

Conversation 1
1 Water from the spring can make you look younger.
2 The idea that water from the spring can make you look younger is just a trick to make money.
3 The claims about the water might be partly true.

Conversation 2
4 Rubbing the statue will definitely bring good fortune and wealth.
5 Rubbing the statue is a harmless gesture.
6 Rubbing the statue is a way to show respect.

Language focus: expressing doubt

1 🔊 1.60 Put the words in the box in the right sentences from the listening to make phrases that express doubt. Then listen and check.

think	believe	unlikely	face	doubt	come

1 Oh _____ on, it's nonsense.
2 Do you really _____ water can make you look younger?
3 Sorry, but I find that a bit hard to _____.
4 Let's _____ it, you could say that about any spring or fountain.
5 I _____ it somehow.
6 It's _____ to do any good either.

2 Listen again to the way the speaker says the sentences in exercise 1. Work with a partner and practise repeating the sentences with the same intonation.

3 🔊 1.61 Listen to the word 'Really?' spoken with three different kinds of intonation. Write which speaker (1–3) expresses …

- interest
- surprise
- doubt

Then listen again and repeat.

Speaking

Work with a partner and choose **one** of the tasks.

A Choose one of the places on page 45. Tell your partner about it. Your partner expresses doubt.

Swap roles and do the role-play again.

B Think of a place you know which is supposed to have magical properties and tell your partner about it. Your partner expresses doubt.

Swap roles and do the role-play again.

Global voices

Warm up

1 Look at the list of different 'mysterious experiences' that people can have. Have you heard of these things before?

- seeing a person or animal disappear suddenly
- thinking about a person and then getting a phone call from that person
- hearing a strange noise at night
- seeing your own body while you are asleep
- having a conversation with somebody and thinking you had that conversation before
- meeting someone for the first time but feeling like you know them
- seeing strange lights in the night sky

2 Look at the list again. For each experience decide if it is:

1 mysterious but probably has a normal explanation
2 mysterious, with no explanation possible
3 not mysterious

Listening

1 🔊 1.62–1.65 Listen to four people talk about mysterious experiences they have had. Match each speaker to one of the experiences in Warm up exercise 1.

Gülgün, Turkey
Kang Sik, South Korea
Charlotte, England
Matthew, US

2 Work in pairs. Listen again and take turns explaining what these things from the people's stories mean.

1	Gülgün	*a girl*	*ten hours*
2	Kang Sik	*once or twice a month*	*his body*
3	Charlotte	*fifteen*	*a field*
4	Matthew	*his feet*	*in the corner of the room*

Language focus: fillers and repetition

1 Match the beginnings of each phrase (1–6) with the end (a–f).

1 I think, er, twice a month I see, um, ...
2 You know, I can't ...
3 In the middle of the night ...
4 ... and it like started at my feet and started coming up ...
5 it was dusk and it did disappear ...
6 and then, then this body of mine ...

a ... and up and up
b ... it didn't run away anyway, it disappeared
c ... you know, with this presence ...
d I can't explain how, how it happened to me ...
e ... it was a night trip. Yeah, and it takes ten hours ...
f ... I see my body when I sleep.

2 In spoken English it's very common to repeat words or phrases and use fillers. Fillers are extra words that give us time to think of what we are going to say next. Look at what the speakers said in exercise 1 again and ...

1 identify any fillers you see (e.g. *anyway, like, you know* ...).
2 identify any repeated words or phrases.

Speaking

1 Have you ever had a magical or mysterious experience? If not, do you know anybody who has? Or perhaps you have read about a mysterious experience or seen a report on TV? Think about what happened: where you were, who was there and why it was mysterious or magical.

2 Tell a partner about your or somebody else's experience. Use fillers if you need time to think while you are speaking.

Gülgün, Turkey   Kang Sik, South Korea   Charlotte, England   Matthew, US

Writing a review

Reading

1 Read Marta's review of *In the sea there are crocodiles*. What is her opinion of the book?

a She thoroughly enjoyed it.

b She enjoyed it but has some reservations.

c She did not enjoy it.

In the sea there are crocodiles, by Fabio Geda, is more than just a best-selling adventure story. It is also a description of a cruel reality that millions of people all over the world still have to face every day.

This is the third book by Geda, who is fast becoming one of Italy's most important contemporary novelists. It tells the true story of Enaiatollah Akbar (Ena), an eleven-year-old Afghan boy, and his search for a new life and family. Ena, who was forced to flee his village because of tribal warfare, arrived on the Pakistani border with his family. After his father's death, Ena was abandoned by his mother and left without relatives and without money.

Ena decided to set off in search of a new life, and for the next five years he had to survive only on his courage and optimism, which shine out from every page of this spell-binding book. Always in danger of being attacked or captured and following a series of amazing ups and downs, he earned enough money to make his way across Pakistan, Iran and Turkey. After crossing the sea from Turkey to Greece in an inflatable dinghy, Ena finally arrived in Italy, where he found a new family, and the love that he had lost during his childhood. Then, at the age of eighteen, he met Fabio Geda, who helped him put his incredible story into words.

This was a captivating book that I could not put down. The narrative is exciting and absorbing, so that you have to read to the end to see what happens to Ena. But more than that, the book depicts universal human realities such as love, loss, pain and endurance. The crocodiles in the title refer to the fears that Ena had to overcome when he was crossing the sea to Greece. The book ends on a happy note but it will also leave you reflecting on the topical issues of war, violence, and migration, and hoping that a solution will be found for the millions of Enas in this world.

2 Are the statements true (*T*) or false (*F*)?

1 The book is based on real events.

2 It has an unhappy ending.

3 Ena's parents both died.

4 Ena travelled from Afghanistan to Italy by sea.

5 The book recounts many exciting adventures.

6 Ena was afraid at times.

7 Ena saw crocodiles from the inflatable dinghy.

8 The book will give you a lot to think about.

3 Would you like to read this book? Why / Why not?

Writing skills: connecting sentences

A Relative clauses

Use relative clauses with *who* to give extra information.

*This is the third book by Geda, **who** is fast becoming one of Italy's most important contemporary novelists.*
*Geda, **who** is fast becoming one of Italy's most important contemporary novelists, has written a new best-seller.*

1 Where are commas used in the sentences?

2 Find two more examples of clauses with *who* in the review.

3 Insert *who* in the sentences below. Put commas where necessary.

1 The book is written by Fabio Geda has already won two literary prizes in Italy.

2 Enaiatollah is called Ena by his family and friends was born in a small Afghan village.

3 Geda works with deprived children met Ena soon after he arrived in Italy.

B Noun phrases

Connect nouns with other noun phrases.

*'In the sea there are crocodiles', **the latest book by Fabio Geda**, is more than just a best-selling adventure story.*
*It tells the true story of Enaiatollah Akbar (Ena), **an eleven-year-old Afghan boy**.*

Match the two halves of the sentences.

1 The book was written by Fabio Geda,

2 The first part of the book is set in Nava,

3 During his travels Ena meets Hussein Ali,

a the village where Ena lived with his mother.

b a prize-winning Italian novelist.

c another Afghan refugee.

C *after* + gerund or noun

Use ***after* + gerund** or **noun** to connect two sentences with the same subject.

After arriving on the Pakistani border, he decided to set off in search of a new life.
After his father's death, Ena was abandoned by his mother.

Connect the sentences using *after*.

1 Ena crossed the sea from Turkey to Greece. He finally arrived in Italy.
2 Ena had a series of adventures. He found a new family.
3 Geda heard the story. He decided to put it into words.
4 You will read the book. You will see the world in a new light.

Preparing to write

Tell a partner about a book you have enjoyed, recently or in the past. Answer these questions.

- What is the title of the book and who is it written by?
- What is special or important about the book?
- What happened in the book?
- What topics or themes are dealt with?
- Would you recommend the book? Why / Why not?

Writing a review

- It is *a novel / based on a true story / the autobiography of X / a biography of X*
- It tells the story of … / It is narrated by …
- It describes the life of refugees / It depicts universal realities/ It recounts his adventures
- It is set in *present-day Afghanistan / 18th century Italy*
- I thoroughly recommend this *exciting / fascinating / moving / captivating / spell-binding / magical* novel

Writing

Write the review based on the questions discussed with your partner. Arrange your ideas in paragraphs.

Study skills

Preparing to read or listen

Before you read or listen in English, it is helpful to **have a clear purpose**. For example, you could listen or read:

to understand the gist (general meaning)

to find specific information

to gain a detailed understanding

to learn new language

1 Work in pairs and discuss the questions.

1 Look again at the texts in this unit of *Global*. What were your purposes for reading or listening?
2 Think about a time when you have read or listened to English outside the classroom recently. What was your purpose?

If you **predict** the content and language of a text before you read or listen, it often makes it easier to understand.

2 Read the following suggestions for using predictions, and choose the three you like best.

- ★ Look at the headline or pictures of a reading text to predict what it is about. Write down, or discuss with a friend, what you know about the topic. Read to check your predictions.
- ★ Write down five questions that you expect the text will answer. Then listen or read and try to answer the questions.
- ★ Write down five words that you expect the text will contain. Then listen or read to check.
- ★ To improve your listening, first read a newspaper article in your own language or in English, and study the vocabulary. Then listen to the same news story on the TV, radio or Internet.
- ★ Read reviews and summaries before watching a film or reading a book in English.
- ★ Listen to a recording and stop at different points to see if you can predict what the speaker will say next.

Compare your ideas with a partner.

Parents & Children

Vocabulary and Speaking

1 Look at these words used on a website forum to describe parenthood. Which words focus on the challenges? Which words focus on the rewards?

amazing	challenging	crazy	exciting
exhausting	expensive	fun	incredible
life-changing	miraculous	noisy	
relentless	rewarding	stressful	
underestimated	unpredictable		

2 Work in pairs. Choose two or three words and discuss what you think parents meant by them. What would you add?

3 Match the words (1–8) with the words (a–h) that have a similar meaning. Use a dictionary.

1	bring up	a	monitor
2	praise	b	believe in
3	punish	c	ignore
4	tell off	d	discipline
5	check up on	e	compliment
6	trust	f	indulge
7	spoil	g	raise
8	neglect	h	criticise

4 Choose four words in exercise 3. Write examples of each type of parent behaviour without using the words in exercise 3. Swap with a partner. Write the correct word.

It's when parents phone their children all the time, or read the messages on their mobile.

5 Discuss one statement with a partner.

- Teachers are more important today in a child's upbringing than their parents.
- It is easier to be a grandparent than a parent.
- Parents are not as strict as they used to be.

Reading

1 Are parenting manuals popular in your country? Do you think good parenting is something that can be learned from a book or is it instinctive?

2 Read the information about an American childcare manual and its author. How do you think the different editions of the book might have been influenced by the changing times?

3 Read two extracts from the 1946 and 1998 editions of *Baby and Child Care*. Answer the questions.

1 How did Dr Spock's ideas about fathers and entertainment change over the years?
2 What do you think of his advice? Is this advice universal? Is it relevant in your country or culture?

Extend your vocabulary – metaphors: relationships

Relationships between people are like physical connections.

We're a very close family.

My parents split up / broke up after I left home.

My parents separated when I was small.

My sister and I were inseparable when we were younger.

My parents have a strong bond.

We're all very attached to each other in my family.

Cracks appeared in our relationship after we got married.

Money problems caused deep divisions in the family.

1 Put the examples above in two lists:
Having a good relationship is like being joined to somebody.
Ending a relationship is like breaking it.

2 Talk about people in your family or in families you know, using the expressions above.

Baby and Child Care

Fathers

1946: Some fathers have been brought up to think that the care of babies and children is the mother's job entirely. This is the wrong idea. You can be a warm father and a real man at the same time. Of course, I don't mean that the father has to give just as many bottles or change just as many diapers as the mother. But it's fine for him to do these things occasionally. He might make the formula on Sunday.

1998: Men, especially the husbands of women with outside jobs, have been participating increasingly in all aspects of home and child care. There is no reason why fathers shouldn't be able to do these jobs as well as mothers. But the benefit may be lost if this work is done as a favour to the wife, since that implies that raising the child is not really the father's work but that he's merely being extraordinarily generous.

Entertainment

1946: Conscientious parents often dread comic strips and comic books, thinking that they ruin their children's taste for good reading, fill their minds with morbid ideas, keep them indoors, interfere with homework and waste good money. All these accusations have a bit of truth in them. But when children show a universal craving for something, whether it's comics or candy or jazz, we've got to assume that it has a positive, constructive value for them. It may be wise to try to give them what they want in a better form, but it does no good for us to cluck like nervous hens.

1998: There is a darker side to the world of computers. I'm speaking about the majority of computer games. Most of these are variations on the theme of kill the bad guys. The best that can be said of them is that they may help promote eye-hand coordination in children. The worst that can be said is that they sanction, and even promote, aggression and violent responses to conflict.

Writing

1 Work in small groups. Make a list of the topics that you think need to be included in a childcare manual.

Rules about computer games, etc.
Role of fathers

2 Write at least three tips which you would pass on to new parents.

Useful phrases

- It's fine for / to …
- There is no reason why you shouldn't …
- You can / might …
- It may be wise to …
- It does no good for / to …

3 Swap your tips with another group. Give your opinion of the other group's tips.

Glossary

formula (*noun*) – milk for babies made from powder

Dr Benjamin Spock
(1903–1998) was an American pediatrician and the author of the hugely influential *Baby and Child Care*, published in 1946. In Dr Spock's lifetime the book went through seven editions, sold over 50 million copies and was translated into 39 languages.

Parents & Children

Reading and Speaking

1 Read the four quotations about names and naming. Which quote …

1 talks about the suitability of the same name for different stages in life?   *Sp.4*

2 emphasises the influence of names?   *Sp2*

3 questions the motives and consequences of name giving?

4 points out that the person is more important than the name?

2 Work in pairs. Discuss the quotes and answer the questions.   *Sp1,*

- How important do you think a name is?
- Do you think it is good for a child to have an unusual name?   *Sp3*
- What effect do you think it has on a child to have an unusual name? Do you know any examples?   *Sp.5*

> **Does the name you give your child affect his life? Or is it your life reflected in his name? In either case, what kind of signal does a child's name send to the world — and most important, does it really matter?**
> (Steven D. Levitt and Stephen J. Dubner,

[handwritten note: MO / 49   Chicago / 2 children - girls / Harvard → lawyer]

... name ... er of ... . But ... let go ... I have ... lity to ... ity.

... ve call ... as

> **From antiquity people have recognised the connection between naming and power.**
> (Casey Miller and Kate Swift, feminist writers)

Vocabulary and Listening

1 Look at the words in bold. Take it in turns to explain their meaning to a partner.

1 Her name's Mercedes but we call her by her **nickname** 'Meche'.

2 In some countries names are gender specific, but **unisex names** are common in many cultures, for example in India.

3 The Brontë Sisters all wrote under male **pseudonyms**.

4 Parents often give their children a relative's name as a first or **middle name**.   *Sp 1*

5 Actors and singers sometimes give themselves **stage names**.

6 Some cultures use **patronymics** and **matronymics** instead of a surname or family name.

7 Women in Spain normally keep their **maiden name** when they marry.

8 Most people use an invented **username** rather than their real name in internet forums.

2 🔊 1.66–1.70 Listen to five people talk about names. Which of the names in bold in exercise 1 do the speakers talk about?

3 Listen again and match the topics a-e to the speakers (1–5).

a using the same first name as a mark of respect   *Sp. 4*

b unusual names   *Sp. 1*

c ancestry   *Sp. 3*

d changing one's family name   *Sp. 5*

e order of family names and given names   *Sp.*

4 Work in pairs. Choose two questions and discuss.

- What influence does the state have on names in your country? Can parents name a child anything they wish?
- Is it usual in your country or culture for women to keep their maiden names on marrying?
- Do you have a nickname? When did you get it? Where does it come from?
- Do you have an interesting username that you use on the internet? How did you choose that name?

Grammar and Pronunciation

present/future habit (handwritten)

*A parent **will usually pass on** their first name to their children as a family name. People **will often** ask me about my name.*

regular (handwritten)

1 Work in pairs. Read the sentences above from the listening and answer the questions.

1 Underline the adverbs of time used with the words. Do the sentences refer to past, present or future time?

2 Do the sentences refer to a particular occasion or regular behaviour?

2 Complete the sentences with *will / won't* and the correct verb from the box.

be christened	call	mostly use
not often address		typically give

In Russia parents (1) _____ a child three names. A child (2) _____ with a first name, a patronymic and a surname. Today people (3) _____ you by your first name and your patronym because that sounds rather formal. People (4) _____ your first name but your parents and / or people who know you well (5) _____ you by your diminutive, a sort of informal family name. Pasha is the diminutive for Pavel, for example.

3 🔊 1.71 Listen. Underline *will / won't* in the sentences where it is stressed. Then choose the correct option for the rule below.

1 Here in Germany women **will keep** their own names.

2 In some countries, the state **won't allow** parents to give their children uncommon names.

3 She **won't accept** that I'm all grown up.

4 Some parents **will insist on giving** their children strange names.

- stress *will / won't* when the statement is *a statement of fact / a criticism*

4 Look at these sentences by parents. Decide if they are a criticism or a statement of fact. Then check with a partner: take turns to read out a sentence with the correct stress.

1 He just won't eat vegetables. *criticism\ annoyance* (handwritten)

2 She just won't tidy her room up. *" "* (handwritten)

3 She will often play basketball after school. *fact* (handwritten)

4 He'll usually go out on a Friday night. *fact* (handwritten)

5 They will leave their clothes lying all over the floor. *criticism* (handwritten)

6 She will usually cook once a week. *fact* (handwritten)

5 Complain to a partner about your children's / partner's / a friend's annoying habits. Use the correct stress.

My daughter <u>will</u> throw her clothes on the floor.

Ⓖ **Grammar focus** – explanation & more practice of *will* for present habits on page 140

Speaking

Work in pairs and choose **one** of the tasks below.

A Prepare a short presentation about naming customs in your country. Think about:

- number of names
- origin of first names: traditional, family, creative names …
- middle names – customary? another first name, a further family name or a patronymic?
- family names: from mother or father? any common names?

Give your presentation to another group.

B Prepare a short presentation about your own name. First make notes:

- Does your first name have a meaning?
- Is your first name a traditional name, a modern name or one your parents invented? Are you named after somebody?
- Is your family name common in your country?
- Do you like your name? What other name would you have preferred?
- Do you have family members with interesting names?

Tell the rest of the group.

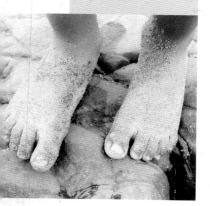

Writing

1 As part of a project about memory, people were asked to submit their earliest memories online. Read the ones at the bottom of these pages. Which ones …

- make you smile / make you feel sad?
- tell you something about the person?
- make you think of a similar memory?

2 Match the quotations at the bottom of the pages to the senses in the box. Do the writers make you feel / see / … the things they describe?

hearing	sight	smell	taste	touch

3 Write about a childhood memory using one of these beginnings:

Touching …	Listening to …	Smelling …
Looking at …	Eating / Drinking …	

Reading

1 Read *Now here, now there* by Molly Wizenberg about a childhood food experience. Answer the questions.

1 Was the childhood experience positive or negative?
2 What experience did she have 25 years later?

2 Read the text again. Make notes on …

1 why oysters were a part of her childhood.
2 whether her family liked eating oysters.
3 what Molly can remember about the oyster she ate as a child.
4 why she tried another 25 years later.
5 how she felt before she ate this second oyster.

Grammar

*They **would** all **stand around**, eating and sighing.*
*I **used to drink** a lot of milk when I was young.*
*I **used to be** a vegetarian.*
*I **didn't use to eat** meat.*
*I **tried** oysters **once** but I didn't like them.*

- to talk about repeated actions or habits in the past that don't happen now we use *would* or *used to*
- to talk about past states or conditions that have changed, we only use *used to*
- we don't use *would* or *used to* when we talk about a specific past event or to describe something that happened a fixed number of times or for a fixed length of time; we use the past simple for these situations

1 Underline more sentences with *used to* and *would* in the text.

2 Complete the text with *would* or *used to*. Sometimes both are possible.

When I was a child we (1) _____ (visit) my grandmother most days. She (2) _____ (live) just around the corner and whenever we visited her she (3) _____ (always / give) us fantastic food. She (4) _____ (often / make) *kibbeh* (minced lamb mixed with bulgar wheat and spices). I (5) _____ (love) this. My grandmother (6) _____ (serve) it with thick pieces of onion. I (7) _____ (not like) raw onion, so I (8) _____ (eat) the *kibbeh* with pieces of flat bread. I've never tasted anything like it since.

G **Grammar focus** – explanation & more practice of *used to*, *would* & past simple on page 140

Listening to my **parents fight** while **I hid** underneath a table.

Crawling along the hall with holes in my dungarees, feeling the carpet and lino on my **bare knees.**

Eating a **worm.**

Trying to wash **marker off my tongue** with a bar of soap.

Playing on the hill behind my friend's house … the dirt smelling like **clay.**

Now here, now there

I have two half brothers who live on the East Coast, and when I was a kid, if they came home for the holidays, they used to bring a Styrofoam cooler of oysters. My father would get out his knife and shucking glove and lean against the kitchen counter, flicking grit and shells into the sink as he went, and they would all stand around, eating and sighing, making the noises that people make when they eat oysters.

I don't know how old I was that night, but I think I must have been about six. I stood next to my father while he shucked, and he leaned down and gave me an oyster, a fat one, an enormous one, amoeba-like, dripping with brine. I have no memory of eating it. I must have forgotten on purpose. But I do know that I ate it, approximately, if nearly choking can be considered eating, and that it took me 25 years to eat another.

Twenty-five years! When I get freaked out about something, I get freaked out. The look of an oyster, the texture, the choking thing: I was alright with the idea of never eating a second.

But last year a cook at my restaurant shucked three oysters and put them on a plate. Then he dared me. I was tempted to punch him in the face. I was not pleased. I picked up an oyster, stared at it, and felt like I was going to cry.

I made everyone look away, and then I ate it. Only one, and it was tiny, but I ate it. I chewed and everything. I didn't die. And when I swallowed, the flavor rang around my mouth the way the ringing of a bell ricochets inside a cathedral, now here, now there. It tasted like seawater and melon and wet rocks. I didn't even hate it. I almost liked it.

Molly Wizenberg is the writer of the food blog *Orangette* and author of *A Homemade Life: Stories and Recipes from My Kitchen Table*. She lives in Seattle, where she and her husband own the restaurant Delancey. Molly likes peanut butter, meatballs, sausage, French apple turnovers, chocolate, ice cream, and nectarines – although preferably not all at once.

Vocabulary

1 Using a dictionary to help you, which of these words describes the texture of oysters?

> crunchy   dry   smooth

2 Which of these words describes how oysters taste for most people?

> bitter   delicious   spicy

3 Decide if these words describe texture or taste.

> bland   chewy   disgusting   lumpy
> soggy   sour   sticky   greasy

4 Choose a word or words from exercises 1–3 to describe …

> unripe oranges   food cooked in too much oil
> old fish   food without herbs and spices
> fresh vegetables

Glossary

shuck (*verb, AE*) – to remove the shell
grit (*noun*) – very small pieces of stone or sand
brine (*noun*) – water that contains a lot of salt
ricochet (*verb*) – to move from one surface to another

5 Work in pairs. Describe the taste and texture of your favourite food and a food or dish you can't stand.

Speaking

Think of foods you regularly ate in your childhood (at home, at your grandparents, at school or on holiday). Then tell a partner about your childhood eating habits. Use *would* or *used to* and some of the words to describe food in Vocabulary exercise 1.

Being on the beach with hot rocks on my feet.

Looking at the legs of the dining room table and chairs as though they were trees in a forest.

Drinking warm milk, watching the rain fall.

Standing in my grandmother's dining room on a faded oriental rug.

Watching potatoes turn round in the microwave.

A bee stinging me when I tried to hold it.

Taking a bath in a porcelain sink and feeling the cold faucet on my back.

Part 4

Listening and Speaking

1 You are going to listen to a lecture which starts off with the words 'Every child, every generation is a product of their times.' Do you think this statement is true?

2 Work in pairs and decide which things you think give a generation their identity. Rank the list below in order of importance (1–7). Then compare with another pair.

the political situation
the economic situation
important historic events
scientific and technological developments
population trends
fashion
music

3 🔊 **1.72** Listen to the lecture and answer the questions.

1   What generation is being discussed? When were they born?
2   Which of the things in exercise 2 has shaped this generation, according to the speaker?

4 Listen again. Are these sentences true (*T*) or false (*F*)?

Generally speaking, this generation …
1   is fairly selfish.
2   is independent.
3   can do several things at once.
4   lacks new ideas.
5   crosses national boundaries.
6   is loyal to employers.

5 Discuss **one** of these questions with a partner.

• Do you see yourself as belonging to a particular generation? What characterises this generation?
• How do you think the generation born between 2000 and 2020 will be different?

Extend your vocabulary – prefixes with *self*

self-control	self-centred
self-esteem	self-confident
self-pity	self-conscious
self-respect	self-righteous

1 Which of the nouns and adjectives have a positive meaning, which have a negative meaning, which are neutral?

2 Pick the word which best fits the descriptions below.
1   'He has such an ego! He thinks everything is about him!'
2   'Poor girl. She's so worried about how she looks and what people think of her.'
3   'It's about not showing you're angry even when you are.'
4   'To listen to him you'd think he'd never done anything wrong in his life.'
5   'It's no good feeling sorry for yourself.'

Grammar

> They are not **used to** standing on their own feet.
> They are still **getting used to** sending emails.

1 Complete the sentences with *older generations* or *members of generation Y*. According to the speaker …

1   _____ are not used to standing on their own feet.
2   _____ are still getting used to sending emails.
3   _____ are used to multitasking.
4   _____ have had to get used to consumerism.

2 Complete the rules about *be used to* and *get used to*.

> • to talk about a situation which you are comfortable with, you use _____ + verb + _____ or noun
> • to talk about a situation you are becoming or have become comfortable with you use _____ + verb + _____ or noun

3 Rephrase the phrases in red using the correct form of *be used to* or *get used to*.

> Different generations of workers in the workplace can cause conflict. Older generations (1) **have no problem with working** long hours and weekends and (2) **are familiar with taking** orders from a boss. However they can have trouble (3) **becoming accustomed** to new technology. Middle-aged workers as a rule (4) **find it easy to do** tasks without supervision. However, due to the uncertain economic situation in some countries, they have had to (5) **adapt to not having** a permanent job. The younger generation (6) **knows how to work** in teams. But many are new to the workforce and will have to (7) **learn how to function** in a work environment. Members of generation Y (8) **are in the habit of getting** results quickly, so they need tasks broken down into manageable stages.

4 Work with a partner of a similar age and complete the sentences about your generation.

1 My generation is used to ...
2 We are still getting used to ...
3 We haven't got used to ...
4 I don't think we'll ever get used to ...

G **Grammar focus** – explanation & more practice of *be used to* / *get used to* on page 140

Pronunciation

1 🔊 **1.73** Listen to words from the listening which contain consonant clusters (two or three consonants) at the beginning. Repeat the words.

creative	**fl**exible	**pr**evious	**sp**oilt	**spr**ead
strong	**sw**itch	**thr**oughout		

2 🔊 **1.74** Work in pairs. Complete the missing consonants in these clusters at the end of words with the letters from the box. Then listen and repeat.

cts	fth	gth	lt	mpt	nks	nt	nth
pth	th						

1 It's a difficu_ _ situation, a generation gap.
2 He's worked here for three mo_ _ _s.
3 He started on the fi_ _ _.
4 He's made a good atte_ _ _ to do the job.
5 But he's out of his de_ _ _.
6 I went to great len_ _ _s to help him.
7 He thi_ _ _ he knows more than me.
8 He expe_ _ _ respect because of his age.
9 I gave him a few hi_ _s.
10 Then I had to tell him a few tru_ _s.

Speaking

1 Walk around the class. Ask questions to *find someone who ...* (Take care to pronounce consonant clusters clearly.)

Find someone who ...
* has a page on a social networking site.
* used to watch black and white TV.
* learnt to use computers in primary school.
* has worked for one company throughout most of their life.
* expects to retire in the next ten years.
* can't get used to using DVD players.
* is used to sending text messages regularly.
* uses instant messaging.
* has never attempted to blog.
* remembers watching Armstrong's moon landing on TV.

2 Tell the class if you were surprised by any of the answers.

3 Do you think there is such a thing as 'the generation gap'? Explain why or why not.

Function globally moving off topic

Warm up

Look at the photos above. Working with a partner, try to find a way you could link these images together into a conversation.

Listening

1 🔊 **1.75–1.78** Listen to four short conversations. Tick (✔) the topics you hear from the list below. There are two extra topics you don't need.

an Italian friend
a situation at the airport
a sandwich bar
a dinner for staff
the cinema
a party

2 Each of the topics in exercise 1 was the **first** topic of one of the conversations. Listen again. What was the **second** topic in each conversation?

Language focus: changing the topic

1 The following are key words the speakers used to change the topic of conversation. Can you remember the whole phrase?

speaking (2 words)   *speaking of*
reminds (3 words)
way (3 words)
forget (3 words)
just remembered (5 words)

2 🔊 **1.79** Listen to the phrases to check your answers. Then repeat the phrases, adding your own ideas.

Speaking

Work in pairs, A and B. You are going to talk about various topics. A: start with the first topic on the left.

B: try to change so you both speak about the second topic.

A: listen to B and then try to change to the third topic.

SOMETHING YOU REMEMBER FROM CHILDHOOD → YOUR PARENTS → YOUR MOTHER'S OR FATHER'S BIRTHDAY → YOUR BIRTHDAY → A NICE PRESENT YOU RECEIVED → PRICES ARE GOING UP

Global English

Learning to talk
by David Crystal

When do children start to talk? If you ask a group of parents when this happened, most will say 'around twelve months of age'. They will probably even remember what the children said. Many parents keep a diary of their child's 'first words'.

We can never predict what a first word is going to be. Often it's the name for 'mummy' or 'daddy', but it could just as easily be the word for an animal or a favourite toy. Everything depends on what has most captured the child's attention. But one thing is certain: after the first word, others come quickly. By 18 months, most children have learned about 50 words. By two, the total has risen to around 200.

Early words are actually one-word sentences. One of the first features of language a child learns well is to control the rise and fall of the voice to make the difference between stating and questioning. In English, *daddy* with a high rising tone means 'is that daddy?' *Daddy* with a high falling tone means 'There's daddy'. Of course, only very basic meanings can be communicated using intonation alone. So it soon becomes necessary to learn some grammar.

In English, grammar chiefly means learning to put words in different orders. Children have to see that *mummy push* is different from *push mummy*. They start practising such changes at around 18 months. By two, they have learned the basic patterns of word order, and we hear them saying such things as *man kick ball* and *where daddy go*?

What are the parents doing, all this time? They're acting as teachers. Here's a typical exchange between a mother and child:

Mother: What's that?
Child: Dog.
Mother: That's right, it's a dog. A big black dog.

The mother is doing what teachers do when they want their students to learn: she's reinforcing the correct answer. Notice too how she shows the child some new grammar at the same time – by putting *dog* into a longer sentence – and also how she points the child in the direction of some new vocabulary. Parents always have an active role to play in their child's language learning.

Warm up

1 Read the following examples of an English child's early language. Put them in order from youngest to oldest.

___ No mummy!
___ I don't want cake.
___ I no want.
___ I don't want.
___ Mummy?
___ Mummy

2 Do you think a child's language develops in the same way in your language?

Reading

1 Read *Learning to talk* and put the paragraph titles in order.

___ Correcting words
___ The first words
___ Word order
___ Words come quickly
___ Words or sentences?

2 Read the text again and answer the questions.

1 What determines a child's first words?
2 How can one word constitute a sentence?
3 What is the difference between a high rising tone and a high falling tone?
4 What is the most basic element of English grammar?
5 How do parents teach children to talk?

3 Each of the following sentences has one error in word order. Without looking back at the text, correct the error.

1 Parents even will probably remember what the children said.
2 Everything depends on what has captured most the child's attention.
3 So soon becomes it necessary to learn some grammar.
4 In English, grammar chiefly means learning to put words in orders different.
5 The mother is doing what teachers do when they want to learn their students.

Speaking

1 Work individually. Choose **two** of the questions below and think of your answers.

- What were your child or children's first words? How old were they?
- Is it a good or bad thing for young children to be exposed to many languages?
- Do children learn English at school? When do they start? Do you think this is a good thing?
- Who is most responsible for the way a child speaks, in your opinion: parents, teachers or friends?

2 Work in pairs. Compare your answers to exercise 1.

Writing an article

Reading

1 Read Paulina's article about her upbringing. Choose the best title:

> Thanks, Mum and Dad!
> Why punishment does not always work
> The importance of table manners

There are always two sides to any situation. In the case of my upbringing, it was neither completely strict, nor completely lenient because my parents were totally different in their views on discipline. For my mother, everything was black and white; she had clear rules about how we should behave, and there were punishments if we did not obey. My father, on the other hand, was always calm and incapable of telling us to do something that we didn't agree with. Sometimes I used to complain to him about my mother and he would try to explain her reactions. I think this has taught me how to deal with conflicts and reach a compromise.

Something that I learnt from both my parents was the importance of having respect for other people. I remember one day when we were travelling on a bus and I sat down while other people were standing. She shouted at me 'Get up immediately! You have young legs and you don't need to sit down'. At the time I felt very embarrassed about being told off in public, but now I understand. I think children nowadays have lost that respect and it really irritates me if I see children sitting down while older people are standing.

One area in which we had a lot of rules was table manners. For example, we weren't allowed to start our meal until the oldest person had started. We had to say 'thank you' when our food was served, and eat everything on our plates before we could leave the table. We couldn't make any noise, such as smacking our lips, burping, or stirring our tea or coffee loudly. Worse than that, we were only allowed to have sweets at the weekend, as a special treat if we had been good.

Although my upbringing was perhaps a bit strict compared with modern children, I'm very grateful to my parents for giving me a clear direction in life. Even though I was sometimes punished, I think it has made me a better person. In my view, children need clear rules, but more than that they need to learn how to get on with other people and realise they are not the centre of the world.

2 Choose the correct option.

1 Paulina's parents had *strict / lenient / different* opinions about bringing up children.
2 Her father *often / sometimes / never* used to get angry with her.
3 She found the differences between her parents *confusing / annoying / helpful*.
4 Her family were *relaxed / strict / lenient* about table manners.
5 She *had to / didn't have to / was allowed to* eat everything on her plate.
6 She was *often / sometimes / never* allowed to eat sweets.
7 She thinks punishment *spoiled / helped / damaged* her.
8 She particularly appreciated the *rules / guidelines / treats* her parents gave her.

Writing skills: writing an article for a magazine or website

A Features of a good article

1 Tick (✔) the four features that you think are the most important in a magazine article.

1 An attention-grabbing title.
2 An interesting first line.
3 Colourful or descriptive language.
4 Questions to make the reader think.
5 A style that is neither too formal nor too informal.
6 Personal experiences.
7 Clear and strong opinions.
8 A thought-provoking ending.

2 Work in pairs and discuss your ideas. To what extent has Paulina included these features in her article?

B Giving examples

> Another way to make an article more interesting is to give clear, concrete examples

a ***In the case of*** my upbringing, it was neither completely strict, nor completely lenient.
b ***Take*** my own upbringing, ***for example***. It was neither very strict nor very lenient.
c One area in which we had a lot of rules was table manners. ***For example***, we weren't allowed to start our meal until the oldest person had started.
d We couldn't make any noise, ***such as*** smacking our lips.

1 In which sentences in the examples on page 64 could you use *like* and *for instance*?

2 Complete the sentences with one of the expressions on page 64.

1 My mother was very strict about our studies. _____, we had to do our homework every afternoon before our meal.
2 We sometimes got into trouble because we disobeyed the rules. _____ the day we played football with our friend Martin, for instance.
3 Some parents don't care about what their children do. _____ my father, it was very different.
4 We weren't allowed to eat junk food _____ chocolate or crisps.

Preparing to write

1 Read *Talking about your upbringing* below. Complete the sentences so that they are true for you.

2 Read your sentences to a partner, and ask and answer questions about them.

3 Together, think of a good title for articles describing each of your experiences.

Talking about your upbringing

- My upbringing was *quite strict / very strict / lenient*
- My parents had *clear / a lot of / some* rules about …
- I *wasn't allowed to* …
- I *couldn't* …
- I *had to* …
- Something that I learned from my parents was …
- I'm grateful to my parents for …
- I think this has taught me how to …

Writing

Use your notes and discussion to write an article about your upbringing. Include some of the features of a good article.

Study skills

Developing your speaking skills

Speaking consists of different skills:

fluency — Speaking — range of vocabulary and grammar
accuracy — pronunciation

1 Read the statements about speaking problems. Match each statement to one of the skills above.

1 I speak too slowly because I am translating from my language.
2 Sometimes people can't understand my accent.
3 I know the rule when people correct me but I still make the same mistakes.
4 I often pause to think about what I want to say.
5 Sometimes I feel frustrated because I can't express my ideas in detail.
6 I wish I sounded more like a native speaker.
7 I've never learned the rules so my grammar is often incorrect.
8 I only know one way to make requests. I need to know more, for different situations.

Work in pairs and discuss your ideas. Do you share any of these problems? Which of the skills do you need to improve most?

2 Here are some strategies for improving speaking. Which skill or skills do you think each one develops?

- ★ Record yourself speaking. Play the recording and note your errors. Then do the task again.
- ★ Do the same as above, but this time plan more varied words and grammatical structures.
- ★ Work with a pronunciation website or CD.
- ★ Ask your partner or friends to correct you.
- ★ Rehearse conversations in English in your head.
- ★ Before having a conversation, plan words and phrases that you could use.
- ★ Listen to a recording by a native speaker and copy their pronunciation. Then practise speaking as you listen to the recording.
- ★ Memorise dialogues and useful conversation expressions.

3 Work in pairs. Choose two strategies to try out.

Power & Money

Reading and Pronunciation

1 Look at the pictures of two famous public speakers. Do you know who these people are? Can you think of any others?

2 Read *Quote me on that!* and match the halves of famous quotations. Which ones do you like most?

3 🔊 2.01–2.08 Listen to the quotations. Pay attention to:

- the stressed words (the words in large type)
- the pause between each part of the quote
- the intonation

Repeat the quotations.

4 Practise saying the ones you like out loud.

Quote me on that!

1 Ask me my three main priorities for government, and I tell you: ... *b*

2 Being powerful is like being a lady. *f*

3 Hate the sin ... *d*

4 I was born in the slum, ... *h*

5 If you talk to a man in a language he understands, that goes to his head. *g*

6 In the end we will remember not the words of our enemies ... *c*

7 We do these things not because they are easy ...

8 Where we are met with cynicism, and doubt, and those who tell us that we can't ... *a*

a we will respond with that timeless creed that sums up the spirit of a people: yes, we can. **Barack Obama**

b education, education, education. **Tony Blair**

c but the silence of our friends. **Martin Luther King**

d love the sinner. **Mahatma Gandhi**

e but because they are hard. **John F Kennedy**

f If you have to tell people you are, you aren't. **Margaret Thatcher**

g If you talk to him in his language, that goes to his heart. **Nelson Mandela**

h but the slum was not born in me. **Jesse Jackson**

Listening and Speaking

1 Read the introduction to a talk. What is it about?

> **The POWER of Words**
> How do successful people get things done? The power of words might be part of the answer. In this short presentation I will examine what rhetoric is and the use of three main rhetorical techniques that are frequently used to make a message more powerful.

2 🔊 2.09 Listen to the first part of the talk and answer the questions.

1 What is rhetoric? Why was it important?
2 Is rhetoric still a popular subject? *No*
3 Why does Professor Atkinson think it is still important? *Alive + well today Essential part of good p... spee...*
4 How is the word 'claptrap' used in rhetoric? *To get applause*
5 How does the speaker explain that these techniques are not difficult? *people already the without thinki...*

3 🔊 2.10 Listen to the second part of the talk. What are the three main techniques the speaker mentions?

4 Look back at the quotations in Reading and Pronunciation exercise 2. Find examples of the three rhetorical techniques referred to in the listening.

5 Decide how much you agree with the sentences. Then discuss in pairs.

- Speaking in public is very difficult.
- Good speakers manipulate their audience with rhetorical techniques.
- There are many good public speakers in my country.
- People should learn how to speak in public.

Grammar

1 Identify the passive form in each of these sentences from the presentation. How is the passive formed?

> *In ancient Greece people in formal education were taught rhetoric and little else. It was considered of great importance. People were thought to be more powerful if they were able to employ good rhetoric. Nowadays, rhetoric is no longer widely taught. Claptraps are techniques that are used by politicians to prompt applause.*

2 Look at these four short texts. Change the lines in italics to the passive voice. Omit *by* + agent if it isn't necessary.

1 *People view him as one of the most powerful speakers of modern times.* From the moment Barack Obama began his race to become America's president *people noticed his way with words.* On the night of November 4th, 2008 *the people of the United States elected Obama as President.* That night he made one of the most famous speeches in modern history, the famous 'Yes we can' speech.

2 We are sorry to announce that *the management has made the decision* to cut five positions this year. This was not by choice, but by necessity. These are difficult times. In addition, *we will not replace staff who leave.*

3 Last night *someone broke into the office.* We think it was a person who works here. *This person stole some office equipment,* and *he or she broke a window. Our insurance company will cover the costs,* but *we are going to open an internal investigation.*

4 *We made mistakes. We did not listen to you. Something hurt people's feelings.* For these reasons, we apologise. *We will not repeat this situation.*

3 Complete the rules about using the passive. Use the examples in exercise 1 to help you.

- use the passive when the action or object of the action is ~~more / less~~ **more** important than the subject
- use the passive ~~to take~~ / *avoid* responsibility
- use the passive when the *subject* / ~~object~~ is known to everyone
- use the passive when the *subject* / ~~object~~ is unknown
- use *by* / ~~for~~ + agent when we want to mention the agent

G **Grammar focus** – explanation & more practice of the passive voice on page 142

Writing and Speaking

1 You are going to prepare and deliver a part of a very short speech. Turn to page 128 and follow the instructions.

2 When you are finished, decide which words you want to stress most and where you are going to pause. Practise saying your speech to yourself and try to learn it by heart.

3 Work in small groups. Give each other your speeches. How can you improve the way you say them?

Power & Money

Part 2

Speaking & Grammar
Causative *have* / *get*

Reading
Masters of the Universe?

Vocabulary
Adverb phrases

Speaking and Grammar

1 Work in pairs. Read the sentences and discuss the questions.

> *He gets his breakfast and newspaper brought to him in bed.*
> *He has his clothes ironed every morning.*
> *He has his other meals cooked for him.*
> *He has his house cleaned three times a week.*

- How would you describe a person like this?
- Do you know anyone like this?

> We **had / got** the house repainted. (*a painter did it for us*)

- use the structure *have / get* + something + past participle to talk about when someone else does something for us or to us

2 Change the sentences so they have the same meaning.

1 Someone washes his car.
2 Someone guards his house.
3 Someone waters his garden.
4 Someone takes his children to school.
5 Someone dry-cleans his shirts every day.
6 Someone cleans his shoes.

3 Discuss in pairs. Which of these things would you like to have done for you? What other things would you like to have done for you? Would this make you happy?

G **Grammar focus** – explanation & more
practice of *have / get* on page 142

Reading

1 Read about a book with a character like the man in Speaking and Grammar. Read *The Masters of the Universe?* and answer the questions. *Plastic dolls / Bankers*

1 What are the Masters of the Universe?
2 Do you think the man is happy? Why or why not?

2 Read the text and decide if these sentences are T (true) or F (false). Then underline the parts of the text that helped you decide.

1 The Masters of the Universe live in America. *F Eternia*
2 There was a comic of the Masters of the Universe. *T*
3 Tom Wolfe wrote a book about the Masters of the Universe. *F Wrote about a banker*
4 Sherman McCoy makes $50,000 with one phone call. *T*
5 Sherman McCoy believes he and a few others have become new Masters of the Universe. *T*
6 The Wall Street bankers struggled with crime-ridden neighbourhoods. *F*

3 Find the bold words in the text. Then answer the questions. Use a dictionary to help you.

1 If you do something **in your euphoria** are you excited or bored?
2 Does a **crime-ridden** neighbourhood have a lot of crime or has it got rid of crime?
3 Is something that is **sumptuous** expensive or cheap?
4 Is a **handful** of people a lot of people or only a few?

The Masters of the Universe?

The Masters of the Universe were originally a set of brightly-coloured plastic dolls for children made by an American toy company in the 1980s. Led by the blond, muscled He-Man, the Masters of the Universe went about their lives on the planet *Eternia* fighting their arch-enemy and saving humanity from destruction. At their most popular, the franchise included toys, comics, television shows and even two feature-length films about the fantastical heroes.

In 1987 the American novelist and journalist Tom Wolfe wrote a book called *The Bonfire of the Vanities*. It told the story of a powerful New York banker named Sherman McCoy. McCoy is a multi-millionaire who makes a fortune buying and selling bonds on Wall Street, the financial capital of the United States. One day at home, after making a $50,000 commission by making one phone call, he sees his daughter's Masters of the Universe toys. In his euphoria, he thinks to himself that he and a handful of other bankers have become just that – masters of the universe. Their power has no limits.

The expression quickly entered popular culture as a reference to the real men and women who worked on Wall Street in the late 1980s and 1990s and were living the high-life. While the rest of New York's inhabitants struggled with unemployment and crime-ridden neighbourhoods, the Masters of the Universe had it all: large salaries and million-dollar bonuses, sumptuous penthouse apartments, chauffeur-driven cars and a luxury lifestyle. But how long could it last?

Vocabulary

1 Put the words in the box into categories a–c below.

a words that have a similar meaning to *naturally*
b words that have a similar meaning to *unexpectedly*
c words that have a similar meaning to *very unexpectedly and surprisingly*.

Miraculously c Needless to say a
Obviously a Oddly b Of course a
Remarkably c Strangely b

Glossary

bond (*noun*) – a document given to someone who invests money in a government or company, promising to pay back the money with interest

commission (*noun*) – an extra amount of money that you have to pay to a bank or other organization when they provide a service for you

2 Choose the correct option to complete the text.

The Bonfire of the Vanities was a bestseller in the United States. Many felt that it perfectly represented the spirit of Wall Street and the greed of the 1980s.

(1) *Oddly / Needless to say*, many Wall Street bankers were not insulted by the book. In fact, they were proud of the term 'Masters of the Universe' and of the power that they held.

(2) *Obviously / Remarkably* this situation and attitude continued for twenty years after the publication of the *Bonfire of the Vanities*, even as more and more people were getting poorer.

(3) *Of course / Miraculously*, everything changed in the stock market crash of 2008, in large part because of the reckless attitude of the same bankers. In the words of the *Financial Times*, the Masters of the Universe became 'the new villains in town'.

(4) *Needless to say / Strangely*, fewer young people were attracted to banking after this.

3 Choose two of the questions below and write your answer in two or three sentences. Use one of the adverbs in exercise 1 in your answer.

- Do you think power corrupts people?
- Do bankers hold too much power in today's society?
- 'Behind every powerful man is a powerful woman.' Is this true?

Tom Wolfe is a journalist and novelist. He was born in Virginia, USA in 1931. Power is a recurring theme in his books.

The Bonfire of the Vanities was Tom Wolfe's first novel. It tells the story of the rise and fall of Wall Street banker Sherman McCoy.

Part 3

Reading
*Ten facts about ...
lotteries*

Grammar
quite

Writing
Problem-solving

Reading

1 Choose two of these questions to ask and answer with a partner.

- How many lotteries do you know about in your country?
- Do you know countries where lotteries are popular?
- What do you think about lotteries?
- Would you ever spend money on a lottery?

2 Read *Ten facts about ... lotteries*. Which facts do you find most interesting?

3 The facts below come from three different sources:

a an encyclopaedia article about lotteries

b a business article about the benefits of lotteries.

c a website about gambling addiction and the dangers of lotteries

Read the facts again and decide which fact probably came from which source.

4 Do you think lotteries are a good or a bad thing? Why? Tell a partner.

Ten facts about ...
lotteries

1 The concept of a lottery goes back to ancient times. There were recorded examples of lotteries in ancient China, Greece and Roman societies. In Ancient Rome, lotteries were organised to raise money for city repairs and were used quite often as entertainment at dinner parties. *encyclopaedia*

2 The English word *lottery* comes from the Dutch word *loterij*, which is derived from the Dutch word *lot* meaning *fate*. The *staatsloterij*, the lottery of the Dutch state, is the oldest lottery still running. *encyclopaedia*

3 The majority of modern lotteries are run by governments who use the money for various projects. They are a form of voluntary tax. *business*

4 The national lottery of Britain has created quite a number of millionaires (some say over 1,500), and on average three people win a prize almost every second. *business*

5 Contrary to what most people believe, many very large lottery prizes are not given in one big payment. This is especially the case in the United States, where winners have the choice of an annual payment or a lump sum. The lump sum can often be quite low, or at least lower than the advertised jackpot. *encyclopaedia*

6 Lotteries exploit poor people. Families with very low incomes often spend quite a lot more on the lottery than those with high incomes. Sales of lottery tickets also go up in difficult economic times. *addiction website*

7 It is generally believed that Spain's *El Gordo* Christmas lottery is the world's largest lottery. The winning number is printed on multiple tickets, which are then sold in fractions, meaning that *El Gordo* prizes are usually split between the multiple winners. *encyclopaedia*

8 The chances of winning a lottery are very small. A lottery ticket buyer (in the US) is 5 times more likely to be eaten by a shark, 6,000 times more likely to be hit by a car and 500,000 times more likely to die in an airline crash. *addiction webs*

9 Lottery projects have been quite valuable as a source of funds for many government projects. In Britain the first decade of the modern national lottery showed many positive results. It funded major projects in the arts, and money from lotteries was used to help various health and education projects. *business*

10 A lottery is a form of gambling. All experts agree that gambling is addictive, so lotteries are also addictive. *addiction website*

Grammar

1 Find all the examples of *quite* in the reading text about lotteries. What words come after *quite*? adjective/noun

> ... *were used* **quite** *often as entertainment* ...
> ... *created* **quite** *a number of millionaires* ...
>
> *Quite* can have different meanings:
> - it means *fairly* when in front of gradable adjectives or adverbs. *It's quite difficult to win the lottery.* (it's difficult to an extent)
> - it means *to some degree* in front of some verbs. *I quite like them.* (I like them to a degree)
> - it means *totally* in front of some verbs. *I quite agree.* (I totally agree)
> - in front of ungradable adjectives, *quite* means *completely*. *It's quite impossible to predict the winning number.* (it's completely impossible)
> - in American English, *quite* means *very*. *He is quite rich.* (he is very rich)
> - *quite* can also be used in front of quantifiers, e.g. *a lot, a bit, some* to emphasise the amount. *He won quite a bit on the lottery.* (more than a bit)

2 The word *quite* has been taken out of these sentences. Insert it in the most suitable place.

1 A typical American can spend a lot of money on lotteries, about $100 a year – more than on prescription drugs and reading material.
2 I don't understand why people buy lottery tickets.
3 The day of the Spanish lottery is amazing. Everything stops for the draw.
4 It's rare for there to be scandals in modern lotteries.

3 Look at these statements about money. Choose three sentences and for each highlighted term, write the sum of money *you* think is appropriate.

I had a coffee at that new café on the corner and it was really quite cheap. _____
They won quite a large sum of money on the lottery. _____
When he retired, his colleagues gave him quite an expensive watch. _____
He's only ten years old, but he already gets quite a lot of pocket money. _____
I work in a shop and the wages are quite normal for my country. _____

4 Compare your answers with a partner. Where do you agree? Where do you disagree?

Ⓖ **Grammar focus** – explanation & more practice of *quite* on page 142

Writing

1 Work in pairs. Choose **one** of the situations below.

A You are good friends. A: you need some money for a trip you need to make to another country. Explain the situation to B and ask him/her to lend you the money.

B You are from the same family. You have discovered that you have both inherited a large sum of money from a distant relative. How are you going to divide the money? How are you going to spend it?

C You work in the same office. You both bought a lottery ticket together. The ticket was a winning ticket but B lost the ticket. A: you don't believe him/her. B: explain what happened.

2 Now turn to page 128 and follow the instructions.

Power & Money

Part 4

Reading

*Economics for Everyone:
A Short Guide to the
Economics of Capitalism*

Extend your vocabulary
Metaphors: money

Vocabulary
Collocations

Reading

1 Work in pairs. Brainstorm as many words connected to money as you can in five minutes. Then compare your list with another pair.

2 Read the following first line from a book called *Economics for Everyone: A Short Guide to the Economics of Capitalism*. Do you agree with the author? Do you think he agrees with his second statement? What do you think his argument will be?

> Most people think economics is a technical, confusing, and even mysterious subject. It's a field best left to the experts: namely, the economists.

3 Read the rest of the text on page 73 and check your answer. What does the author suggest we do? *We should listen more to other professions / and less to economists*

4 Read the text again. Find the following:

1 Two arguments that everybody should have something to say about economics.
2 Six examples of why the author thinks economists are not to be trusted.

5 The author uses stronger language to make his points. How does he express the following ideas?

1 Economists use technical jargon.
2 Economists try to explain theories which are difficult for people to understand.
3 Economists think they know more than other people.

6 Do you agree with the author? Do you know any economists?

Extend your vocabulary – metaphors: money

In English, money is often viewed as food which gets eaten or shared. Money is also seen as a liquid.

1 Look at the sentences below. What has happened to the money in each one?

1 Buying a car <u>took a huge chunk out of</u> our savings.
2 The university fees <u>swallowed up</u> most of my grant.
3 The company made large profits and the workers <u>wanted a slice of the pie</u>.
4 The government is <u>pouring money</u> into education.
5 We are having <u>a problem with cash flow</u>.
6 They <u>splashed out</u> on a new television.
7 You're buying a new car? That's just <u>pouring money down the drain</u>.

2 Choose two of these expressions and make your own sentences.

Economics for Everyone

In reality, economics should be quite straightforward. After all, economics is simply about how we work. What we produce. And how we distribute and ultimately use what we've produced. Economics is about who does what, who gets what, and what they do with it.

At that simplest, grass-roots level, we all know something about the economy. And so we should all have something to say about economics.

Moreover, because we interact, cooperate, and clash with each other in the economy, economics is a social subject. It's not just technical, concrete forces like technology and productivity that matter. It's also the interactions and relationships between people that make the economy go around.

■ ■ ■

Unfortunately, in my view, most professional economists don't think about economics in this common-sense, grass-roots context. To the contrary, they tend to adopt a rather superior attitude in their dealings with the untrained masses. They invoke complicated technical mumbo-jumbo – usually utterly unnecessary to their arguments – to make their case. They claim to know what's good for the people, even better than the people themselves do. They take great pleasure in expounding theories that are counter-intuitive and puzzling to the rest of us. They present themselves as interpreters of a mysterious realm which average people cannot hope to comprehend. And since they study things

that are measured in billions or even trillions of dollars, their sense of importance grows – in their own eyes, and in others.

That's why we see economists on the television news every night. We almost never see anthropologists, biologists, social workers, nutritionists, or architects on the nightly news. Perhaps we should hear more from those other professions, and less from the economists. Their advice might actually be more important to our long-term economic well-being than that of the economists.

Vocabulary

1 Match the two sentence halves.

1 Have you got any **loose**
2 Ok, let's **settle**
3 They inherited a **small**
4 My parents gave me some extra **pocket**
5 This part of the country has always been **desperately**
6 After her life story was made into a film she became **extremely**

a **fortune** when their grandfather died.
b **poor**. They have nothing.
c **rich** and famous.
d **change**? I've only got large notes.
e **the bill**. I have to get back to work.
f **money** for the weekend.

2 Replace the words in exercise 1 numbers 1–6 with the words in the box below so the phrases have the same meaning.

considerable	dirt	filthy	pay	spare
spending				

3 Think of at least four questions about money that you could ask a partner. Include one collocation from above for each question. Then ask another student your questions.

Jim Stanford is the author of *Economics for Everyone: A Short Guide to the Economics of Capitalism.* He is one of Canada's best-known economists, who writes regular columns for several Canadian newspapers.

a b c d

Warm up

1 Look at the pictures. What favours are these people doing for their friends, neighbours and colleagues? Make a list of other common favours you might ask somebody to do?

2 Work in pairs. Ask and answer the questions.

1 Do you feel comfortable asking favours? How do you feel when someone asks you for a favour?

2 When was the last time you asked somebody to do you a favour? What was it?

3 When was the last time somebody asked you to do them a favour? What was it? Did you grant the favour or did you have to refuse it?

Listening

1 🔊 2.11–2.14 Listen to the four conversations. For each conversation, note down:

* what you think the relationship between the people is (friends, family, neighbours etc)
* where they are
* what favour is being asked

2 Listen again. How does the person asked react? Does he / she grant or refuse the favour?

Language focus: asking for a favour

1 Look at these three ways of asking for a favour. Which is the most direct?

I was wondering if you could help me with something?
Can you do me a favour?
Do you think I could borrow …?

2 Complete the table with the phrases in the box.

Since you put it that way …
Go on then.
Sorry, I'm afraid I can't.
Sure, no problem.
Well, perhaps in that case…
Yes, of course.
Yes, I can do that.
I'm really sorry but …

Granting a favour	Refusing a favour

Speaking

Work with a partner. Take it in turns to role-play asking for a favour and giving a reply.

* as two friends
* as two acquaintances or colleagues

Use your list of favours from Warm up exercise 1 and expressions from Language focus exercises 1 and 2.

Global voices

Warm up

1 Look at these sayings about money. Have you heard them before? Do you know what they mean? Do you think they are true or useful?

1 Money doesn't grow on trees.
2 Take care of the pennies and the pounds will take care of themselves.
3 Money is the root of all evil.
4 Money talks.
5 A fool and his money are soon parted.
6 Money isn't everything.

2 Tell the class if any of these sayings translate into similar sayings in your language.

Listening

1 🔊 2.15–2.20 Listen to people describing how their parents taught them about money. Who talks about …

1 saving money *Magdi*
2 spending money *Ahmet/Mieke Douglas*
3 borrowing money *Eamon*
4 the importance of money *Isadora (but indirectly all)*

Ahmet, Turkey *learnt by himself at boarding school*
Eamon, Ireland *never borrow money*
Mieke, Belgium *pocket money (limited)*
Magdi, Sudan *take care of pennies and pounds...*
Isidora, Greece *Money isn't the most important thing*
Douglas, Scotland ———

2 Listen again and answer the questions.

1 Which speakers learned indirectly about money, through actions rather than words? How?
2 Can you match any of the sayings in Warm up exercise 1 to any of the speakers?

Language focus: substituting lists

1 Look at the examples from the listening. The phrases in bold are used in spoken English to substitute for items on lists. Do they refer to specific or <u>unspecific items</u>?

1 I had to buy the things I wanted with my pocket money and if I didn't have enough, I had to get a holiday job **or whatever**.
2 I had to learn by myself how to spend my time, how to allocate my money to different hobbies, **that sort of thing**.

2 Decide which of the phrases below can be used in a similar way to the phrases in exercise 1.

in that way
something like that ✓
or whatnot ✓
and so on ✓
now and again
and other things ✓
or so
stuff like that ✓

3 Tell your partner about the things below. Say two or three things and use a phrase in exercise 2 to substitute for other items on the list.

- what is in your bag
- what sports you do
- what food you like
- what personality traits annoy you

Speaking

Work with a partner. Tell your partner how you learned about money. What did your parents tell you about money? What advice did they give you? What habits or experiences as a child helped you deal with money?

Ahmet, Turkey   Eamon, Ireland   Mieke, Belgium   Magdi, Sudan   Isidora, Greece   Douglas, Scotland

Writing a report (2)

Reading

1 Read Aleixandre's report on the financial situation of Brazil. What is his opinion?

a   There is a deep financial crisis in the country.

b   There are problems, but also advantages.

c   Most people have few financial problems.

2 Find evidence in the text to support these statements.

1   Some Brazilians have a lot of money, and some have very little.

2   The economy in Brazil is becoming stronger.

3   High inflation caused an increase in consumer spending.

4   Buying food is not a problem for most Brazilians.

5   Most consumer goods are expensive in Brazil.

6   The majority of people do not earn a lot of money.

7   It can be extremely expensive to buy goods on credit.

8   Many Brazilians owe money to banks or credit card companies.

3 Which of the facts in the report are true for your country?

Writing skills: giving reasons and describing consequences

reason   consequence
Charges on credit cards are about 12% each month, so once you are in debt it is hard to get out.

1 Read the report again. Complete the statements with words and phrases from the box.

as a result	as	consequently	since	so

1   Until very recently, the inflation rate in Brazil was extremely high. _____, Brazilians stopped saving money.

2   Brazil is the fifth largest country in the world in terms of area, _____ our food production is plentiful. _____, the cost of food is very low.

3   _____ the majority of Brazilians do not have a high income, they usually need help from a bank.

4   _____ most Brazilians are not used to saving money, many of them end up in debt.

Brazil is the richest South American country in terms of GDP and it is currently one of the fastest growing economies in the world. However, there is a huge gap between the rich and the poor, and the financial situation is not easy even for ordinary Brazilians. In particular, we have problems related to consumer spending, bank interest rates, and debt.

Until very recently, the inflation rate in Brazil was extremely high (sometimes 80% per month). As a result, Brazilians stopped saving money under their mattresses and started investing in consumer goods. Now, inflation is under control and the cost of living is generally not too high, but we have acquired a habit of spending and a desire for a higher standard of living.

Brazil is the fifth largest country in the world in terms of area, and so our food production is plentiful. Consequently, the cost of food is very low and most people can afford to buy enough to eat. However, the cost of consumer goods is extremely high. New cars, in particular, are very expensive and it is not easy to find cheap second-hand cars.

As the majority of Brazilians do not have a high income, they usually need help from a bank in order to fulfil their consumerist dreams. From then on, for people who take out a loan, it is the start of a long and complicated journey to meet their financial obligations. To take one example, the interest on a loan to buy a new car could be, on average, about 1.5% per month. And it is even worse when people take out a 100% loan to buy an item. In some cases, they could end up paying three times the original price of the goods.

Bank interest rates are extremely high for borrowers, but very low for savers. Since most Brazilians are not used to saving money, many of them end up in debt. Moreover, credit card charges are about 12% each month, so once you are in debt it is hard to get out. However, if you take care of your finances and spend prudently, you can generally live very well in Brazil.

2 Answer the questions.

1 Which words or phrases in exercise 1 are used to **join** sentences?
2 Which words or phrases could be replaced by ...
   a *because*?   b *because of this*?

3 Match the reasons with the consequences.

1 Since the price of petrol is extremely high,
2 There is little agricultural land in my country. As a result,
3 As it is very easy to take out loans,
4 The economy in my country is very strong. Because of this,
5 Young people cannot afford to buy a house, and so

a many of them end up living with their parents.
b we enjoy a high standard of living.
c many people cannot afford to run a car.
d a lot of people end up in debt.
e we have to import a lot of food.

Preparing to write

1 Read *Describing finance*. Make notes on the situation in your country.

2 Work in pairs. Exchange information and ideas about the financial situation in your country, explaining reasons and consequences. Talk about some of the following:

- The cost of living and prices of goods.
- Spending patterns.
- Borrowing, debt and credit cards.
- Banks and saving.
- Other interesting facts.

Describing Finance

- The *cost of living / price of food / inflation rate* is *high /low*
- Most people *can / cannot* afford to buy *a house / consumer goods*
- There is a *huge / large / small* gap between the rich and the poor
- Most people have a *high / low* standard of living and a *high / low* income
- *Salaries / Bank interest rates / Credit card charges* are *high / low*
- Many people *take out a loan / end up in debt*

Writing

Write a report on how people in your country manage their finances, based on your discussion with your partner.

Recording and learning vocabulary

1 Work in pairs and discuss the questions. Then read the information in the box.

- Where and how do you normally record vocabulary?
- What information do you record?

When you record a word in your vocabulary notebook, you can include different information. For example:

- definition
- pronunciation
- grammar
- register
- translation
- example sentence
- connotation
- derivatives
- collocations and expressions
- compounds

2 Look at the spidergram for *power*. Which of the information listed above is included?

phonetic spelling of *power* /paʊə/
力
power shower, power cut, power station
Power
The government has too much power
countable or uncountable noun
have power over s.o., be in power, take power
powerful (adj), powerless (adj), empower (vb)

3 Read about different ways to remember vocabulary. Put a tick (✔) next to ones you have tried, and an arrow (→) next to ones you would like to try.

- ★ When you want to learn a new word or expression, write it in a true sentence about you.
- ★ Read through your vocabulary notebook every evening, and again at the end of each week and each month.
- ★ Take out your notebook and read it at different times of the day (e.g. on the bus, in a queue).
- ★ Test yourself by making vocabulary cards with a word or expression on one side and information (e.g. a translation or definition) on the other.
- ★ Put vocabulary cards in different places in your house (e.g. by your bed or computer).
- ★ Invent stories in your head to link words you have learned recently.
- ★ Make links between new words and words in your language (e.g. with a similar pronunciation or spelling).

4 In small groups, share ideas for learning vocabulary that you have used.

Rhyme & Reason

Reading and Pronunciation

1 Read the information about the novel *The Golden Gate*. What is special about it? What would be the challenges of writing a novel in this way?

> *The Golden Gate* is a novel in 690 verses by Vikram Seth. The novel follows the relationships of a group of young people who live in California. Each verse has fourteen lines and the same rhyming scheme and rhythm.

2 🔊 2.21 Read and listen to the three verses on page 79 and answer the questions. Explain your answers with examples from the text.

1 Who are the two people? Do they know each other?
2 Where are they? What are they doing there?
3 How do they feel about the meeting?
4 What do they think of each other?

3 Listen to the three verses again. Underline the pairs of rhyming words in each verse.

4 Work in pairs. Take turns to read out the pairs of rhymes.

Waiting, dating. Trieste, …

Check that you understand all the words.

5 Write down the rhyming scheme (the lines that rhyme with each other) in each verse. Use a new letter for each new rhyme. Start like this:

A, B, A, B, C, C, …

6 Work in groups of three. Read out one verse each, paying attention to the rhymes but also to the meaning and rhythm of the verses.

7 Answer the questions.

- Do you ever read poetry? Do you have a favourite poet?
- Can you recite any poetry by heart?
- Who are the most famous poets in your country? Are they classical or contemporary poets?
- What sort of role does poetry play in your country?

Extend your vocabulary – ways of saying *beautiful*

good-looking *for men and women who are nice to look at*

attractive *for men and women who are good-looking and who appeal to you, physically*
I find him/her very attractive.

beautiful, lovely *for children and (usually female) adults who are extremely good-looking*

handsome *(usually) for men who have strong, regular features*

pretty *for women and girls who are good-looking in an ordinary way; men and boys who are good-looking in a feminine way*
The band was just another bunch of pretty boys.

gorgeous *for men and women who are very attractive; beautiful children (rather informal)*
He looked absolutely gorgeous in a suit.

striking *for men and women who are attractive in an interesting or unusual way*

cute *for small, sweet children*
Ahh, isn't her little brother cute!
    for attractive men and women (informal)
Where did you find that cute guy?

1 Which words do Liz and John use to describe each other in the poem?

2 With a partner, look through the photos in this book. Can you find any photos which you would describe using these adjectives?

The Golden Gate

On Sunday morning, groomed and waiting,
John sits in the Cafe Trieste.
A canny veteran of blind dating,
(Twice bitten, once shy), it is best
To meet, he reckons, far from drama,
In daylight: less romantic, calmer,
And, if things should not turn out right,
Convenient for ready flight.

At noon, the meeting hour appointed,
A tall fresh-faced blonde enters, sees
The suited John. 'Excuse me, please …
(A little hesitant and disjointed) … Would
you be – John?' John smiles. 'Correct.
And you're Elizabeth, I suspect.'

'She's lovely,' John thinks, almost staring.
They shake hands. John's heart gives a lurch.
'Handsome all right, and what he's wearing
Suggests he's just returned from church …
Sound, solid, practical and active,'
Thinks Liz, 'I find him quite attractive.
Perhaps …' All this has been inferred
Before the first substantive word
Has passed between the two. John orders
A croissant and espresso; she
A sponge cake and a cup of tea.
They sit, but do not breach the borders
Of discourse till, at the same time,
They each break silence with, 'Well, I'm –'

Both stop, confused. Both start together:
'I'm sorry –' Each again stops dead.
They laugh. 'It hardly matters whether
You speak or I,' says John: 'I said
Or meant to say – I'm glad we're meeting.'
Liz quietly smiles, without completing
What she began. 'Not fair,' says John.
'Come clean. What was it now? Come on:
One confidence deserves another.'
'No need,' says Liz. 'You've said what I
Would have admitted in reply.'
They look, half smiling, at each other,
Half-puzzled as if to say,
I don't know why I feel this way.

Vocabulary and Pronunciation

1 Read the explanation of homophones. Which pairs of words below are **not** homophones?

> Homophones are words which have the same pronunciation but different spellings and different meanings.
> For example:
> piece, peace
> buy, bye
> sure, shore

1	flower, flour	5	close, clothes
2	you're, year	6	axe, acts
3	size, sighs	7	grown, groan
4	allowed, aloud	8	whole, hole

2 Find these words in *The Golden Gate* extract. What do they mean? Work with a partner. Say the words aloud and write a homophone for each word.

be	hour	fair	meet	passed
right	two	whether		

3 Write three sentences with a word or its homophone from exercise 2. In pairs, take it in turns to read a sentence. Your partner identifies the word and says which spelling and meaning the word has.

A: He asked me whether I was going to the party.
B: Whether with 'wh', meaning 'if'.

Writing

1 You are going to continue the story in *The Golden Gate* in an eight-line verse, starting like this:

John and Liz talk for hour upon hour, …

Brainstorm ideas about what could happen in the verse.

2 Now think of words which rhyme with your ideas.

3 Work in pairs or alone and write your verse. Use the same rhyme scheme as in the first eight lines of each verse in *The Golden Gate*.

4 Read your verse to a partner or another pair. Give your partner(s) feedback on their verse: is it interesting / sad / funny? Does it rhyme well and have a good rhythm?

Vikram Seth is an Indian poet, novelist, travel writer, biographer and children's writer who has lived in England, the US and China. He is best known for his epic novel *A Suitable Boy*.

Rhyme & Reason

Part 2

Vocabulary

1 Look at the adverts. Brainstorm possible slogans for each advert, in small groups.

2 Look at the advertising expressions in the box below. Which pairs are …

1 people who are affected by advertising?
2 words used to advertise something?
3 methods of advertising a product?
4 part of a product's identity?

brand name / logo	slogan / jingle
commercial / billboard	
consumers / target audience	

Puffin Biscuits, 1956

American Optical, 1959

3 Work in pairs. Take it in turns to explain the differences between each pair of words in exercise 2. Use a dictionary to help you.

4 Complete the explanation with words from exercise 2. Then tell the class your opinion of product placement.

> Product placement is paying a film or TV company to show a (1) _____ product or its (2) _____ in a film or TV programme or even in video games. It has been shown to be a very effective way to reach a particular (3) _____. Product placement, however, is controversial because it is a very hidden form of advertising – unlike watching (4) _____ on TV. (5) _____ are often unaware that they are the focus of an advertising campaign.

Listening

1 Work in pairs. Answer the questions.
• What memorable adverts have you seen recently? Why were they memorable?
• Can you remember any advertising slogans and what the brand name of the product was?

2 2.22 Listen to an advertising executive talking about what makes a good advertising slogan. Complete his tips.
1 Include the _brand name_ in the slogan.
2 Make the brand name _rhyme_ with another word in the slogan.
3 Use a rhyme but _without_ the brand name itself rhyming with another word.
4 Mention a key _benefit_ of the product.
5 Include something that sets the product apart from its _competitors_

3 Match the slogans below with the tips in exercise 2. Then listen again and check.

a **Taste. Not waist.**
(low-fat food products)

b **Savour the flavour of Belgium.**
(Belgium)

c **Everything you want from a store and a little bit more.**
(a supermarket)

d **The flavour of a Quaver is never known to waver.**
(Quaver crisps)

4 Look at your slogans from Vocabulary exercise 1: do they follow any of the tips in the listening? Try to write a slogan for one of these products with these tips in mind.

5 Can you think of any slogans for global brands that don't use rhyme? Why are they effective?

Grammar

1 Read the sentences from the listening. Complete the rules with the correct option in bold.

*Note, however, that when the brand name is not the rhyme, the slogan doesn't evoke **such** a strong identification with the product.*
*The slogan implies that other newspapers are not **such** exciting reads.*
*The slogan implies that because Safeway offers **so** many products and services, other supermarkets are simply not as good.*
*A slogan should be **so** memorable that it leaves the key message of a brand in the mind of the target audience.*

- the words *so* and *such* in these sentences have a similar meaning to **slightly / very**
- **so / such** is used with adjectives and adverbs
- **so / such** is used with quantifiers such as *much / many* and *little / few*
- **so / such** is used with noun phrases
- **that / to** is used with *so* and *such* to introduce a consequence or result

2 Rewrite these sentences using *so* or *such* so that the meaning stays the same.

1 This jingle is so annoying.
This is _____.

2 Advertising agencies come up with such weird ideas sometimes.
The ideas that advertising agencies come up with are _____.

3 Nobody could remember the slogan because it was too long.
The slogan was _____.

4 I saw a fantastic commercial yesterday. I couldn't stop thinking about it.
I saw _____.

3 Pick one of the topics in the box. Finish these sentences. Then read two or three sentences to a partner, explaining in more detail what you mean.

| advertising | health |
| materialism and greed | work-life balance |

1 Nowadays there are so many …
2 Unfortunately there are so few …
3 Some people are such …
4 Some people are so …
5 Our world is …

G **Grammar focus** – explanation & more practice of *so* / *such* on page 144

Speaking

Work in small groups. Turn to page 129 and follow the instructions.

Rhyme & Reason

Reading and Speaking

The *Last Word* is a website produced by the *New Scientist* magazine where people ask questions about everyday science. Other readers answer questions and vote for the best answers.

1 Look at the list of questions below. They were all asked on the *Last Word* website. Which do you think are the most interesting? Can you answer any of them? Tell the class.

1 Is it possible to drink snake venom and survive?
2 Why does skin squeak on glass?
3 Does anything eat wasps?
4 Why does a millipede have so many legs?
5 Why does soap go mouldy?
6 Why is monosodium glutamate so popular in Chinese and Japanese cooking?

2 Work in groups of three.
A: read the two texts on page 83.
B: turn to page 129 and read the texts.
C: turn to page 130 and read the texts.
Underline the key words or information in the questions and answers. Use a dictionary if necessary.

3 Tell your partners about the main information in the texts using your underlined key words and information. Ask each other questions if you don't understand.

Useful phrases

- I didn't quite understand what you meant by …
- Could you run through that one more time?
- Could you explain the bit about … more slowly?
- Hang on a minute, could you go over that again?
- So, in other words …

Grammar

1 Read the sentences from the reading texts. Complete the rules.

The book **says** snake venom **is** deadly.
My biology teacher **told** the class it **was** possible to drink snake venom and survive, because it **would be broken down** by the digestive process.
He wanted to know **why** his skin squeaked on the glass.
A colleague wondered **if** anything ate wasps.

We usually report **statements** with 'He said' or 'He told me'.
- when the reporting verb is in the _____ tense there are no changes to tenses
- when the reporting verb is in the _____ tense, some tenses change into the past and *will* changes into *would*

We usually report **questions** with 'She asked' or 'She wanted to know'.
- in questions with question words we use the question word and statement word order (not *do* or *did*)
- in *yes/no* questions we use _____ / *whether* + statement word order
- tenses in questions follow the same rules as in reported statements

2 Complete the sentences. Sometimes more than one answer is possible.

1 My mum told me that a neighbour's daughter _____ (*catch*) pneumonia because she _____ (*go*) outside with wet hair.
2 My dad told me that children who _____ (*sit*) too close to the TV _____ (*go*) blind.
3 My mum told me that if the wind _____ (*change*) when I _____ (*look*) angry, my face _____ (*stay*) like that.
4 My grandma told me that she _____ (*know*) a boy who _____ (*have*) such dirty ears that potatoes _____ (*grow*) in them.
5 My dad told me that chewing gum _____ (*stay*) in your stomach for seven years.

Puzzling questions and scientific reasons

I've been reading a book about poison and it has raised two questions. When I was at school my biology teacher told the class it was possible to drink snake venom and survive, because the venom is a protein and it would be broken down by the digestive process. Yet the book says snake venom is deadly if taken orally. Who is right? And is it possible to build up a tolerance to arsenic?
(Darren Fowkes)

I have watched a Zambian snake expert milk the venom from a live puff adder into a wine glass and drink it with no ill effects.

Snake venom is a complex mix of proteins, varying from species to species. Whatever the type, the venom has to enter the bloodstream to have an effect. That is why snakes bite with hypodermic-like fangs. If you swallow venom, provided you have no cuts in your gastrointestinal tract, the proteins will be broken down into harmless amino acids and absorbed, like the products of all protein digestion.

Arsenic is an entirely different matter. Being an element, it is not affected by the digestive process. It is poisonous in doses of as little as 65 milligrams and the poisoning can arise from a single large dose or from repeated small doses – for example, by inhaling arsenical gases or dust, or drinking contaminated water.

There have been various accounts of people acquiring tolerance to poison by repeated small doses. In the 2nd century BC, King Mithridates IV was reputed to have used this method so successfully that when he tried to commit suicide by swallowing poison after defeat in the Battle of Pompey he failed. However, the physiological basis for such a tolerance has never been ascertained.
(Alistair Scott)

I was stumped this morning. My three year old son was wiping something from the window with his bare hands and wanted to know why his skin squeaked on the glass. I didn't have a clue. Does anybody else?
(Dawn Hanna)

The skin does not make a noise. The glass on the other hand does. Any material, from paper to titanium, is capable of vibrating. Glass is no exception. In a pane of glass there are, as in any other material, definite harmonic series, and the type of rubbing will determine the 'note' or harmonic generated.

Not only fingers cause glass to squeak. When cleaning with detergent and newspaper, the glass will squeak louder and with finer pitch control. If you move the paper slowly, you will hear a moan that, on a large enough piece of glass, sets the whole pane vibrating. Move it more quickly and you will produce a tone guaranteed to set a mouse's teeth on edge.
(Martin James)

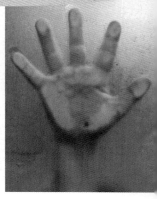

3 Did your parents tell you any similar things when you were a child?

4 You looked after your friend's daughter who asked lots of questions. Tell your friend what his daughter asked you.

G **Grammar focus** – explanation & more practice of reported statements & questions on page 144

How much does the sky weigh?

Where has the sun gone?

Did somebody paint the grass green?

Will my ears grow all my life?

Are you coming again tomorrow?

Why did my rabbit die?

Vocabulary

1 Look at these idioms from the text.
Do they refer to knowing or not knowing something?

I was stumped this morning.
I didn't have a clue.

2 Now look at these sentences. Mark them 'knowing' or 'not knowing'.

1 '**She's a mine of information** on many things, especially events in the area.'
2 'He practises constantly until he **knows** all the notes **by heart**.'
3 'I'm sick of being served by people who **don't have the faintest idea about** the products they're selling.'
4 'When it comes to food, he certainly **knows what he's talking about**.'
5 'Don't worry. She **knows** that area **like the back of her hand**.'
6 'Unfortunately **he's** completely **out of his depth** in front of a large audience.'

3 Who could the people in exercise 2 be talking about? Match the sentences to a person in the box.

> a chef   a keen musician   a mountain climbing guide
> a university lecturer   shop assistants   the local librarian

4 Work in pairs. Choose **four** of the expressions in exercise 2 and make sentences about yourselves or people you know.

Part 4

Reading and Speaking

1 Look at the picture on the left. Who do the objects belong to? Have you read books about this character? What do you know about him?

2 Read *Reasoning backwards* below. What is the meaning of the word *reason* in the quotation?

3 What is the speaker saying about reasoning? Are the statements true (*T*) or false (*F*)?

1 Most people reason backwards – they work out how things happened from a result.
2 Reasoning backwards can also be called reasoning 'analytically'.
3 Most people can work out what the result of certain events will be.

4 How do you solve puzzles or difficult situations: do you rely on reason or do you rely on your feelings or intuition? Does it depend on the situation? Give examples.

Listening

1 🔊 2.23 The quotation is from the novel *A Study in Scarlet*. Listen to an extract and choose the correct options.

1 Watson finds out about Sherlock Holmes's job *by reading about him in a newspaper / by reading an article written by Holmes.*
2 Watson thinks Holmes's ideas are *very impractical / very practical.*
3 Holmes is a private detective who takes on *cases from private customers / cases that the police and private detectives can't solve.*
4 At the beginning Watson thinks Holmes is *clever and admirable / intelligent but arrogant.*
5 Watson's opinion of Holmes changes because Holmes *correctly guesses Watson's previous occupation / correctly guesses the messenger's previous occupation.*

2 Read the sentences about Holmes below. Then listen again. Tick (✔) the special skills that Holmes says he has.

1 He rarely needs to visit the scene of the crime.
2 He has a good knowledge of crime cases.
3 He has a special intuition for crime.
4 He knows immediately when somebody is lying.
5 He has strong powers of observation.

3 Do you think detectives today solve crimes in the same way?

Reasoning backwards

'In solving a problem of this sort, the grand thing is to be able to **reason** backwards. That is a very useful accomplishment, and a very easy one, but people do not practise it much. In the everyday affairs of life it is more useful to **reason** forwards, and so the other comes to be neglected. There are fifty who can **reason** synthetically for one who can **reason** analytically … Let me see if I can make it clearer. Most people, if you describe a train of events to them, will tell you what the result would be. They can put those events together in their minds and argue from them that something will come to pass. There are few people, however, who, if you told them a result, would be able to evolve from their own inner consciousness what the steps were which led up to that result. This power is what I mean when I talk about **reasoning** backwards or analytically.'

The 56 Sherlock Holmes stories and 4 novels were written by Arthur Conan Doyle (1859–1930).

Grammar

1 Complete the sentences with the correct name: Holmes or Watson. Use the audioscript on page 155 to help you.

1 _____ complained that the article in the magazine was rubbish.

2 _____ accused the article writer of being a fraud.

3 _____ refused to believe that it was possible to tell somebody's job by looking at them.

4 _____ admitted he had written the article.

5 _____ claimed to be able to solve crimes without seeing the scene of the crime.

6 _____ insisted on knowing more about his friend's occupation.

7 _____ assured his colleague that he knew the profession of the man in the street.

8 _____ begged the messenger to tell them his former profession.

2 Underline the reporting verbs in the sentences in exercise 1 and look at the structures that follow them. Then work in pairs and add the verbs to the correct rule.

- + (*that*) + clause   _____
- + *to* + infinitive   _____
- + object + (*that*) + clause   _____
- + object + *to* + infinitive   _____
- + prep + -*ing*   _____
- + object + prep + -*ing*   _____

3 Look up these reporting verbs in your dictionary. Add them to the correct group in exercise 2. Some verbs can take more than one pattern.

agree   confirm   deny   mention
promise   remind

4 Read what a modern-day police inspector said at a press conference. Report what she said for a newspaper story using the reporting verbs from exercises 2 and 3. Different verbs are possible.

A serious crime took place this morning in the city centre.

We have been unable to trace the people involved so far.

We will do everything in our power to find them.

Remember that this incident took place in broad daylight in a busy street.

We would like to ask members of the public: please, please contact us if you saw anything unusual.

G Grammar focus – explanation & more practice of reporting verbs on page 144

Writing

1 You are going to write the newspaper article for the incident in Grammar exercise 4. First decide what sort of incident it was, who the people involved were and how it took place. Make detailed notes. Think of a good headline.

2 Write your article. Include your reported sentences from Grammar exercise 4 and report any other information you think the inspector might have mentioned. Swap articles with a partner and read your partner's article.

a b c d

Warm up

Look at the statements below with the class. What are they trying to say? Do you agree?

Advertising is legalised lying. (HG Wells)

Advertising is the very essence of democracy. (Anton Chekhov)

Listening

1 Look at the four adverts above. What are they about?

2 🔄 **2.24** Listen to two people. Which advert(s) are they talking about?

3 Listen again. Write down the arguments mentioned for and against these adverts.

Language focus: stating another point of view

1 🔄 **2.25** Listen to these sentences from the listening. Which of the phrases in the box are used in these sentences to state another point of view?

mind you though, ...   nevertheless ...
on the other hand ...   even so, ...   after all, ...
all the same, ...   still, ...

1 _____, they're pretty harmless compared to some adverts.
2 But _____, it's just taking advantage of people's insecurities.
3 OK, but _____, it's so hard to ignore them.

2 Listen again. Repeat the intonation of the phrases. Then repeat the whole sentence.

Speaking

1 Work in pairs. Choose **one** of the topics below (or think of your own topic) and together brainstorm a list for and against this topic.

computer games
speed limits and speed cameras
minimum wage
adoption
dress codes in the workplace
genetically modified foods
social networking sites

2 Now talk about your topic:
- State one of your arguments.
- Your partner gives another side of the argument using one of the phrases in Listening exercise 1.
- Introduce another argument in support of the first.
- Your partner replies with another counter argument – and so on.
- Do this as quickly as you can.

3 When you have finished choose another topic. Swap roles and do the same again.

Global English

The appeal of rhyme
by David Crystal

Rhyme is always noticed in English. You may even hear someone comment on it, if a rhyme unexpectedly appears in a conversation. 'Ooh, you're a poet and you didn't know it!' What's the reason for this?

Words rhyme when they end with the same vowel sounds (as in *me* and *tea*) or the same sequence of vowels and consonants (as in *cat* and *mat*, or *ready* and *steady*). In the English tradition, the beginning of the words must be different. It doesn't feel comfortable to say that *ready* rhymes with *ready*.

The longer the rhyming sequence, the more effective the rhyme. A popular word game is to find really long rhymes. Is there a word in English that rhymes with *nomination*? *Domination*. With *harmonious*? *Euphonious*. People also enjoy hunting down words that don't have any rhymes at all. For example, no word in English rhymes with *silver*.

We learn to love rhymes at a very early age. Some of our earliest linguistic memories are of nursery rhymes: *Jack and Jill / went up a hill* ... And we played with rhymes in the street, while bouncing a ball against a wall, or while skipping ('Three six nine, the goose drank wine ...').

So why are rhymes so effective in English? The answer is partly to do with the structure of the language. Words in English don't usually end with the same sounds. So when we do make them end in the same way, the effect is really noticeable.

Not all languages go in for rhyme. Languages which have a lot of inflections, such as Latin, avoid it, because in everyday speech many words rhyme already. 'My good friend' is *amicus bonus meus* (if a man) or *amica bona mea* (if a woman). Rhyming loses its appeal if everyone does it all the time. English is a language with very few inflections, so words don't naturally rhyme.

Rhymes are fun, and they sound nice, but they can be useful too. What do we do if we want to remember something really well? We rhyme. 'Thirty days hath September / April, June and November ...'

Glossary

inflection (*noun*) – a change in the basic form of a word to show something such as tense or number

Warm up

Look at the list of words below. Organise the words into three groups. How did you decide?

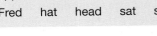

appeal   bread   cat   feel
Fred   hat   head   sat   steal

Reading

1 Read *The appeal of rhyme* and answer the questions.

1 How can words rhyme in English? Name two ways.
2 Why is rhyme so effective in English?
3 What kinds of languages avoid rhyme?

2 Read the text again. Are the sentences below true (*T*) or false (*F*) according to the author?

1 For a good rhyme in English, the beginning of the word must be the same.
2 Children use rhymes when they play games.
3 Similar sounds at the end of words are common in English.
4 A language with many inflections is fun to rhyme with.
5 Rhymes are fun but can cause problems when remembering things.

3 Cover the text. Look at the sentences below. Can you remember what the correct preposition is?

1 What's the reason *for / about* this?
2 People also enjoy hunting *up / down* words that don't have any rhymes at all.
3 And we played with rhymes (...) while bouncing a ball *at / against* a wall ...
4 Not all languages go *out / in* for rhyme.
5 Latin avoids rhyme because *in / for* everyday speech many words rhyme already.

4 How many words can you think of that rhyme with the following?

reader   cloud   sing   black   eat   nation

Speaking

Work in pairs. Choose **one** of the tasks below.

A Take the words in Reading exercise 3 and make them into a poem.

B Think of all the irregular verbs in English you know. Make a list of the past forms. Then organise these irregular verbs according to how they sound. Try to make a rhyme to remember this list.

Reading

1 Read Maxim's information sheet about his workplace and answer the questions.

1 Who do you think it is written for?
2 Do you think Pegasus is a small, medium-sized or large company? Why?

Welcome to Pegasus!
Here is some information to help familiarise you with the facilities.

Opening hours
The building is open between 8 a.m. and 6 p.m. (and 5 p.m. on Fridays). If you need to work outside these hours, you will need to make arrangements with Angela.

Transport
Unfortunately, there are no car parking facilities; however, there is a cycle rack just in front of the entrance where cyclists can lock their bikes.

Photocopier
To use the photocopier, you will need a personal code – please ask Martin for this. In order to save trees, please only make copies when strictly necessary, and make double-sided copies where possible. Put waste paper in the recycling bin. If the copier jams and you can't fix it, or if you run out of paper, see Martin.

Kitchen
There is a kettle in the kitchen for making tea or coffee; tea, coffee, sugar and biscuits are provided in the cupboard for staff to use. There is also a microwave which staff are welcome to use, and a fridge to store your own food and drink. Please label your food and throw it away if it starts to go off. N.B. Remember to wash and put away your dishes after use!

Leaving the building
If you are the last person to leave the building, please do the following:
• Make sure that all the windows are locked and the blinds are pulled down.
• Check that the computers and photocopier are switched off.
• Switch off the lights and close all the doors.
• Set the alarm – instructions for doing this are on the wall, next to the alarm.

Smoking
Please do not smoke anywhere in the building. Smoking is permitted in the yard behind the building, and there is a small shelter that smokers can use in the event of rain.

Thank you for your cooperation.

2 Answer the following questions from new staff at the company.

1 Is it possible to stay to work overtime in the evenings?
2 What should I do if the photocopier jams?
3 Are there recycling facilities?
4 Where can I park my car?
5 Do you provide coffee-making facilities?
6 What can I do about lunch?
7 How do I set the alarm?
8 Is it possible to smoke at work?

Writing skills: punctuation

1 Add punctuation to the following extracts from the information sheet:

1 The building is open between 8 am and 6 pm and 5 pm on Fridays
2 Unfortunately there are no car parking facilities however there is a cycle rack just in front of the entrance where cyclists can lock their bikes
3 To use the photocopier you will need a personal code please ask Martin for this
4 If the copier jams and you cant fix it or if you run out of paper see Martin
5 There is a kettle in the kitchen for making tea or coffee tea coffee sugar and biscuits are provided in the cupboard for staff to use
6 NB Remember to wash and put away your dishes after use
7 If you are the last person to leave the building please do the following
8 What should I do if the photocopier jams

2 Match the punctuation with the names.

1	.	a	question mark
2	,	b	brackets
3	:	c	full stop
4	;	d	comma
5	–	e	apostrophe
6	( )	f	colon
7	?	g	semi-colon
8	!	h	exclamation mark
9	'	i	dash

3 Which punctuation in exercise 2 is used in these situations?

1 To ask a question.
2 To end a sentence or show abbreviations.
3 After something important or amusing.
4 To separate items in a list, parts of a sentence or after an adverb.
5 To separate information from what comes before or after.
6 To show possession or contractions.
7 To connect related sentences.
8 To introduce items in a list.

4 Add punctuation to the following passage. Remember to use capital letters to start a new sentence.

> if you want to eat out there is an excellent restaurant just round the corner make sure you book in advance it accepts the following credit cards Visa MasterCard Diners Club and American Express it serves vegetarian food however it is a bit limited you must try the House Pizza its delicious

Preparing to write

1 Work in pairs. Imagine you are going to use your partner's house while he / she is away. Write the questions you would ask. For example, ask about what facilities there are, where to find and how to operate things in the house, what you need to do while your partner is away.

2 Ask and answer the questions with your partner. Give extra information where necessary.

Giving instructions

- Please *make sure / ensure / check* that …
- Please *switch off the lights / do not open the blinds*
- If you want to …, you will need to …
- *You can / You are welcome to / Please feel free to* use the microwave
- Unfortunately it is not possible to *use the washing machine / get internet access*
- N.B. Remember to / Do not forget to …

Writing

Write an information sheet for someone who is visiting your house while you are away. Use sub-headings for each section, and bullet points for lists, as in Maxim's information sheet.

Dealing with unknown words

When you meet an unknown word in a reading text, you can decide to …

- ignore it.
- look it up in a dictionary immediately.
- look it up in a dictionary later.
- try to guess the meaning.

1 What do you normally do when you meet unknown words? If you use more than one of the above strategies, what are the reasons for your choice? Read the information below and compare your ideas with a partner.

Did you know?

- ★ Looking up every word in a reading text can help develop your vocabulary but it will slow down your reading. If you are skimming a text (reading for general understanding) or scanning (reading for specific information), you do not need to understand every word.

- ★ Research suggests that if you understand most of a reading text, you can often guess the meanings of unknown words from their appearance or from the context.

  Clues from a word's appearance include:

  - Prefixes and suffixes (*mis-, re-, -ism, -ant*)
  - Compounds (*good-looking, daylight*)
  - Similarities to other words (*ascertain – certain*)
  - Similarities to words in your language

2 Work in pairs. Can you guess the meaning of these words?

colour-blind	downhearted	manual	guidance

3 Now read the words in a context. Does the context help you understand the meaning and word class (e.g. noun, verb)?

The 100-page manual provides detailed guidance on how to use the computer.

Traffic lights are dangerous for me because I'm colour-blind.

Don't get too downhearted – you can easily take the exam again.

Dreams & Reality

Reading and Speaking

1 Imagine you hear someone say the following sentence:

I'm living the American Dream!

What kind of life do you think they have?

2 Read the text about the phrase 'The American Dream' and answer the questions.

- In your own words, what do you think the author means?
- Do you think this is a good dream?
- Is this what people usually mean when they talk about the American Dream?

The American Dream
is the dream of a land in
which life should be better
and richer and fuller for everyone,
with opportunity for each according
to ability or achievement … It is not
a dream of motor cars and high wages
merely, but a dream of social order in
which each man and each woman shall
be able to attain to the fullest stature of which
they are innately capable, and be recognised
by others for what they are, regardless of the
fortuitous circumstances of birth or position.
James Truslow Adams, The Epic of America (1931)

Glossary
fortuitous (*adjective, literary*) – lucky
attain (*verb*) – to reach

Listening

1 2.26–2.32 Listen to seven Americans answer the question *Is there an American Dream? If so, what is it?* Which speakers are optimistic about the American Dream? Which are pessimistic?

2 Listen again and match each speaker to an opinion below.

1 ___ People chase the American Dream but they never get it.
2 ___ People's lives now are not as good as in the past.
3 ___ The American Dream is a good idea for parents to teach their children.
4 ___ We need to take care of the environment and stop consuming so much.
5 ___ Work hard, play hard and buy lots of things.
6 ___ You can be anyone and do anything you want.
7 ___ You have to be rich to live the dream.

3 Work in pairs. Choose **two** of the groups of questions and discuss.

- Is it enough to work hard and want something to get it? If not, what other factors are important?
- One speaker mentions a 'dream of a simple life'. What kind of life do you think that would be?
- Is the idea of 'the American Dream' unique to America? Why? / Why not?
- Could this be the national dream in your country? In any other countries?
- Is it a good idea for a country to have a national dream?

Extend your vocabulary
metaphors: the mind

In English, your mind is like a container, with thoughts being stored there or going in and out. You can have a closed or an open mind; you can empty your mind or fill your mind with ideas.

Match the two halves of the sentences.

1 I have a suspicion, at the back of my mind, that …
2 My parents had this idea fixed in their heads that …
3 An illusion that many people have in their minds is that …
4 If I need to relax and empty my mind, I usually …

a life was always much better in the past.
b he's not really telling me the truth.
c I would become a successful lawyer or doctor.
d go for a run in the park.

Grammar

providing that
provided that

*You can live the American Dream **providing** you have a lot of money.*
***Even if** you pass the exam, you might not pass the course.*
*You will not do well **unless** you try.*
*You will not do well **if** you don't try.*

so/as/as

- *providing, as long as, unless* and *even if* can all introduce conditional clauses
- *providing* and *as long as* can replace *if*; *providing* means only if a certain thing happens or is done
- *unless* means the same as *if not*; *You will not do well unless you try = You will not do well if you don't try*
- *even if* is an emphatic way of saying *if*; *even if* means that although something happens or may be true, another situation remains the same

1 Choose the correct option in the sentences from the listening.

1 It is possible to live the American Dream *unless / as long as* you have lots of money.
2 *Providing / Even if* you work hard and really want something then you will get it.
3 *As long as / Unless* you work hard, and teach your children right, then things can get better.
4 *If / Unless* we stop buying and consuming and polluting so much we're going to destroy the environment that makes the American Dream worth living.
5 Most people cannot have the American Dream, *providing / even if* they work very hard all their lives.

2 Make three sentences you agree with and three sentences you don't agree with using the words in the table.

You Your children	can will can't won't	make lots of money be unhappy be happy have a good life live longer	if unless providing as long as even if	you your parents they	work hard. are rich. are poor. are smart. are beautiful.

Speaking

Work in pairs. Choose **two** of the tasks below and discuss.

A What would be a good national dream for your country? Create two suitable sentences.

B What did your parents say to you to encourage you to work or study harder?

C What would / do / did you say to your children to encourage them to do better?

G **Grammar focus** – explanation & more practice of conditional structures on page 146

Dreams & Reality

Speaking

Read the following quotations about dreams by four writers. For each quotation, discuss with a partner what you think it means and what sort of dreams they are talking about. Which quotation do you like the best?

1 'The supreme object of life is to live. Few people live. It is true life only to realize one's own perfection, to make one's every dream a reality.'
Oscar Wilde

2 'I have dreamed in my life, dreams that have stayed with me ever after, and changed my ideas; they have gone through and through me, like wine through water, and altered the colour of my mind.'
Emily Brontë

3 'You see things; and you say, "Why?" But I dream things that never were; and I say, "Why not?"'
George Bernard Shaw

4 'Dreaming is an act of pure imagination, attesting in all men a creative power, which *if it were available in waking, would make every man a Dante or Shakespeare.*'
F.H. Hedge

Grammar

1 Read the last quote in the Speaking section again and answer the questions.

1 Look at the clause in italics. What form is the first verb?
2 Is this a real or unreal situation?
3 What is the verb form in the second part of the clause in italics?
4 What other verbs can we use instead of *would* here? How does it change the meaning?

2 What is the difference in meaning in these sentences?

1 If I dared to dream, my life would be different. *Pres*
2 If I had dared to dream, my life would be different. *Past* *Pres*
3 If I had dared to dream, my life would have been different. *Past* *Past*

3 Complete the three sentences below with your own ideas.

- If I … my life would be different.
- If I had … my life would be different.
- If I had … my life would have been different.

4 Turn to page 130 and follow the instructions.

G **Grammar focus** – explanation & more practice of unreal conditionals on page 146

Reading

1 🔊 **2.33** Read the information about Edgar Allan Poe and then read and listen to the poem *A Dream within a Dream*. Choose the best summary.

a The writer feels worried and uncertain about his future. He has had a dream about the sea which he finds difficult to interpret.
b The writer feels sad and frustrated. The whole of his life feels like a dream and he is losing everything that is important to him.
c The writer feels optimistic and full of hope. He is certain that his dreams of a happy and wealthy future are going to be fulfilled.

2 Choose the correct meanings of these words. Use the poem to help you. Then compare with a partner.

1 part from
  a meet   b leave
2 avow
  a confess   b complain
3 deem
  a decide   b think
4 roar
  a noise   b stillness
4 creep
  a rush   b move slowly
5 grasp
  a hold loosely   b hold firmly

3 Work with a partner and discuss the questions.

First verse:
1 Who do you think the writer is parting from? In what way?
2 What does this person think about the writer's life? What does the writer think?

Second verse:
3 Where is the writer?
4 What is he trying to hold on to? What is happening to it?
5 What do you think is 'the pitiless wave'?

4 Do you like the poem? Why or why not?

Vocabulary

1 Match the two halves of the sentences.

1 I *wonder*
2 I can't really *picture myself*
3 When I was young I would *pretend*
4 I *suppose that*
5 At work, I will often *daydream*
6 I sometimes *fantasise*

a as a teacher.
b *about* telling my boss what I really think.
c *that* I speak fluent English.
d *to* be a rock singer.
e *what* it would be like to live in another country.
f winning the lottery would make life easier.

2 Choose **three** of the phrases in italics from exercise 1 to make true sentences about yourself.

Edgar Allan Poe

(1809–1849) was an American writer and poet. He is best known for his stories of mystery and horror and has been called the father of the modern detective story.

A Dream within a Dream **was published in the year of Poe's death. His short life was one of chaos and personal misery and the cause of his death remains unclear.**

A Dream within a Dream

Take this kiss upon the brow!
And, in parting from you now,
Thus much let me avow-
You are not wrong, who deem
That my days have been a dream;
Yet if hope has flown away
In a night, or in a day,
In a vision, or in none,
Is it therefore the less gone?
All that we see or seem
Is but a dream within a dream.

I stand amid the roar
Of a surf-tormented shore,
And I hold within my hand
Grains of the golden sand-
How few! yet how they creep
Through my fingers to the deep,
While I weep- while I weep!
O God! can I not grasp
Them with a tighter clasp?
O God! can I not save
One from the pitiless wave?
Is all that we see or seem
But a dream within a dream?

Dreams & Reality

Vocabulary and Pronunciation

1 Look at these opinions about documentaries. Do you agree or disagree with the speakers?

1 I like knowing that in a documentary what I'm seeing happened **for real** rather than in the imagination of some scriptwriter.

2 I prefer to watch documentaries because I'm more interested in **the real world** than in fiction.

3 Even documentaries are often scripted. Some are so heavily edited that they completely **distort reality** by only showing certain aspects.

4 The storylines of a lot of soap operas or drama series are so over the top that they **bear no relation to reality** at all.

5 Documentary makers are still trying to create 'good TV' so you can never be sure if you're seeing **the real thing** or a set-up.

6 **In reality**, there sometimes isn't much difference between fiction series and documentaries.

2 Match the phrases in bold in exercise 1 (1–6) with the correct meanings (a–f) below.

a change things so that they are no longer true
b something that is authentic and genuine, not a fake
c the true situation is …
d what happens in real life
e actually
f aren't at all like the real situation

3 🔊 2.34 Listen to the opinions in exercise 1. Mark which words are most stressed and where there is a pause. Then decide which opinions you agree with most and read those out to a partner.

4 Work in pairs. Make up a dialogue (for example, about soap operas or crime series) using at least three phrases from exercise 1. Read it out to another pair or to the class, paying attention to pronunciation.

Listening and Speaking

1 Do you like to watch nature documentaries? Why or why not? Are they popular in your country? Is their popularity linked to a particular age group?

2 Look at the quotation below from Sir David Attenborough, a well-known presenter of natural history documentaries. Discuss the questions.

1 Why might it be difficult to tell the truth in nature documentaries? What particular problems might there be when trying to film animals and their habits?
2 How might natural history film-makers lie? What kind of tricks might they use?

> **Reputable natural history film-makers do not lie. They tell the truth. But telling the truth is a simplification. It is often very difficult to tell the truth.**
> *David Attenborough*

3 🔊 **2.35** Now listen to a report about nature documentaries. Tick (✔) the methods used to distort reality in the two films.

White Wilderness (1958)   *Arctic Warrior (1997)*

	White Wilderness (1958)	Arctic Warrior (1997)
1 using captive or trained animals	☐	☐
2 filming in a zoo	☐	☐
3 filming in a different habitat	☐	☐
4 staging a scene with human intervention	☐	☐
5 showing false facts about animal behaviour	☐	☐

4 Listen again. Make notes about exactly how the film-makers used the methods in exercise 3.

5 Now answer the questions.
- How did the film-makers justify portraying something as the real thing when in actual fact it wasn't?
- What is your opinion of their arguments?
- Do you think the end justifies the means when it is for an educational purpose?

Extend your vocabulary – verbs used with *truth* and *lies*

1 Match the verbs in the box to the two nouns. Which verbs can go with both nouns?

expose	face	learn	make up
reveal	stretch	tell	

_____ the truth.
_____ lies.

2 Write four sentences about films and film-makers. Use a different expression with *truth* or *lies* in each sentence.

Speaking

1 Work in pairs. A: turn to page 126. B: turn to page 133.
First read your paragraph. It contains three deliberate 'lies' or factual mistakes which are underlined.

2 Read the paragraph out to your partner. Your partner should listen carefully and stop you when they think they hear a 'lie'. Continue reading to the end unless your partner asks you to stop. If your partner has missed one or more 'lies', read the paragraph again.

Useful phrases

- Stop! / Hold on! / Hang on a minute!
- Could you just repeat that sentence?
- That sounds wrong. / That can't be right. / You said …, so … is a lie. It should be …

3 Write your own paragraph on a subject that interests you. Include at least three 'lies' similar to those in the texts in exercise 2. Read out your paragraph to your partner as above. Tell your partner how many 'lies' there are.

Dreams & Reality

Reading

1 What is a 'memoir'? Who usually writes memoirs?

2 Now read the blurb from the cover of a book of six-word memoirs and answer the questions.

1 What story did Ernest Hemmingway tell in six words? Retell it in your own words.

2 Who wrote the six-word memoirs in this book?

3 What do these six-word memoirs aim to do?

When Ernest Hemmingway famously wrote 'For Sale: baby shoes never worn', he proved that an entire story can be told using half a dozen words. When the online storytelling magazine SMITH asked readers to submit six-word memoirs, they proved that a whole life can be told this way too. From small sagas of bittersweet romance to proud achievements and stinging regrets, these true tales relate the diversity of human experience in bite-sized pieces.

3 Read *Reality check*. Which memoir do you empathise most with? Why?

4 Work in pairs. Read the memoirs again and answer the questions. Which memoir …

• is the funniest?
• is the saddest?
• is the the most difficult to understand?
• is your favourite?

Grammar

1 Look at these wishes and regrets. Match them with six memoirs in *Reality check*.

1 **I wish I had grown** a bit more.
2 **If only I had found** somebody to share my life with.
3 **I should have done** something with my life.
4 **It's a pity I wasted** my youth.
5 **I don't regret getting** an education but **I wish it hadn't** cost so much.
6 **My biggest regret is that** I didn't marry the person I really loved.

2 Look at the regrets in bold in exercise 1. Work in pairs. Write the structure used in each one.

1 *I wish* + past perfect (*had* + past participle)
2 …

3 Complete these regrets. Use a suitable verb.

1 I'm late for work again. I should _____ earlier.
2 I've still got a headache. I wish I _____ an aspirin.
3 Do I look OK? It's a pity I _____ time to iron my shirt.
4 I don't regret _____ my old job but I miss my colleagues.
5 It's never quiet in our house. My biggest regret is _____ my son that drum kit.
6 We had a terrible argument. If only I _____ those awful things.

4 Write speech bubbles for these photos. Write at least two sentences for each using the structures in exercise 1. Compare your speech bubbles in pairs or in a small group. Who has the funniest?

G **Grammar focus** – explanation & more practice of wishes & regrets on page 146

Reality check

Never should have bought that ring.
Paul Bellow

Rich in degrees and student loans.
Barb Piper

Followed rules, not dreams. Never again.
Margaret Hellerstein

Someone had to pay the bills.
David Kuizenga

Found true love, married someone else.
Bjorn Stromberg

Quit uni, had baby, now bored.
Samantha Ng

Young, skinny, ridiculed. Old, skinny, envied.
Phil Sweet

Marked time till 55, reborn thereafter.
Doug Fraser

Afraid of everything. Did it anyway.
Ayse Erginer

Never really finished anything, except cake.
Carletta Perkins

Born bald. Grew hair. Bald again.
A. J. Jacobs

I thought I would be taller.
Lisa Brown

Divorced twice, lived happily ever after.
Susan Guyaux

Dreamed of endless love. Awoke alone.
Mohammad Fatayerji

Thought I would have more impact.
Kevin Clark

Vocabulary

1 Complete the collocations about experiences in life. Check your answers in the text *Reality check*.

1   pay the b_____
2   live h_____ e_____
    a_____
3   follow r_____
4   have an _____
5   mark t_____
6   find t_____ l_____
7   quit u_____

2 Match each pair of words below with the correct verb in exercise 1. Use a dictionary if you are unsure.

1   your job / smoking
2   happiness / your feet
3   the penalty / your way
4   advice / a dream
5   an occasion / the start of something new
6   a lie / for the moment
7   a responsibility / a ball

3 Work in pairs or in a small group.
* Write the verbs and nouns from exercises 1 and 2 on small pieces of paper and put them face down on your table.
* Take turns to turn over two pieces of paper.
* When you see a correct collocation, make a sentence that is true about your life.

Writing

Work in pairs and choose **one** of the tasks below.

A Write you own six-word memoir. Then read it to a partner. Explain the memoir in more detail. What was good or what did you regret? Your partner should make a personal comment on your story.

B Pick one of the memoirs in the reading. Expand the memoir into a paragraph using the first person: explain what happened and what you regret. Read it to your partner. Your partner should say how well the paragraph communicates the ideas in the memoir.

a   b   c

Warm up

Look at the photos. Write what the person on the other end of the line could be saying: write two or three different things for each person. Then compare your ideas with a partner.

Listening

1 2.36–2.37 Listen. Match the conversations to two photos. What is the surprising news that they have just been told.

2 Listen again. How did the two people react to the news? Tick (✔) their reaction.

		Speaker 1	Speaker 2
1	pleasantly surprised	☐	☐
2	unpleasantly surprised	☐	☐
3	ecstatic	☐	☐
4	speechless	☐	☐

Language focus: giving surprising news

1 Look at these ways of telling somebody some surprising news.

Which phrases are quite formal? Which are quite informal?

1 I have some good / interesting news.
2 Believe it or not …
3 I'm very pleased to be able to tell you …
4 You won't believe this but …
5 Guess what! You'll never believe it …
6 This might sound strange but …
7 This might come as rather a surprise but …
8 Have you heard about / that …?

2 2.38 Match the replies on the left to one with a similar meaning on the right. Listen and check. Then listen again to the speaker's intonation. Practise saying the replies in the same way.

1 Really?   a That's wonderful news!
2 No way!   b I don't know what to say.
3 Wow!   c I don't believe it.
4 I'm speechless.   d Are you serious?

Speaking

1 A: Look at the upside down prompts below. Tell B who you are in each situation and then give him / her the news using an expression from Language focus exercise 1. B: React to the news using an appropriate expression from Language focus exercise 2.

2 Swap roles. B: look at the upside down prompts below.

A:
1 You are B's best friend. You are going to marry the person you met on holiday two weeks ago.
2 You are B's mother. You have decided to sell most of your possessions and donate the money to the local cats' home.
3 You are B's boss. B has been successful in their bid for promotion and will receive a large pay rise and other benefits.

B:
1 You are A's partner. You have booked a surprise romantic holiday for A and yourself as a birthday treat.
2 You are A's boss. You are going to send A on a team-building course which involves parachuting, sailing and mountain climbing.
3 You are A's neighbour. You have heard that the council is going to abolish property tax on all homes in the area.

Global voices

Warm up

1 A survey of five- to seven-year-olds revealed these dream careers. What do you think the top five dream careers were for boys and the top five for girls? One career was chosen by both girls and boys.

> fireman   doctor   footballer   vet   nurse
> archaeologist   dancer   policeman   teacher

2 Look at page 131 for the answer.

Listening

1 🎧 2.39–2.45 Listen to people talking about their biggest dream as a child. Match the dream careers to the speakers. Who doesn't talk about a dream career? What were their childhood dreams?

a paramedic
b football player
c teacher
d university professor
e tennis player

Dilamar, Brazil   ____
Judy, Australia   ____
José, Spain   ____
Karina, Russia   ____
Javier, Spain   ____
Alison, England   ____
Mingyu, South Korea   ____

2 Listen again and answer the questions.

1 Whose dream came true?
2 Who is on the way to fulfilling their dream?
3 Who had to give up their dream?
4 Whose dream was only a childhood wish?

3 Which of the dreams did you relate to most?

Language focus: repetition

Look at these sentences (1–3) from the listening. Match them with the type of repetition (a–c).

1 [It] was very popular to become a football player because it's your main interest you know. It's the main thing you, you think about.
2 That's my dream, that was my dream as a child.
3 I'm here, in England, work like uh … like … like a cleaner.

a repetition of the same words, to gain thinking time (often with words like *er* or *uh*)
b repetition to correct a mistake
c repetition of the same idea, to explain or expand on something

Speaking

1 Work with a partner. Tell your partner about your biggest dream as a child. Explain why it was your dream at that time. Tell your partner if you fulfilled that dream and how. If you didn't fulfil your dream, explain why.

2 Then decide what your biggest dream is today. Write it on a piece of paper. Then collect the papers and give them out again. Read out the dream on the paper you have been given. The class guesses who it could be.

Dilamar, Brazil   Judy, Australia   José, Spain

Karina, Russia   Javier, Spain   Alison, England   Mingyu, South Korea

Writing a formal letter of complaint

Reading

1 Read Erik's letter. Is he complaining about:

a a faulty item?

b poor service?

c unsatisfactory facilities?

8, Warren St,
Manchester M14 0EU

The Manager,
Telstar Electricals,
17, Purley Way,
Croydon CR9 2FZ

August 7th 20___

Dear Sir / Madam,

1 I am writing *with regard to* a Samsung Q 330 laptop that I ordered online from your company on 5th July (reference number 81406530). Unfortunately there have been *several* problems with this order, and I am *extremely dissatisfied* with the inefficient and unhelpful service I have received so far.

2 First of all, when I received an email confirmation of the order, I was told that you would contact me within 48 hours to arrange a time and date to deliver the computer. However, four days later I still had not heard from you. When I *telephoned* Customer Services, I was told that the computer was out of stock, and that they did not know when it would be in stock again. I *therefore* asked them to refund the money and they promised that they would do this within 3 to 5 working days. In the meantime, I bought a laptop from another company.

3 Yesterday I checked my bank statement and was shocked to see that the money I paid had still not been refunded to my account. *Moreover*, as I have paid for two computers, my bank account is now overdrawn and I have to pay interest charges. Finally, when I telephoned Customer Services again they *informed* me that they could not give me a refund because I had placed the order over 30 days ago. They also offered to deliver the laptop next week, but as you will *appreciate*, I *no longer* need this product.

4 This situation has caused great inconvenience, *not to mention* financial problems. I would therefore be grateful if you could cancel my order immediately, and refund the money I paid for the computer as well as the interest charges on my bank account within 7 working days.

I look forward to hearing from you,

Yours faithfully

E Olsen

Erik Olsen

---

2 Complete Erik's notes for his letter.

SERVICE - (1) _____ and unhelpful.

DELIVERY - They promised to contact me (2) _____.

PHONE CALL 1 - They told me computer was (3) _____.
- They promised to (4) _____.

YESTERDAY - Discovered that they (5) _____.
- My bank account is (6) _____.

PHONE CALL 2 - They said that they (7) _____.
- They offered to (8) _____.

REQUEST - (9) _____.
- (10) _____.

Writing skills: a formal letter

A Follow the rules for writing a formal letter

Choose the correct options.

1 Write your *name and address / address* in the top right-hand corner.

2 Write the recipient's *name and address / title, name and address* in the top left-hand corner.

3 Write the date in *the top left hand corner / the top right hand corner*.

4 Start your letter with *I am writing … / This letter is …*

5 Finish your letter with 'I look forward to *hear / hearing* from you'.

6 If you start with 'Dear Sir / Madam', end with *Yours sincerely / Yours faithfully*.

7 If you start with 'Dear + Name', end with *Yours sincerely / Yours faithfully*.

8 Write your full name *below / above* your signature.

B Use formal words and phrases

Match the words and phrases below with formal ones in italics in the letter.

1 as well as _____
2 understand _____
3 told _____
4 lots of _____
5 accordingly _____
6 really fed up _____
7 don't now _____
8 also _____
9 about _____
10 called _____

C Use *this* to talk about something you have already mentioned

Explain the meaning of *this* in the following phrases.

1 *this* order (paragraph 1)
2 do *this* (paragraph 2)
3 *this* product (paragraph 3)
4 *this* situation (paragraph 4)

Preparing to write

1 Think about something that you would like to complain about, e.g. an item you have bought, poor service, or unsatisfactory facilities. Make notes like Erik's in Reading exercise 2.

2 Using your notes as a guide, describe the situation to a partner.

Making a complaint

- I am writing to *complain about / express my dissatisfaction with* …
- Unfortunately there *has been a problem / have been several problems* with …
- I am extremely *dissatisfied with / annoyed about* …
- This has caused *great inconvenience / several problems*
- I would be grateful if you could *refund the money / look into the situation / send a replacement*

Writing

Write a letter of complaint based on your notes and the situation you described. Follow this structure:

Paragraph 1: Say why you are writing
Paragraphs 2 and 3: Explain the problem(s)
Paragraph 4: Say what action you want

Study skills

Examination strategies

1 Work in pairs and discuss the questions.
- Have you ever taken an important English exam?
- What did you have to do in it?
- How did you prepare for it?

2 Work in pairs. Say whether you agree or disagree with these statements and discuss your ideas.
- Taking an exam can provide motivation to improve your English.
- Passing an external English exam is necessary in today's world.
- Preparing for an exam is a good way to improve your English.
- Focusing on an exam can prevent natural language learning.

3 Read the exam tips below and match each to one of the headings.

Revision strategies   Doing the exam
Preparing for the exam

- ★ Read the instructions slowly, at least twice.
- ★ Do practice papers in timed conditions.
- ★ Make a revision timetable.
- ★ Always check both sides of the exam paper.
- ★ Keep an eye on the clock.
- ★ Leave enough time at the end to check your answers.
- ★ Do a little revision every day.
- ★ Get plenty of sleep the night before the exam.
- ★ Find out what exactly the exam is designed to test.
- ★ Arrange revision sessions with friends.
- ★ Divide your time equally between questions that have the same marks.
- ★ Take plenty of breaks and do things to relax and have fun.

4 Compare your ideas in small groups. Do you have any other tips to add to each heading?

Rise & Fall

Writing

1 Think of the most impressive or beautiful building in your town or a town nearby. Write a short paragraph describing this building for an English travel brochure. Your paragraph must have at least three sentences.

2 Work in pairs. Compare your paragraphs.

Reading

1 Look at the photos of the two buildings on page 103. Do you know either of them? Where do you think they are? What could they be used for?

2 Read *Higher and higher* about two of the world's tallest buildings. Where do you think the text comes from?

a   the buildings' respective websites
b   a newspaper article about tall buildings
c   a criticism of construction in the 21st century

3 Read the texts again. Which building …

1   is in a city that has become an international centre?
2   mentions the possibility of eating there?
3   claims to be a symbol of progress for a region?
4   mentions technological uses of the building?
5   claims to be an example of countries working together?
6   claims to be a top tourist destination?

4 Read the texts again and find different ways the authors have expressed the following ideas:

1   that no other tower is like theirs
    world's tallest, incomparable, …
2   that their tower is wonderful
    a living wonder, a stunning work of art, …

5 Look at the paragraph you wrote about a building in your city. Rewrite your paragraph to make it a longer description, using language from exercise 4 to help you.

Vocabulary

1 Complete the table with the correct form of the words. Use the reading text to help you.

noun	adjective
	precedented
symbol	
region	
	global
prosperity	
	comparable
inspiration	
	ingenious
	possible
architecture	

2 Complete the sentences with the correct form of the word in brackets.

Welcome ladies and gentlemen to the
(1) _____ (*open*) of this city's greatest
(2) _____ (*architecture*) achievement.
This building is more than a simple skyscraper
it is a (3) _____ (*symbolic*) of our modern
city. This (4) _____ (*wonder*) tower
will be an (5) _____ (*inspire*) to us all,
and it stands as an (6) _____ (*precedent*)
(7) _____ (*commit*) to the progress and
future of this country.

Higher and higher:
the rise and rise of the world's tallest buildings

The world's tallest building. A living wonder. A stunning work of art. An incomparable feat of engineering. *Burj Khalifa* is all that. In concept and execution, *Burj Khalifa* has no peer.

More than just the world's tallest building, *Burj Khalifa* is an unprecedented example of international cooperation, a symbolic beacon of progress, and an emblem of the new, dynamic and prosperous Middle East.

It is also tangible proof of Dubai's growing role in a changing world. In fewer than 30 years, this city has transformed itself from a regional centre to a global one. This success was not based on oil reserves, but on reserves of human talent, ingenuity and initiative. *Burj Khalifa* embodies that vision.

Mr Mohamed Alabbar, Chairman, Emaar Properties, said: '*Burj Khalifa* goes beyond its imposing physical specifications. In *Burj Khalifa*, we see the triumph of Dubai's vision of attaining the seemingly impossible and setting new benchmarks. It is a source of inspiration for every one of us in Emaar. The project is a declaration of the emirate's capabilities and of the resolve of its leaders and people to work hand in hand on truly awe-inspiring projects.'

Defining the Toronto skyline at 553.33m (1,815ft 5in), the *CN Tower* is the World's Tallest Tower, ... a record it has held for over three decades. As Toronto, Ontario and Canada's most recognisable ... icon, the *CN Tower* is an internationally renowned architectural triumph, an engineering Wonder of the Modern World, a world-class entertainment and dining destination and a 'must-see' for anyone visiting Toronto. Each year, over 1.5 million people visit Canada's National Tower to take in the breathtaking views and enjoy all the *CN Tower* has to offer.

In 1995, the *CN Tower* was classified as one of the Seven Wonders of the Modern World by the American Society of Civil Engineers. Canada's Wonder of the World shares this designation with the Empire State Building, the Chunnel under the English Channel, the Golden Gate Bridge in San Francisco, Itaipu Dam on the Brazil/Paraguay border, the Panama Canal, and the North Sea Protection Works off the European coast.

Since the *CN Tower* opened, Canadians and tourists from around the world have made the trip to Toronto to celebrate this marvel of engineering. Besides serving as a telecommunications hub, the *CN Tower* provides a wide range of unique attractions, exhibits and food and beverage venues.

Over the years, millions of dollars have been invested in expanding and revitalising the *CN Tower* to continue to provide visitors with a world-class experience.

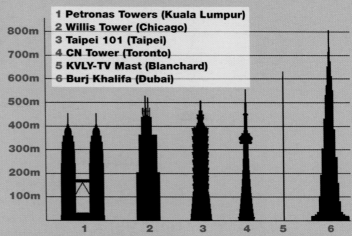

1 Petronas Towers (Kuala Lumpur)
2 Willis Tower (Chicago)
3 Taipei 101 (Taipei)
4 CN Tower (Toronto)
5 KVLY-TV Mast (Blanchard)
6 Burj Khalifa (Dubai)

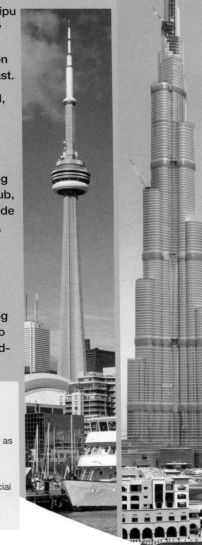

Speaking

1 How much do you agree with the sentences below? For each sentence mark your opinion from 1 (completely agree) to 5 (completely disagree).

I would feel worried about living on a high floor of a skyscraper.	1 2 3 4 5
A skyscraper is a sign of wealth and modernity.	1 2 3 4 5
Tall buildings are ugly, unsafe and unnecessary.	1 2 3 4 5
It is not natural for people to live close together in tall buildings.	1 2 3 4 5
Building tall buildings is simply human arrogance.	1 2 3 4 5

2 Work in pairs. Choose at least four of the sentences above and compare your answers. Is your partner generally in favour of or against skyscrapers?

Glossary

benchmark (*noun*) – a standard that you can use for judging how good or bad other things are

emblem (*noun*) – something that is generally accepted as a symbol of a quality, idea, or principle

exhibit (*noun*) – (AMERICAN) an exhibition

renowned (*adjective*) – famous and admired for a special skill or achievement

to have no peer – better than anyone or anything else

Rise & Fall

Vocabulary

Work in pairs. Decide which of the words below can be used with the verb *rise*. Explain to a partner what each correct collocation means. Use a dictionary to help you.

> a bird   a cake   a lift   a problem
> children   prices   salaries   stress
> tension   the sun   the temperature
> the tide   your spirits   your voice

The sun rises. It means it gets higher in the sky in the morning.
A ... doesn't rise. It ...

Listening

1 Look at the photo of a phoenix and describe what you can see. Do you know what happens to the bird according to legend?

2 🔊 2.46 Listen to the story of the phoenix and check your answer in exercise 1.

3 Listen again. Decide if the sentences are true (*T*) or false (*F*).

1 The sun told the phoenix that it would never die.
2 The phoenix lived for six hundred years in a desert.
3 The phoenix began to lose its strength.
4 It landed in the desert and built a nest.
5 The sun shone down on the phoenix and burnt it to ashes.
6 The same phoenix rose from the ashes.

4 Work in pairs and answer the questions.

1 According to the listening, what does the phoenix represent today?
2 Is the phoenix used as a symbol in your culture? Give examples.

Extend your vocabulary – words beginning with *re-*

What does the prefix *re-* mean in these words? Where is the stress – on the prefix or the verb or both?
The phoenix was reborn.
It rebuilds its nest in the palm tree.

1 Explain the meaning of these common words with *re-*. Use a dictionary if necessary.

> recharge   reconsider   recycle
> refill   refuel   re-release
> reschedule   reset   resit

2 Match each of the verbs above to an object below.

> a CD   a cup   a decision
> a machine   a meeting   an exam
> a plane   newspapers
> your batteries

3 Pick three of the expressions (verbs and objects) and make questions for your partner.

Grammar

1 Look at these sentences from the listening. Underline the phrasal verbs. Work with a partner and take turns to explain the meaning.

1 Glorious Phoenix, you shall be my bird. I shall look after you and you shall live forever!
2 The phoenix flew for a long time before it came across a hidden desert.
3 The phoenix asked the sun to give it its strength back.
4 The phoenix thought the situation over and decided to return to the place of its origin.
5 It picked up pieces of bark and all kinds of fragrant leaves.
6 After a while the flames died down. Only a heap of silvery-grey ash remained.
7 It set off for the faraway desert again.
8 The rising phoenix has come to stand for rebirth, change and survival.

2 Some phrasal verbs are followed by an object and some have no object. Which ones in exercise 1 don't have an object?

3 Look at the phrasal verbs in exercise 1 that have objects. Circle the object. Then read the rules in the box and decide which verbs are 'separable'.

- most phrasal verbs are separable: that means the object can go between the verb and particle (*fill* a form *in*), or after the verb and particle (*fill in* a form).
- however, if the object is a pronoun, it always goes between the verb and particle (*fill it in*).
- some phrasal verbs are non-separable: the verb and particle always come before the object (*deal with* a problem)
- your dictionary shows you if verbs are separable or non-separable.

4 The metaphor of the rising phoenix is often applied to survivors: people who have 'risen from the ashes' to rebuild their life in some way.

Put the sentences about survivors in the correct order, paying attention to the position of objects. Sometimes there are two possibilities.

Survivors are people who …

1 … through experiences have gone very difficult
2 … pick have had to up and start again themselves
3 … after have learnt look themselves to
4 … difficulties have when a positive attitude across they come
5 … carefully before acting over the possibilities think
6 … in search of are set off new challenges prepared to

G **Grammar focus** – explanation & more practice of phrasal verbs on page 146

Speaking

Tell your partner about somebody you know, somebody you have heard about or somebody in a film who survived a difficult experience.

Useful phrases

- One of my relatives once …
- A good friend of mine experienced …
- I recently read a story in the news about somebody who …
- I once heard about a woman who …
- Do you know the film about the man who …?

Speaking

Work in pairs. Choose three of these groups of questions and discuss.

- Did you study history at school? Did you enjoy it?
- Do you think young people in your country know enough about their history?
- 'History is written by the winners.' Do you agree with this statement? Can you think of exceptions?
- What would you say was the most important historical event in your country in the past five hundred years?
- 'Those who forget history are doomed to repeat it.' What does this quote mean? Do you think it's true?
- Have you ever felt you were witnessing history? When? What happened?

Reading

1 In history classes when you were at school, did you learn anything about the Roman Empire? What do you remember?

2 Read *Ten Ways to Fall*. Match each 'way' to a title below. There is one extra title you do not need.

Aliens destroyed it	**Its people were poisoned**
Disease killed it	
It destroyed its environment	Politics destroyed it
It had economic problems	**Technology finished it**
It got too big	The Empire never fell
It lost its values	There were too many foreigners

3 What do you think of the theories in the text? Which ones sound most plausible to you? Why? Which of these theories could also be about fears for the decline in today's society?

Vocabulary

1 Rewrite the following sentences so they have the same meaning, using the words in bold.

1 The size of the empire led to its fall (**due to**)
2 The Romans couldn't protect themselves against external enemies, which led to their decline. (**trigger**)
3 These problems caused farmers to move to the cities. (**result in**)
4 The Roman Empire declined as a result of a rise in immigration. (**lead to**)
5 The empire had grown very large and so it was hard to keep roads functioning properly. (**consequently**)

2 Look at the following 'historical mysteries'. Have you heard of any of these?

In the 8th and 9th century, the **great Maya civilisation** of Central America **suddenly collapsed**.

In 1937, while making a **round-the-world flight**, the woman aviator Amelia Earhart disappeared over the Pacific Ocean. Her plane was **never found**.

In 1872, the merchant ship the Marie Celeste was **found adrift** at sea in excellent condition, with a full cargo but **not a single person** on board.

In the 1970s several **large, circular marks** appeared in different crops around the United Kingdom. These **'crop circles'** were very large and had complex patterns.

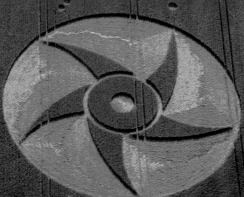

TEN WAYS TO FALL

Theories on the decline of one of the world's greatest empires

For over three hundred years historians have obsessed over the fall of the Roman Empire. At its height it covered most of Europe and North Africa and lasted for more than a thousand years. So how and why did it end? Some historians have estimated that there are more than 200 theories for the fall: here we address the top ten …

I _____

Many historians believed that the Roman Empire grew too quickly. Due to its size, it was hard to keep everything functioning properly, especially the network of roads and the military. Consequently the Romans could not protect themselves against external enemies, which led to their decline.

_____

Others argue that the Roman Empire – particularly the military – declined as a result of a rise in immigration. Many soldiers from other lands were brought into the Roman army, leading to a lack of obedience and decadence in the society in general.

II _____

There is another theory that the Romans, as they became richer and more powerful, became more corrupt. According to this theory, the Romans became weaker people from the inside, which resulted in a weakening of the Empire on the outside too.

IV _____

Because of the size of the Empire, it needed money. The economy was in part based on slave labour and the Romans did not trade enough with other lands. Much of their money came from tax collection. However, the taxes grew so high that the population eventually turned against its leaders.

V _____

There are theories that developments in technology are the main driving forces of history. According to this, the invention of the horseshoe in the first decade of the 2nd century AD played a decisive role in ending the military rule of the Romans, whose army mostly moved on foot. This triggered the fall of the Empire.

VI _____

The Roman Empire suffered a severe plague in 165 AD. For years, smallpox and measles ravaged the population. Some historians report that around half of the population was killed by illnesses.

VII _____

One theory holds that the Empire collapsed because of endless civil wars between different political groups in Rome for control of the Empire. This weakened the military and the society in general. Rome was unable to defend itself against its external enemies.

VIII _____

This theory says that gradual environmental problems including deforestation and excessive irrigation caused population and economic decline. Human activity caused fertile land to become desert and resulted in the extinction of various species of animals. These problems led farmers to move to the cities, which became overpopulated.

IX _____

The Romans did a lot of cooking in lead pots and drank out of lead cups. Poison leaked out of these into their food and drink in very small quantities, but over a period of time had an effect on the people that contributed to the fall of their Empire.

X _____

Finally, this theory states that the Roman Empire never really ended, rather it kept changing into other Empires.

3 Choose one of the mysteries (or use another historical mystery of your own). Think of reasons why this happened. Write your ideas, using the language in exercise 1. Try to make your reasons sound as believable as possible.

4 Read your situation and explanations to a partner. Which explanations sound most believable?

Glossary

collapse (*verb*) – to suddenly fail or stop existing

corrupt (*adjective*) – doing dishonest, illegal, or immoral things in order to gain money or power

decadence (*noun*) – behaviour that is considered immoral because it concentrates too much on pleasure

plague (*noun*) – any serious disease that spreads quickly to a lot of people and usually ends in death

ravage (*verb*) – to destroy something or damage it very badly

Rise & Fall

Reading and Speaking

1 Think about weddings that you have attended. Were they serious or fun occasions? Have you ever been to a wedding where there was an unexpected event?

2 Read the information about the novel *Behind the Scenes at the Museum* on page 109. Then read the extract and answer the questions.

1 What mood is Sandra in?
2 What has Ted done? Is he sorry?
3 Who is Beatrice? What does she think of Ted?

3 Read the extract again. Underline words and phrases that helped you answer the questions in exercise 2.

4 What do you think happens next? Work in pairs and make notes about the next possible scene. Try to think of as many details as possible. Tell another pair your ideas.

Listening and Vocabulary

1 🔊 **2.47** Listen to what actually happens in the next scene of the novel. Did you have similar ideas?

2 Put the events in the right order.
—— His feet **slip** under him and he **collapses**.
—— He almost **trips over** a bridesmaid.
—— He **lurches** towards the wedding cake.
—— He tries to regain his balance.
—— He **lands** in the wedding cake.
—— He **loses his balance**.
—— He tries to back away from Beatrice.

3 Look at the verbs in bold in exercise 2. Match them with the definitions below. Use a dictionary if necessary.

1 to move suddenly in an uncontrolled way
2 to be unable to stand and stay steady
3 to come down to a surface after falling through the air
4 to fall down suddenly
5 to hit your foot on something and fall
6 to move quickly across a surface

4 Work with a partner. Tell your partner about a fall you (or somebody you know) had. It could be an embarrassing experience or a more serious accident.

5 Discuss the questions with a partner.

1 Did you find this extract funny, shocking or sad?
2 What did you think of the behaviour of Ted, Sandra and Beatrice? Can you imagine people behaving like this at a wedding in your country?
3 Did you feel sympathy for any of the characters?
4 Do you think you'd like to read the rest of the book? Why or why not?

Grammar

> … Ted **tries to** back away …
> … in an attempt to **avoid crushing** her …

- some verbs are followed by *to* + verb and some verbs are followed by the *-ing* form
- sometimes the same verb is followed by both *to* and *-ing* with a difference in the meaning of the verb

1 Look at the sentences below. Work with a partner and explain what the verbs mean in each pair.

1 Ted **tried telling** the truth to his wife.
He **tried to tell** the truth to his wife.

2 The men **stopped to watch** the match.
Ted **stopped lying** and told the truth for once.

3 I **forgot to take** my camera.
I'll never **forget seeing** him fall.

4 **Remember to show** me photos of the wedding!
Do you **remember hitting** your husband?

Behind the Scenes at the Museum

And it's a free kick to West Germany. One minute to go, just sixty seconds …

The tension coming out of the TV lounge is visible, like the smoke of gunfire. I hurry on my way, only to be confronted by a seething bride. 'Have you seen Ted?' she demands in a very vexed way.

'Ted?'

'Yes, Ted – my so-called husband!' Sandra twirls round, surveying the corridors of the hotel like a snapping crocodile. 'Where are they all?' she asks, a puzzled look on her face.

'All who?'

'The men.'

I watch with interest as enlightenment dawns slowly on Sandra's face. She gives a little scream of frustration and stamps her satin foot. 'The World Cup! I'll kill him.'

…

All the men who had previously disappeared are suddenly herded back into the reception by Sandra and her mother. Beatrice remains by the door, standing guard. 'In the TV lounge,' she says loudly by way of explanation to the rest of the wedding party. 'That's where they were – watching the football.' The commentary drifts in after them through the open door. *There's Ball running, there's Hurst – can he do it?* The men stand rooted to the spot, craning to hear. *He has done! – yes – no,* their faces twist in agony. *No, the linesman says no! … It's a goal! It's a goal! Oh, the Germans have gone mad at the referee!* The men go mad at Sandra.

She is unaffected. Her eyes are like arrow slits as she turns to Ted in disgust. 'Aren't you ashamed, isn't your wedding day more important than the World Cup?'

Ted can't help himself somehow. Until this moment of his life lies have fallen from his lips like rain, but on this occasion, this very public, important occasion, we watch in horror as he drops, like a parachutist without a parachute, onto the hard rock of truth.

'Of course not', he says, 'It's the Final!'

Whack! goes Sandra's hand against his cheek. 'Sandra,' Ted whines in a feeble attempt at mollification but Sandra is white-hot now. 'We haven't had any speeches,' she screams at him.' We haven't had any toasts, we haven't cut the cake. What kind of a wedding do you call this?'

'You're just riff-raff!' Beatrice's voice booms out as she elbows her way towards her new son-in-law, handbag at the ready.

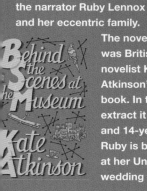

Behind the Scenes at the Museum tells the story of the narrator Ruby Lennox and her eccentric family.

The novel was British novelist Kate Atkinson's first book. In this extract it is 1966 and 14-year-old Ruby is bridesmaid at her Uncle Ted's wedding to Sandra.

2 Read the story about another fall. Choose the correct option.

I'll never forget (1) *to fall / falling* off my bike when I was twelve. I was trying (2) *to impress / impressing* the boy next door by doing some stunts. I'd tried (3) *to do / doing* the same stunt before but never in front of an audience, and unfortunately it went horribly wrong. I forgot (4) *to brake / braking* slowly and I remember (5) *to fall / falling* headfirst into a huge puddle. I stopped (6) *to do / doing* bike stunts after that.

Speaking

Work in pairs. Choose **two** of the things below and tell your partner.

Something …

- you'll never forget doing
- you'll always regret doing
- you never remember to do
- you've never tried but would like to do
- you've stopped doing

G Grammar focus – explanation & more practice of verbs with *-ing* & *to* on page 146

Function globally conceding points in a discussion

Warm up

1 Look at the photos. What educational achievements and skills are necessary in today's world?

2 Read the two arguments about educational standards. Tell a partner what your reaction is to what you have read.

Dumbing down

Educational standards have fallen. Most people today seem to lack even a basic grasp of geography or scientific processes, let alone any knowledge of literature and the arts. Popular entertainment such as television and the internet has contributed widely to the overall dumbing down prevalent in the twenty-first century.

'Clevering up'

Many people have a wider range of knowledge today. Most people are familiar with thousands of subjects, even though many might not have a deep grasp of them. The ability to process large amounts of information, think fast and adapt quickly to new situations is what counts in the 21st century knowledge economy – not useless facts that have been learned by heart.

Listening

1 2.48–2.49 Listen to two conversations. Answer the questions for each one.

1 Who starts the discussion – the man or the woman?
2 What are they talking about?
3 Who concedes the other might be right?

2 Listen again. Decide if the sentences are true (*T*) or false (*F*).

1 The man thinks schools aren't as good as they used to be.
2 The woman agrees some young people aren't very good at maths.
3 The woman thinks algebra is important outside school.
4 The woman thinks a changing world requires new skills.
5 The woman thinks if you can use the internet, you don't need to know anything.

Language focus: conceding points in a discussion

1 Look at these sentences from the listening. Underline the phrase that indicates the speaker is conceding a point to the other speaker.

Man: What do they teach them in schools nowadays?
Woman: All right, all right, calm down. Admittedly, some people today don't seem to be able to do maths in their heads …

2 Make phrases with a similar meaning to the phrase above by completing them with a word from the box.

point	true	right	may	something

There's _____ in what you're saying.
I suppose / guess you're _____.
I take your _____.
You _____ be right.
It may well be _____ that …

Speaking

1 Work in pairs.

A: Prepare some arguments for this topic: 'Academic qualifications are the key to success in life.'

B: Prepare some arguments for this topic: 'The best education is the one you get through experience.'

2 A: Present your arguments for your topic. B: Listen and respond. Concede points using the phrases above. Then swap roles and do the same again.

Global English

The **rise** and **fall** of English?
by David Crystal

Why does a language become used internationally, or even – as in the case of English – globally? A surprising number of people think it's something to do with the language itself. They say that English has become a world language because it's more beautiful than other languages, or because it has a simpler grammar or vocabulary.

The reason is none of these things. Notions such as beauty are impossible to pin down. And, as any student of *Global* knows, English has quite a complex grammar and a very large vocabulary! There are also aspects of English which make it more difficult to learn than some other languages, such as its irregular spellings. Yet this hasn't stopped its rise as a global *lingua franca*.

A language becomes a world language for one reason only: the power of the people who speak it. But power can be of many different kinds, and it's important to see which kinds of power fostered the growth of English over the centuries.

English started on its international career during the Middle Ages, when it moved from England up into Scotland and across the sea into Ireland. Soon after, it crossed the Atlantic, and then the Indian Ocean and beyond. Here we're talking about political and military power. When the British Empire became a global reality, English was described as 'a language on which the sun never sets'.

But military power is not enough, as political fortunes rise and fall. Today, English is still a world language, though the British Empire is a thing of the past. Three other kinds of power helped maintain its position. During the Industrial Revolution, we see the power of knowledge: English became the main language of science and technology. During the 19th century, we see it associated with economic power: if 'money talks', then the language it was chiefly talking about was that of the pound and the dollar. And during the 20th century, we see it as the language of cultural power, used in everything from transport to advertising, from pop music to the internet.

Some people think that other languages could never match this combination of circumstances. But there is only one rule when it comes to talking about the rise and fall of languages: never say never.

Warm up

Why does a language become an international language? Read the options below and tick (✔) the ones you agree with.

- Because it is simple
- Because it is beautiful
- Because of power
- Because of money

Reading

1 Read *The rise and fall of English*? How does the author answer the question in the Warm up? How does he specify his answer?

2 Which statements can you infer from the text? Mark them with a tick (✔).

1 Many people have different views to the author about why English is a global language.
2 The author had trouble learning English.
3 English began in England.
4 English destroyed many other languages as it spread around the world.
5 During the Industrial Revolution, all scientists spoke English.
6 England and the United States had a lot of financial power in the 19th century.
7 The author is sure English will always be powerful.

3 Find these words in the text. Then decide which is the best synonym.

1 to pin down   a to understand exactly   c to postpone
         b to explain
2 to foster   a to leave alone   c to stop from
         b to help develop   developing
3 to maintain   a to change   c to develop
         b to keep the same
4 chiefly   a completely   c mostly
         b a little

Speaking

Work in pairs. Choose **two** of the sets of questions below and discuss.

- Is English an important language in your country? Do children learn it at school? How long has it been important?
- What other languages are important in the world? If you could speak another two languages, which ones would they be?
- Do you think it's unfair that English is an international language? Would you prefer it to be another one? Which one?
- Is it a good idea for everyone in the world to speak the same language? What could be some of the problems in this?

Writing a proposal

Reading

1 Read Gemma's proposal for improving student facilities on her university campus. What three facilities does she recommend improving?

Introduction
The purpose of this report is to make recommendations on ways to improve the student facilities on the university campus. I have recently completed a post-graduate degree course at the university and overall was very satisfied with the experience. The university campus is large and attractive, and it provides excellent libraries, lecture halls and IT services. However, some of its student facilities could be greatly improved, as outlined below.

Restaurants and cafés
First of all, there are not enough restaurants on the campus offering cheap, healthy food. Prices are very high in most places, and the majority of students cannot afford to eat there regularly. The only cheap restaurants on the campus just sell fast food and on top of that they are very large and noisy. Similarly, there are not enough cafés equipped with wi-fi where students can sit down and work while enjoying a cup of tea of coffee.

Sports facilities
Another area in which improvements could be made is the provision of sports and fitness facilities. At present there is a sports centre with a small gym and a few tennis and badminton courts, but these are often booked up, and moreover the annual subscription is very high. This is not satisfactory for such a large campus and students are entitled to expect better facilities.

Suggestions
I suggest firstly that the university should provide cheaper and healthier restaurants on campus, including some specifically for graduate students. This would enable them

to meet and discuss research with their peers while having lunch or dinner and in this way foster a sense of community. Secondly, it should open more cafés with wi-fi so that students could relax and study at the same time. Thirdly, I recommend extending the fitness facilities so that all students could exercise regularly on campus. I also suggest reducing the subscription. With better facilities students would not only have a healthier and more pleasant life, but their performance in their studies would also improve.

2 Read the proposal again and complete the chart.

	Problem(s)	Suggested improvement(s)	Reason(s) for improvement
Restaurants			
Cafés			
Sports facilities			

Writing skills: writing a proposal

A Making suggestions
1 Choose the best way to make a suggestion.

1 The purpose of this report is to *make / do* recommendations on ways to improve the facilities.
2 Student facilities *could / can* be greatly improved.
3 I suggest *the university to provide / that the university should provide* cheaper restaurants.
4 I recommend *extending / to extend* the fitness facilities.
5 I suggest *reducing / to reduce* the subscription.
6 It *should / has to* open more cafés equipped with wi-fi.

2 Check your ideas in Gemma's report.

3 Complete the suggestions (1–5) below using information from the notes.

- Accommodation fees too high
- No drinks machine in the common room
- Student common room needs redecorating
- Not enough computers in the IT room
- Gym opening hours too short

1 I recommend _____ the fees.
2 There _____ a drinks machine in the common room.
3 I suggest that the school _____ the common room.
4 The school _____ provide more computers for the IT room.
5 I suggest _____ the gym opening hours.

B Justifying suggestions

> When you make a suggestion, give a reason to justify it.

The university should provide more cafes. **This would enable students** *to meet their colleagues and* **in this way** *foster a sense of community. I recommend extending the fitness facilities and reducing the entrance fees,* **so that** *all students* **could** *exercise regularly.*
With / If students had *better facilities, they* **would** *have a more pleasant life.*

Match the suggestions in A exercise 3 with the reasons below.

a This would enable more students to work on the campus.
b If it were more attractive, students might use it more.
c This would encourage students to exercise more.
d In this way, students could have coffee together during the breaks.
e With lower fees, student numbers would increase.

Preparing to write

Work in pairs. Discuss a school, college, university or workplace that one or both of you know. Make notes on ways **either** to improve student or workplace facilities **or** to increase student numbers.

Describing problems

- *First of all / Firstly*, there are *not enough / insufficient* places to *meet / have coffee*
- *Secondly / Moreover / On top of that*, the libraries are too *noisy / crowded* for students to work in
- *Another / A further* problem is that the common room needs *redecorating / refurnishing / renovating*
- This is *not satisfactory / far from satisfactory / unacceptable*
- Students are entitled to expect *better facilities / lower rents*

Writing

Write a proposal based on the ideas you have discussed. Use sub-headings and follow this structure:

Introduction (purpose of the report / strengths of the institution)
Problems
Suggestions

Improving your grammar

1 Which of these statements best describes your attitude to grammar?

> I find grammar very interesting. I enjoy studying rules and doing grammar practice exercises.

> I dislike studying grammar. I prefer to concentrate on communicating my ideas, even if I make mistakes.

Discuss your answers with a partner. Why is it important to be accurate when you speak or write in English?

2 Read the list of grammar areas below. Tick (✔) the ones in which you sometimes make errors, and add others. To remind yourself, you could:

- look at your corrected homework.
- ask your partner.
- think about when your teacher or another person has corrected your speaking.

Gerunds or infinitives	☐	Formation of verbs	☐
Using correct tenses	☐	Word order	☐
Conditional sentences	☐	Articles	☐
Singular-plural agreement	☐	Prepositions	☐
Countable / uncountable nouns	☐	Other	☐

3 Read the suggestions below, then discuss with a partner how each of you will work on accuracy this week.

- ★ Select an area that you want to improve, and make it your focus for the next week.
- ★ Look at your written work to find examples of errors you have made in this area. Copy the corrections into a notebook, and memorise them.
- ★ Do you understand why the mistakes are wrong? If not, study the rules in a grammar book.
- ★ Write true sentences about yourself using the grammar area. Ask your teacher to check them.
- ★ When you write in English this week, read it to check for mistakes in your chosen area.
- ★ When you speak in English this week, ask a friend or teacher to correct mistakes you make in this area.
- ★ At the end of the week, discuss your progress with your partner.

Vocabulary and Writing

1 Look at the phrases in the box and check that you understand them. Use a dictionary if necessary.

> cry your eyes out
> burst into tears
> weep with joy (or rage, etc.)
> cry tears of rage (or frustration, etc.)
> be bored to tears
> cry with laughter

2 Work in pairs and answer the questions.
- Talk about an occasion when you were bored to tears.
- For what sorts of reasons do people cry tears of rage or frustration?
- Describe an occasion when you or somebody you know burst into tears.

3 Look at the pictures. Describe each of the pictures using the phrases in exercise 1.

4 Work in pairs. Choose one picture in exercise 3 and think of the reasons why the person in the picture is feeling like that. Write a paragraph about what led up to this situation.

Listening

1 Look at a diagram showing how tears are produced. Put the words in the correct place (1–3).

> eyelash   pupil   eyelid

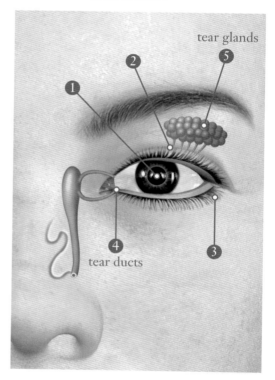

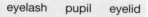

tear glands

tear ducts

2 🔊 2.50 Now listen to a lecture about tears. Where are these tears produced? Decide which is the correct place in the diagram (4 or 5).

> basal tears   reflex tears   emotional tears

3 Listen again and complete the lecture notes. Add other details about each type of tears if you can.

Function of tears
Basal: _____
Reflex: _____
Emotional: _____

4 Work in groups of three. Using your diagram and your notes, take it in turns to explain how **one** type of tears functions.

Grammar

1 Read the rules in the box. Then underline the relative clauses in the sentences from the listening below. Write the sentences as examples in the correct place in the rules.

Their job is to wash out foreign objects that come into contact with the eye.
In addition, cold air or wind, which dry out the eyes, cause the tear glands to produce reflex tears.
Your tear ducts are also connected to your nose, which is why tears sometimes run down into it.
Emotional tears help people to establish a bond with people they care for.

- defining relative clauses identify a thing, person or place; without this information, the sentence isn't complete or doesn't make sense
  Example: *Their job is to wash out foreign objects that come into contact with the eye.*
- in defining relative clauses where the relative pronoun is the object, the pronoun can be left out
  Example: _____
- non-defining clauses add extra information about a person, place or thing; without this information the sentence still makes sense; the clause is separated from the rest of the sentence by commas; the relative pronoun can't be left out
  Example: _____
- non-defining clauses can also give a comment on the whole sentence
  Example: _____
- non-defining clauses are mostly used in formal, written speech

2 Complete the text with relative pronouns where necessary.

> Professor Randolph Cornelius, (1) _____ is an expert in crying, studied tears using an experiment (2) _____ he carried out at Vassar College in the US. He showed participants pictures with people (3) _____ had tears rolling down their face and other pictures in (4) _____ the people's tears had been deleted. The people with tears were clearly identified as being sad, (5) _____ in itself isn't surprising. But when participants looked at the people (6) _____ tears had been deleted, they often couldn't identify their emotions. The experiment, (7) _____ Cornelius repeated several times with the same results, clearly shows what a powerful signal tears give.

3 Complete the sentences with your own ideas.

1 I often get frustrated by things that _____
2 I get angry with people who _____
3 I love doing activities which _____
4 _____, which makes me feel really sad.
5 _____, which usually really cheers me up.

G **Grammar focus** – explanation & more practice of defining & non-defining relative clauses on page 148

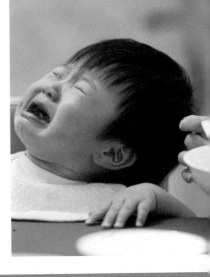

Speaking

1 Work in pairs. Ask and answer the questions in the questionnaire. Give your partner examples or further information.

1 Do you think people cry more or less as they grow older? Why do you think this is the case? Do you see this as being a good or bad thing?

2 In what situations can crying be used to manipulate people?

3 In your country is it more culturally acceptable to cry or not to cry ...
- at a wedding?
- at a funeral?

4 Have you ever cried ...
- at the end of a sad film?
- while reading a book?
- while listening to music?
- at a sports event?

5 Do you think crying makes people feel better? How? In what situations would you encourage someone to cry?

6 Imagine you are on a crowded bus in your country and an adult is crying. How would people feel (embarrassed, sympathetic, impatient?) and how would they react?

Tears & Laughter

Reading

1 Read the information on page 117 about Jane Austen and *Sense and Sensibility*. Look at the book cover. Which of the girls do you think is Marianne? Why?

2 Now read the extract and answer the questions.

1 Why do you think Marianne is sad?
2 Who do you think Willoughby might be?
3 What activities remind her of him?

3 Read the extract again. Tick (✔) the ways in which Marianne shows her grief.

1 she doesn't eat ☐
2 she sleeps late ☐
3 she cries ☐
4 she gets angry with her family ☐
5 she doesn't speak ☐
6 she goes riding alone ☐
7 she walks around the village by herself ☐
8 she plays music she played for Willoughby ☐

4 Explain how Marianne's family react to her behaviour.

5 What do you think of Marianne's behaviour?

Extend your vocabulary – metaphors: strong emotions

Experiencing strong emotions is like being *hit, touched* or *hurt*.
The parting from Willoughby **hit** Marianne really hard.
It **pained** Marianne's family to see her suffering.
Marianne was **touched** by her family's support.
Willoughby's lack of communication **hurt** Marianne's feelings.
When Willoughby didn't want to see her anymore, it **came as a huge blow**.
She was **overcome** by grief.

1 Can you understand this metaphor? What sort of news might provoke emotions so strong that they feel like a physical blow?

2 Can you express emotions in this way in your language?

Grammar

1 Read the examples and the rules in the box. Do you think participle clauses are more common in spoken or written language?

> She was unable to talk and unwilling to take any nourishment, **giving** pain every moment to her mother and sisters.
> She wandered about the village of Allenham, **crying over** the unhappy changes in her circumstances.
>
> • present participle clauses are used to link information so that more information is given in shorter sentences
> • a present participle is used in one clause instead of a subject and a main verb; the subject of the actions must be the same
> • when the participle clause is negative, *not* is used <u>before</u> the participle (*not eating*)

2 The present participle is often used after *before*, *after*, *when*, *while*, *on* and *without*. Find two examples in the reading text.

3 Rewrite the phrases in bold using a participle clause.

Marianne wrote to Willoughby **and she told him** that she was in London. **She didn't hear anything from him**, so she wrote again but again she got no reply. She therefore wrote a third letter **and asked him** to return her notes and a lock of her hair. He did this **and explained** that he was engaged to another person. **When she discovered that** Willoughby was going to marry a rich heiress, Marianne was overcome with grief. Willoughby later told her sister that, **because he feared** he would be disinherited if he married Marianne, he had decided to marry for money.

Sense and Sensibility

They saw nothing of Marianne till dinner time when she entered the room and took her place at the table without saying a word. Her eyes were red and swollen; and it seemed as if she held back her tears with difficulty. She avoided the looks of them all, could neither eat nor speak. After some time, on her mother's silently pressing her hand with sympathy, she burst into tears and left the room.

This depression continued the whole evening. She was without any power over herself. The slightest mention of anything to do with Willoughby upset her in an instant. Her family were most attentive to her comfort but it was impossible for them to keep clear of every subject which her feelings connected with him.

***

Marianne was awake the whole night and she wept the greatest part of it. She got up with a headache and was unable to talk. She was unwilling to take any nourishment, giving pain every moment to her mother and sisters. When breakfast was over she walked out by herself. She wandered about the village of Allenham, crying over the unhappy changes in her circumstances for most of the morning.

The evening passed off in the equal indulgence of feeling. Marianne played over every favourite song that she had been used to play to Willoughby, every piece of music in which their voices had been joined. She sat at the instrument gazing on every line of music that he had written out for her, till her heart was so heavy that no further sadness could be gained. This nourishment of grief continued every day. She spent whole hours at the pianoforte alternately singing and crying; her voice often totally choked by her tears.

4 Match the two halves of the sentences to tell a story.

1 After meeting Lucy at a friend's dinner party
2 But on hearing she had been seeing another man
3 Not wanting to show her I was upset,
4 After a few months, I decided to start doing sport
5 And while out running one day,
6 The problem was I couldn't be with her

a I decided to break off the relationship.
b without thinking of Lucy.
c instead of feeling sorry for myself.
d I met somebody else.
e I pretended not to care.
f we started going out together.

Ⓖ **Grammar focus** – explanation & more practice of present participle clauses on page 148

Glossary

grief (*noun*) – a strong feeling of sadness, usually because someone has died

swollen (*adjective*) – an area of your body that is swollen has increased in size as a result of an injury or an illness

Writing

1 Work in pairs. Choose **one** of the tasks below.

A Rewrite the story in Grammar exercise 3 from Willoughby's point of view.

B Rewrite the story in Grammar exercise 4: add in more details about the characters and the events and add dialogue. You can also change details in the story or change the ending.

2 Read your story out to a partner who did the same task. How similar or different are your stories?

Jane Austen (1775–1817) was an English novelist whose work focused on the questions of courtship, marriage, morals and inheritance. *Sense and Sensibility* (1811) tells the story of Elinor and Marianne Dashwood, two sisters who are very different in personality. Elinor is very practical and sensible and Marianne is very emotional and sensitive.

Speaking

1 Can you remember the last time you really laughed? What was the reason?

2 Look at these proverbs and try to explain what they mean. Can you think of other proverbs about laughter in your language? Tell the class.

> Time spent laughing is time spent with the gods (Japanese)
>
> Much laughter, little wit (Portuguese)
>
> Laugh and the world laughs with you; weep and you weep alone (American)
>
> People show their character by what they laugh at (German)
>
> The teeth that laugh are also those that bite (West African)
>
> He who laughs too much is hiding his grief (Italian)

Listening

1 🔊 **2.51** Listen to the introduction to a TV programme. Who is laughing?

2 🔊 **2.52** Now listen to the lecture. Tick (✔) the points that are mentioned in the listening.

1 The advantages of live laughter. ☐
2 The problems with live laughter. ☐
3 The origins of canned laughter. ☐
4 The problems with canned laughter. ☐
5 The different kinds of canned laughter. ☐
6 Other kinds of fake laughter. ☐
7 Changes in the way people laugh. ☐
8 The disappearance of canned laughter. ☐

3 Look at the statements that you ticked. Listen again and make notes on further details.

4 Work in pairs. Discuss these questions.

- How do you feel about canned laughter?
- Is there more canned laughter on foreign programmes than those from your country?
- Do you agree that humour and laughter have changed and become more subtle?

Extend your vocabulary – ways of saying laugh

1 🔊 **2.53** Match the verbs to the definitions. Then listen to five people laughing and check.

1	giggle	a	start laughing uncontrollably (used in informal speech)
2	chuckle	b	laugh loudly and unpleasantly; old women often laugh like this in stories
3	snigger	c	laugh in a high-pitched voice, often in a silly way or when you are nervous; children and especially girls often do this
4	cackle	d	laugh quietly, especially in a private or secret way; adult men often laugh like this
5	crack up	e	laugh in an unpleasant way, often at something rude or somebody's mistakes

2 All these words for *laugh* can be used as nouns and verbs except one. Which one?

3 Are there different words for these ways of laughing in your language? Do you have words for other types of laughs?

Grammar and Pronunciation

1 Read the examples and the information in the box. What would be the usual way to say the example sentences without emphasis?

> **What** has also changed **is** the way people laugh.
>
> **The thing that** American producers liked most **was** the fact that the laff box allowed them to simulate an audience.
>
> You can emphasise a particular part of a sentence using these structures:
> - *it is / was* + person / thing + relative clause
> - *what / the thing that* + clause + *is / was*

2 🔊 2.54 Listen to the sentences in exercise 1. Mark where there is a pause in the sentence (/). Then listen to the sentences again and mark the words that are stressed most. Finally, listen again and repeat the sentences.

3 Change the emphasis of the sentences in bold. Rewrite them using *What … is / was*. Then compare your sentences with a partner: take turns to read out a sentence, paying attention to pronunciation.

4 Work in pairs. A: read the story on page 126. B: read a different story on page 133. Guess the correct alternatives in each sentence.

5 A: check your story with your partner, paying attention to pronunciation. B: use the correct version of partner A's story to confirm or correct A's guesses.

A: I think it was … who / that …

B: Yes, you're right. / No it was actually … who / that …

Then swap roles and check B's story.

6 Which of the pieces of information in exercises 4 and 5 did you think was most interesting?

ⓖ **Grammar focus** – explanation & more practice of emphasising (cleft sentences) on page 148

Five facts about laughter

1 People don't just laugh when they find something funny, they laugh to show agreement or that they like somebody. **Ordinary social comments cause most laughter.**
What causes …

2 **The difference in the way men and women laugh is particularly interesting.** Women usually produce giggles and chuckles and men produce deeper sounds, often through the nose.
What is …

3 As laughter is a social experience, it is hard to say if laughing is good for your health. **Being with family and friends is probably the most important aspect.**
What is probably …

4 **Many people don't know that laughter can kill.** Some unlucky laughers have had heart attacks and strokes because they laughed so hard.
What many people …

5 People certainly don't lose their sense of humour when they get older. **But the ability to understand complex humour often decreases with age.**
What often decreases …

Part 4

Speaking & Listening
Humour around the world

Reading
Comedy performances around the world

Speaking
Improvisation dialogue

Speaking and Listening

1 What kinds of things make you laugh?

2 In 2001 Professor Richard Wiseman did a year-long research project into humour around the world and the reasons people find jokes funny. Match the reasons (a–c) to the jokes from his research (1–3) below.

Reasons why people find jokes funny …

a it makes us feel superior to people in the jokes who are stupid or unattractive

b it is a way of coping with problems or events in our lives that we find difficult to talk about openly (for example sex, marriage, death)

c it surprises us because of some kind of incongruity (something that is out of place or doesn't fit our expectations)

1 A woman gets on a bus with her baby. The bus driver says: 'That's the ugliest baby that I've ever seen. Ugh!' The woman goes to the rear of the bus and sits down, fuming. She says to a man next to her: 'The driver just insulted me!' The man says: 'You go right up there and tell him off – go ahead, I'll hold your monkey for you.'

2 I said to the gym instructor: 'Can you teach me to do the splits?' He said: 'How flexible are you?' I said: 'I can't make Tuesdays.'

3 A woman told her friend: 'For eighteen years my husband and I were the happiest people in the world! Then we met.'

3 🔊 2.55 Listen to the joke that in Wiseman's research was found to have the most appeal around the world. Count how many people in the class found the joke funny. Which of the reasons in exercise 2 apply to this joke?

Reading

1 Look at the pictures on page 121 showing different types of comedy around the world. Are you familiar with any of these types of comedy?

2 Work in pairs. A: read about types 1 and 2. B: read about types 3 and 4. Make notes about these things:

1 whether the comedy is an old or new form of humour
2 why it is funny
3 which props are used

3 Using your notes from exercise 2, tell your partner about the types of comedy you read about. Then work together to answer these questions.

Which type(s) of comedy …
a involves audience participation?
b can be done silently?
c usually uses no props at all?
d is not scripted?
e is very culturally specific?
f uses current events?

4 Find words and expressions in the text which mean the following:

1 be very unsuccessful (text 1)
2 make decisions quickly in a difficult situation (text 1)
3 a particular way of speaking or moving (text 2)
4 the sound something makes when it hits something with a lot of force (text 3)
5 range of things somebody can do (text 3)
6 happening in a natural way without being planned (text 4)

5 Are the types of comedy in the text known and popular in your country? Is there another type of humour which is popular or connected to your country? How would you describe it?

Comedy performances around the world

1 Stand-up comedy is performed by one person, usually without any props apart from a microphone. It is characterised by a conversational storytelling style and usually comprises a series of humorous stories based on everyday observation or political events. Professional stand-up comics spend hours writing and perfecting their routines before a performance; indeed many spend years performing the same material until they have perfected it. But whether a routine works well or 'bombs' depends very much on the individual audience. Stand-up comics have to be able to think on their feet and react immediately to negative audience feedback.

2 *Rakugo* is a traditional Japanese art of comic storytelling, which has also been called 'sit down comedy'. The comedian or storyteller, who usually wears traditional Japanese clothes, remains seated while performing a monologue with comic punch lines. *Rakugo* goes back to the end of the 17th century and about 300 classic stories are still performed today, along with new stories by contemporary artists. Traditionally, storytellers were male and today there are few female performers. *Rakugo* relies on the skill of the storyteller to portray different characters through clever changes of voice, facial expressions and mannerisms and using only a fan and small towel as props to represent different objects. *Rakugo* stories feature many puns as well as topics and customs which are particular to Japanese culture.

3 Slapstick is a very visual comedy with lots of physical action. The humour often results from comic timing and unexpected events and can be quite violent: tried and tested elements include people falling over, people being hit with various props and pie throwing. Slapstick goes back to mime in Greek and Roman times, but the actual word comes from a wooden instrument used in the Italian *comedia dell'arte* performances in the 16th century: when used to strike somebody

on the bottom it produced a loud whack, much to the delight of the audience. The development of film in the late nineteenth and early twentieth century led to a wider repertoire of jokes and more complex routines. Today many different types of humour feature elements of slapstick.

4 Improvisational comedy (or improv) is an ancient oral art which has been practised throughout history all over the world. It is a form of theatre in which no script is used: the actors make up the plot and dialogue as they go along. Improvisers often ask the audience to name characters and a setting (for example, a blind secret agent and a cricket player at the dentist's) and then they develop short spontaneous scenes within the framework of these suggestions. Good improv results from successful collaboration between participants: improvisers must listen carefully to their partners, accept their ideas and build upon them. The result is that the audience and the actors share a unique experience which can never be repeated. Humour usually arises naturally from the situation.

Glossary

prop (*noun*) – a piece of furniture or small object used in a play or film

pun (*noun*) – a humorous use of a word that has two meanings, or of words with the same sound but different meanings.

punch line (*noun*) – the last few words of a joke, including the part that makes the joke funny

Speaking

Choose **one** of the improvisation tasks below.

A The standard improvisation

Work in pairs. Think of two characters and a place and improvise a scene.

B The dubbed film

Work in pairs. Think of two characters and a place.
Improvise a scene at the front of the class using your characters and place – but don't speak (you can move your mouths as if you are speaking). Two other students sit in front of you and improvise what you are saying – as in a dubbed movie.

C Problem-solving

Work in pairs. Think of a problem; think of an object. Don't tell anybody! Two people (one person from two different pairs) go to the front of the class and present their problem and object. Each person solves the other's problem with his / her object.

A: I've lost my keys and my wife isn't coming home for three hours. I've just bought this shirt ...

B: I got robbed and I've got no money. But I've just found this ball in the street ...

A: Here's my new shirt; you can take it back to the shop and get the money back.

B: Erm ... Take the ball. You can play football until your wife comes home.

Function globally interrupting

a b c d

Warm up

1 Describe the situations in the photos. Where are the people? What are they doing? What do you think their relationship is to one another?

2 Would you consider it appropriate to interrupt in these situations? Explain why or why not.

3 Are there 'rules' concerning status or age about interrupting in your culture? How would you explain these?

Listening

1 🔊 2.56–2.57 Listen to the two conversations. For each conversation, note down …

1 who is speaking.
2 what the speaker is talking about.

2 Listen again. For each conversation, note down who interrupts and why.

Language focus: interrupting

1 Look at sentences from the listening. Underline the phrases used for interrupting.

1 May I interrupt for a moment? Could you just draw the curtains?
2 Just a second, don't you usually cycle to work?
3 Could I just say something here? Are you sure that …
4 I'd like to say something if I may. I think …
5 Wait a minute, how come you didn't notice?
6 Excuse me for interrupting, but what I think the others were trying to say …
7 Hang on, didn't you think it was a bit odd?

2 Put the phrases in exercise 1 on the scale of formal to informal.

Formal	Neutral	Informal
_____	Excuse me …	_____
_____	Sorry, but …	_____
_____		_____
		_____

Speaking

1 Work in pairs. Use appropriate phrases from the Language focus exercise to do the following tasks.

A: B is your friend. Tell him / her a funny or embarrassing story about something that happened to you or a friend (at work, at home, while travelling, when you were at school). Answer all your partner's questions or reply to their comments.

B: Interrupt when you want more information or something isn't clear.

2 Swap roles.

B: A is a new acquaintance that you have met at a conference. Tell him / her about what your job (or course of study) involves or the place you work / study.

A: Interrupt when you want more information or something isn't clear.

Global voices

Warm up

1 What would you say makes somebody a funny (amusing) person? What personality traits do they have? What do they do?

2 Would you describe yourself as a funny person?

Listening

1 2.58–2.63 Listen to people talking about the funniest person they know. For each person write down who the person is and one thing that makes them funny.

Giorgio, Italy   _____
Georgios, Greece   _____
Luisa, Chile   _____
Erik, Sweden   _____
Quirin, Germany   _____
Raphael, Brazil   _____

2 Listen again and check your answers in exercise 1. Add other reasons why the people are funny if you can.

Language focus: *actually*

1 Look at the sentences from the listening and the dictionary entry for *actually*. Which meaning does *actually* correspond to in these sentences?

The funniest person I know is **actually** a person I met.
The funniest person I know is **actually** one of my friends.

> **actually**
> **1** used for emphasising what is really true
> **2** used for emphasising that something is surprising
> **3** (*spoken*) used when correcting what someone has said
> **4** (*spoken*) used for admitting something

2 Write sentences using *actually* to reflect these situations.

1 Emphasise that you have met a famous comedian in reality.
2 Emphasise that you find it surprising that your teacher can tell good jokes.
3 Correct the assumption that you are good at telling jokes. You are not.
4 Admit that you didn't understand a joke that was just told.

Speaking

Work with a partner. Tell your partner who the funniest person you know is. It can be somebody in your family, a friend or a famous comedian. Explain what makes this person funny.

Giorgio, Italy   Georgios, Greece

Luisa, Chile   Erik, Sweden

Quirin, Germany   Raphael, Brazil

Writing a competition entry

Reading

1 Read Miriam's entry for the competition below. Who does she nominate for the award? What do you think is his most important quality?

> **We are looking for a special person to win our Best Teacher Award. If you know a teacher who deserves the award, write and let us know why.**

a _____. All teachers, no matter what they teach, can help you extend your knowledge of different subjects. However, really good teachers do more; they develop students' minds. They teach you to think, use logic, and put theory into practice in real life. In my view, Matthew East is one of those special teachers and so I would like to nominate him for the Best Teacher Award.

b _____. I can honestly say that he has all the qualities I look for in a teacher. His academic record is outstanding, and he has considerable teaching experience. But more than that, he is good at encouraging his students. I felt he believed in me and that inspired me to achieve success.

c _____. One of his main strengths is that he gives very clear explanations, and also gives plenty of examples to illustrate his points. He takes on board his students' interests and so his examples are useful and relevant. Another thing I particularly appreciate about him is that he doesn't mind repeating things if you didn't understand the first time.

d _____. Perhaps his most important quality is his ability to make lessons fun. His lessons are always lively and he has an excellent sense of humour. That makes everyone pay attention, and so the next day you can remember what he was talking about. The last point I would like to highlight is that he is patient and never makes fun of students, which I think is really important in a teacher.

e _____. He is someone who motivates and inspires his students to do well, and so I very much hope you will choose him as the best teacher in your competition.

2 Choose the best first sentence for each paragraph.

1 I met Matthew while I was doing a part-time course in media communication and I loved his way of teaching.
2 A good teacher is not just someone who prepares you to pass exams, but someone who prepares you for life.
3 For all these reasons, I believe Matthew thoroughly deserves the award.
4 Matthew is simply a brilliant classroom teacher.
5 He also has many personal qualities.

3 Find adjectives used to describe:

1 Matthew.
2 his academic record.
3 his explanations.
4 his examples.
5 his lessons.
6 his sense of humour.

4 Do you think Miriam has written a convincing entry? Why / Why not?

Writing skills: a writing checklist

1 Read the following tips about writing. Do you agree?

a Always keep your reader in mind.
b Think carefully about your purpose and how to achieve it.
c Write in an appropriate register.
d Include appropriate content.
e Plan and organise your ideas.
f Make the connections between your ideas clear.
g Use a range of vocabulary, grammar and expressions.
h Remember that accuracy is very important in writing.

2 Match the questions in the checklist below to tips c–h in exercise 1.

1 Have you included a variety of ideas, facts or opinions with examples to illustrate your ideas?
2 Have you used correct spelling, punctuation and grammar?
3 Are your paragraphs clear and of an appropriate length? Have you used topic sentences? Are your first and last sentences clear and interesting?
4 Have you joined sentences with appropriate linkers? Have you used appropriate expressions to link ideas?
5 Have you used varied and more complex grammatical structures and colourful, interesting and varied vocabulary?
6 Have you written in an appropriate style (e.g. formal, informal, factual, personal, entertaining)?

3 Work in pairs and look at Miriam's entry. Ask and answer the questions in the checklist.

4 Work in pairs. Look at a piece of writing you have done recently. Ask and answer the same questions. What could you do differently next time?

Preparing to write

1 Read the competition entry and choose someone to write about.

> **Is there a special person who has inspired or motivated you in your life? Write and tell us about them and how they have inspired you. They could win our *Personal Hero Award!***

2 With a partner, ask and answer about the person you have chosen.

- How did you meet or hear about this person ?
- In what ways is this person special?
- What have they achieved in their lives?
- What are their personal qualities?
- How has this person inspired you?
- Why do you think they deserve the award?

Describing personal qualities

- One of his main strengths is that …
- Another thing I particularly appreciate about him is that …
- I can honestly say that … / But more than that, …
- He is very good at …
- Perhaps his most important quality is his ability to …
- The last point I would like highlight is that …

Writing

Write the competition entry based on your discussion with your partner.

Keeping up your English

1 Complete the sentences to summarise what you have learnt about yourself as a language learner.

1. My strengths in English are _____
2. I have made progress with _____
3. My favourite language-learning activities are _____
4. I learn best by _____
5. New language-learning strategies that I have used successfully are _____
6. I still need to work on _____
7. After this course, I intend to keep up my English by _____

2 Work in pairs and discuss your answers.

3 If you are not planning to continue studying English formally, you can still keep up your English in a variety of ways. Read the suggestions and tick (✔) the ones that you plan to do.

- ★ Find someone who wants to learn your language and arrange to meet for a language exchange.
- ★ Join with other people who want to continue learning English and arrange regular informal meetings for conversation (e.g. at a restaurant).
- ★ Find an Internet pen pal.
- ★ Write a diary in English.
- ★ Create a class website, and visit and contribute to it regularly.
- ★ Watch films and DVDs in English regularly.
- ★ Write a blog in English.
- ★ Read or listen to the news in English every day.
- ★ Subscribe to an English magazine or journal.
- ★ Tune in to satellite TV channels in English or to the radio once a week.
- ★ Buy self-study grammar or vocabulary books and use them regularly.

4 Make two plans for keeping up your English.

> I am going to …
> a _____.
> b _____.

Unit 2, Grammar (page 21)

1 Read the sentences. Then make a question for the words in bold. Begin with the question word provided.

1 A human being has **nine senses**. In addition to the five senses we know about, there is also the sense of heat, the sense of pain, the sense of balance and the sense of body awareness. *How* …?

2 The first invention to break the sound barrier was **the whip**. *What* …?

3 A cup of coffee **has more caffeine** than a cup of tea. *Which* …?

4 Carrots were **originally purple on the outside and yellow on the inside**. *What* …?

2 When you have made your questions, ask them to your partner. How many did your partner answer correctly?

Unit 4, Vocabulary & Speaking (page 49)

1 You need these things, but you don't know the name for them. Describe them to your partner. You start. Begin like this: *Hi, can you help me? I need …*

Useful phrases

- a thing you use to …
- a whatchamacallit for …ing
- the stuff you put on …
- the things that you …
- I can't remember the word for it.

2 Your partner will also explain the following things. When you think you know what the object is, say 'Oh, you mean a …' and say the name.

a belt buckle

Dental floss   **a screwdriver**   **a spatula**

Unit 8, Speaking (page 95)

The earliest known nature documentary was a simple one-minute film called *Cheese Mites* which was first shown in 1903. *Cheese Mites* was about the tiny spider-like insects which live in cheese. The film makers attached a camera to a microscope, which revealed the film's stars <u>flying around</u> in a piece of Stilton cheese. Under the microscope the mites looked like <u>very small</u> crabs. The audience was stunned by the film, which was narrated by one of the <u>mites</u>. Today nature documentaries are a much more complex and costly affair.

What is wrong?
- flying (mites don't fly, they crawl)
- very small (under a microscope they are enlarged so they seem huge)
- mites (film-makers)

Unit 10, Grammar & Pronunciation (page 119)

In 1962 in the African country that is now Tanzania, *three / thirteen / thirty* schoolgirls began to laugh uncontrollably. Within a few months, about $1/3$ / $2/3$ / *all* of the school's students had the symptoms, and the school closed. The laughing fit spread, and eventually affected about *a hundred / five hundred / a thousand* people in Tanzania and neighbouring Uganda. The epidemic lasted for *one / six / twelve* month(s).

Answers to Student B's text
Tickling was used as a method of torture in the past: a victim was tied up so that his *feet* were visible. These were covered with *salt*. A *goat* carried out the torture by licking the substance and causing intense tickling. The licking also caused very painful *blisters*.

Additional material

Phonetic symbols

Single vowels

/ɪ/	fish	/fɪʃ/	(build, business, England, women)
/iː/	bean	/biːn/	(he, key, niece, people)
/ʊ/	foot	/fʊt/	(could, put, woman,)
/uː/	shoe	/ʃuː/	(fruit, rule, through, two)
/e/	egg	/eg/	(breakfast, friend, many, said)
/ə/	mother	/ˈmʌðə/	(arrive, colour, husband, police)
/ɜː/	word	/wɜːd/	(learn, curly, skirt, birthday)
/ɔː/	talk	/tɔːk/	(four, horse, thought, water)
/æ/	back	/bæk/	(fat, cat, catch, bag)
/ʌ/	bus	/bʌs/	(blood, does, enough, onion)
/ɑː/	arm	/ɑːm/	(aunt, heart, laugh, past)
/ɒ/	top	/tɒp/	(what, stop, hot, spot)

Diphthongs

/ɪə/	ear	/ɪə/	(beer, here, Italian, theatre)
/eɪ/	face	/feɪs/	(break, eight, fail, say, they)
/ʊə/	tourist	/ˈtʊərɪst/	(plural, sure, pure)
/ɔɪ/	boy	/bɔɪ/	(noise, toy)
/əʊ/	nose	/nəʊz/	(although, coat, know, no)
/eə/	hair	/heə/	(careful, their, wear, where)
/aɪ/	eye	/aɪ/	(five, buy, die, my)
/aʊ/	mouth	/maʊθ/	(town)

Consonants

/p/	pen	/pen/	(happy)
/b/	bag	/bæg/	(rabbit)
/t/	tea	/tiː/	(ate, fatter, worked)
/d/	dog	/dɒg/	(address, played)
/tʃ/	chip	/tʃɪp/	(natural, watch)
/dʒ/	jazz	/dʒæz/	(age, bridge, generous)
/k/	cake	/keɪk/	(chemistry, kitchen, cake, toothache)
/g/	girl	/gɜːl/	(foggy, dog)
/f/	film	/fɪlm/	(different, laugh, photograph)
/v/	verb	/vɜːb/	(of, very)
/θ/	thing	/θɪŋ/	(thin, think)
/ð/	these	/ðiːz/	(that, those, mother)
/s/	snake	/sneɪk/	(city, message, race)
/z/	zoo	/zuː/	(has)
/ʃ/	shop	/ʃɒp/	(description, machine, sugar)
/ʒ/	television	/ˈtelə,vɪʒən/	(garage, usual)
/m/	map	/mæp/	(summer)
/n/	name	/neɪm/	(sunny, knife)
/ŋ/	ring	/rɪŋ/	(sing, tongue)
/h/	house	/haʊs/	(who)
/l/	leg	/leg/	(hill, possible)
/r/	road	/rəʊd/	(carry, write)
/w/	wine	/waɪn/	(one, why)
/j/	yes	/jes/	(used)

Letters of the alphabet

/eɪ/	/iː/	/e/	/aɪ/	/əʊ/	/uː/	/ɑː/
Aa	Bb	Ff	Ii	Oo	Qq	Rr
Hh	Cc	Ll	Yy		Uu	
Jj	Dd	Mm			Ww	
Kk	Ee	Nn				
	Gg	Ss				
	Pp	Xx				
	Tt	Zz				
	Vv					

Additional material

Unit 1, Reading (page 10)
Student B

Judith Rich Harris, independent investigator and theoretician

I am optimistic about human relationships — in particular, about friendship. Perhaps you have heard gloomy predictions about friendship: it's dying out, people no longer have friends they can confide in, loneliness is on the rise.

But friendship isn't dying out: it's just changing, adapting to the changes in the world. People are discovering different ways of getting together. It may be harder to find a bowling partner but it's easier to find someone to chat with, because there are many more ways to chat.

I have friends whom I know only through email conversations but who are as dear to me as my college roommate and dearer by far than my next-door neighbour. [...] People we have never met before may be important to us in the future. They may become our trading partners or employers. They may become our lovers or our rivals. Or they may simply become our friends.

Unit 2, Reading & Speaking (page 24)

No longer at ease

Back in Nigeria and under pressure from his village and family to succeed, Obi gets a job as administrative assistant to the Inspector of Schools. Although he has an important job, Obi soon has problems with money. He has to pay back his loans to the villagers, send money home to pay for the education of his brothers and sisters, and keep up an expensive lifestyle in keeping with his new job and the expectations of his family.

Obi is forced to borrow money from the bank and from his girlfriend Clara. Clara is from an outcast tribe and although he loves her, he is forced to break the engagement because his parents won't agree to the marriage. During this time Obi refuses to accept the many bribes he is offered although he has terrible money problems. Indeed, he criticises the corruption in Nigeria – an attitude which surprises many of his countrymen who see bribery as a necessary part of daily life.

When Clara finds out she is pregnant and his mother dies, Obi feels depressed and is put under more financial pressure. It is then that the businessman visits Obi and that Obi takes his first bribe.

Unit 4, Reading & Listening (page 46)

The extract is from Chapter One of H.G. Wells' *The Invisible Man*, about a scientist who becomes invisible but cannot become visible again. The book was originally published in 1897. His other famous books include *The Time Machine*, *The War of the Worlds* and *The Island of Doctor Moreau*.

Unit 6, Writing & Speaking (page 67)

1 Choose a topic you would like to talk about. Use the ideas below to help you.

Why learning English is important / necessary
What your city needs
How to stay healthy
What are the most important things in life
Your own idea

2 Prepare a short part of a speech about this topic. Use the phrases below and the techniques discussed in the lesson to help you. Then go back to pages 67.

Useful phrases

- You ask me, why / what / how …? I tell you …
- It isn't …. it is …
- It has been said that … But I am here to tell you that …
- In the end, it really just comes down to three main things: …, … and …

Unit 6, Writing (page 71)

You are going to have your conversation in a written chat. Follow these instructions:

A: take a piece of paper and begin the conversation. Write something to B and give him / her the paper.
B: continue the conversation on the same paper.

- After you have exchanged the paper five or six times, stop.
- Exchange your paper with another pair of students.
- Check each other's paper. How was each problem solved?
- Do you think they found a good solution?

Unit 7, Speaking (page 81)

1 Choose one of the products on the right or think of your own product. Then decide …

- what the special features of your product are.
- who your target audience is.
- what the name of your product is.
- what your advertising image and slogan will be (use the tips from the listening).
- where you want to advertise your product.

2 Explain your ideas to the class. The class says if they think your ideas would be successful and why.

Unit 7, Reading & Speaking (page 82)
Student B: animals

In a recent conversation about food chains, a colleague wondered if anything ate wasps. Someone suggested 'very stupid birds'. Does anyone know any more about this? *(Tom Eastwood)*

The lowly wasp certainly has its place in the food chain. Indeed, the question should possibly be 'what doesn't feed, in one way or another, on this lowly and potentially dangerous insect?'

Here are a few that do, the first list being invertebrates: several species of dragonflies; wasps, usually the larger species feeding on smaller species; beetles and moths.

The following are vertebrates that feed on wasps: numerous species of birds; skunks; bears; badgers; bats; weasels; rats; mice and last, but certainly not least, humans and probably some of our closest ancestors.

I have eaten the larvae of several wasp species fried in butter and found them quite tasty. *(Orvis Tilby)*

I was once idly observing a wasp crawling round the edge of a water lily leaf in my pond, when it paused to drink. There was a sudden flurry of activity when a frog leapt from its hiding place and swallowed the wasp. The frog did not appear to suffer any ill effects, so I captured another wasp, tossed the hapless creature into the pond and waited. The frog was slow on the uptake but there was another disturbance in the water and this time a goldfish snapped up the wasp. The fish, too seemed undisturbed. *(John Croft)*

Glossary

invertebrate *(noun)* – an animal without a backbone

Ever since finding a millipede in my bath, I've wondered why this creature has so many legs. What advantages do they provide and how did it get them? *(Sarah Crew)*

Millipedes and earthworms have similar lifestyles. Both burrow in soil, eating dead and decaying vegetation, but they have evolved very different methods for forcing their way through the soil. Worms use the strong muscles in their body walls to push forward or widen a crevice in the soil. Millipedes however use their legs to push through the soil. The more legs the animal has, the harder it can push.

Millipedes are different from centipedes. They have very large numbers of short legs because long legs would be a liability in a burrow. Centipedes which spend their time on the surface have fewer, longer legs. They have little need to push, but have to run faster than millipedes. *(R. McNeill Alexander)*

Glossary

evolve *(verb)* – develop over many generations as a result of natural selection

liability *(noun)* – someone or something that causes problems

Additional material

Unit 7, Reading & Speaking (page 82) Student C: domestic science

I found a forgotten bar of soap after winter at my home in northern Sardinia. It had grown a coat of mould. How did it grow on soap, which is supposed to keep your hands clean? *(Patrizia Figoli Turcheteti)*

We use soap for cleaning because it is a detergent: a means of emulsifying dirt in water. Its nutritional value is usually irrelevant, but pure traditional soap consists of fatty-acid salts. Because of this, it is completely digestible in modest quantities. You may see a dog eating a chunk of soap because it smells appetisingly of fatty acids. Toilet soap commonly contains surprising amounts of other materials that make it smoother, less aggressive to the skin or simply cheaper to produce. These are all edible too, and moulds are happy to consume them. As long as the soap doesn't contain too much sodium and the air is moist enough, as it well might be in a bathroom, a bar of soap can certainly grow some very contented fungi. *(Jon Richfield)*

I'd been wondering why two bars of soap stored under our bath had been almost completely eaten by a mouse.
(Xiangyu Hu)

Glossary

mould (*noun*) – a fungal growth occurring in warm conditions on food or other organic ma[...]

Monosodium glutamate is a common flavour enhancer that is used widely in Chinese and Japanese cooking. I'd like to know why it is so popular in these cuisines. How does it enhance the flavour of food? *(Michael Stuart)*

Monosodium glutamate or MSG is presumably most commonly used in oriental cooking for traditional reasons. For thousands of years the Japanese have incorporated a type of seaweed known as *kombu* in their cooking to make food taste better. It was not until 1908, however, that the actual ingredient in *kombu* responsible for improvement in flavour was identified as glutamate. Today hundreds of thousands of tonnes of MSG are produced all over the world.

It is widely known that Chinese and Japanese food contains MSG but people don't seem to be aware that it is also used in foods in other parts of the world. In Italy, for example, it is used in pizzas and lasagne and in Britain it can be found in snack foods such as potato crisps and cereals. It is thought that MSG intensifies the naturally occurring fifth taste in some food – the other, better known, four tastes being sweet, sour, bitter and salt. The fifth taste is known as *umami* in Japanese and is often described as a savoury, meaty taste. *(Mark Bollie)*

Does anything eat wasps? And 101 other questions Profile Books, © New Scientist 2005

Glossary

intensify (*verb*) – make greater, stronger or more extreme

Unit 8, Grammar (page 93)

1 Take a piece of paper and write the numbers 1 to 7 on it. Then follow the instructions.

1 write the name of a neighbouring country to yours
2 choose one of the following words: brother, sister, uncle, aunt, grandparent
3 write a large sum of money
4 write a number between 7 and 15
5 write the name of your wife / husband / boyfriend / girlfriend / best friend
6 write the name of a famous person currently alive
7 write the name of a famous person who is not alive now

2 Work in pairs. Exchange your papers. Complete the questions below with the information your partner gave you. Then ask your partner the questions.

IMAGINE ...
7 WAYS YOUR LIFE COULD BE DIFFERENT ...

1 How would your life be different if you had come from _____?
2 What would you do if you discovered you had _____ you had never met?
3 Who would you call first if you won _____?
4 If you could go back to being _____ years old what would you do differently?
5 If you hadn't met _____ how would your life be different now?
6 If you could meet _____ what would you say?
7 If you could have met _____ what would you have told him/her?

Unit 8, Warm up (page 99)

	Girls	Boys
1	teacher	footballer
2	vet	policeman
3	doctor	fireman
4	nurse	archaeologist / scientist
5	dancer	doctor

Unit 3, Speaking (page 30)

ONLY WHEN THE LAST TREE HAS DIED & THE LAST RIVER HAS BEEN POISONED & THE LAST FISH HAS BEEN CAUGHT WILL WE REALISE THAT WE CANNOT EAT MONEY

19TH-CENTURY CREE INDIAN PROVERB

Unit 3, Speaking (page 36) The *Carta Marina*

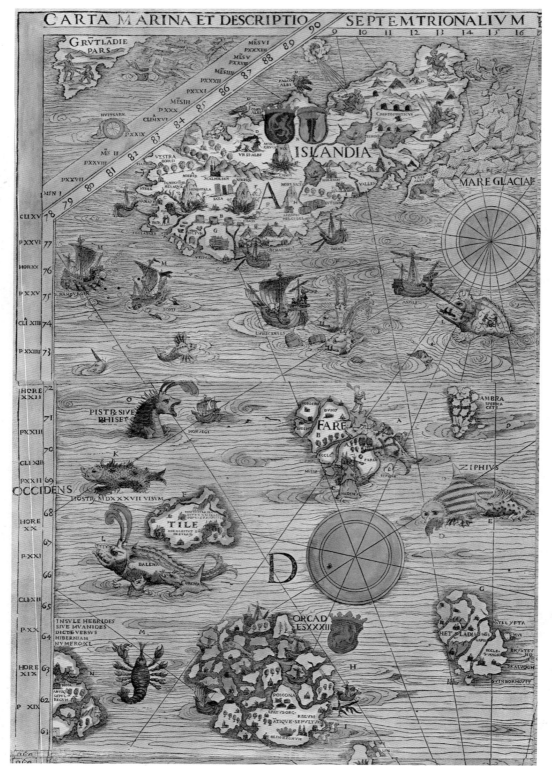

Communication activities: Student B

Unit 2, Grammar (page 21)

1 Read the sentences. Then make a question for the words in bold. Begin with the question word provided.

1 A ton of feathers and a ton of metal weigh **the same amount**. *Which* …?
2 The black box of an airplane (where the data is kept) is **not black, it is orange**. *What* …?
3 When he first sailed across the Atlantic, Christopher Columbus was looking for **India**. *What* …?

2 When you have made your questions, ask them to your partner. How many did your partner answer correctly?

Unit 4, Vocabulary & Speaking (page 49)

1 Your partner will ask you for the following things, but they don't know the name. When you think you know what the object is, say 'Oh, you mean a …' and say the name.

a pencil sharpener

a bookmark

a corkscrew

a usb memory stick

2 When your partner finishes, swap roles. You need these things, but you don't know the name for them. Describe them to your partner. You start. Begin like this: *Hi, can you help me? I need …*

Useful phrases

- a thing you use to …
- a whatchamacallit for …ing
- the stuff you put on …
- the things that you …
- I can't remember the word for it.

Unit 8, Speaking (page 95)

The documentary series *Man vs Wild* which is shown <u>on radio</u> around the world, stars an ex-soldier, who has to survive in the wild – for example in the <u>French</u> desert, on a desert island in the Pacific or in the Sumatran jungle. Reporters have however shown that many of the presenter's nights 'out in the wild' are actually spent in hotels. Other scenes have been clearly staged. In one scene which attracted angry complaints from viewers, the presenter tries to ride a <u>tame horse</u>. In fact, the horse was a domestic horse brought to the site from a nearby ranch. A close up of the horse clearly shows a flash of its horseshoe.

What is wrong?
- radio (has to be TV)
- French (no desert in France)
- tame (context makes it clear it is a wild horse)

Unit 10, Grammar & Pronunciation (page 119)

Tickling was used as a method of torture in the past: a victim was tied up so that his *shoulders / hands / feet* were visible. These were covered with *salt / sugar / honey*. A *sheep / goat / pig* carried out the torture by licking the substance and causing intense tickling. The licking also caused very painful *blisters / bruises / spots*.

Answers to Student A's text
In 1962 in the African country that is now Tanzania, *three* schoolgirls began to laugh uncontrollably. Within a few months, about $^2/_3$ of the school's students had the symptoms, and the school closed. The laughing fit spread, and eventually affected about *a thousand* people in Tanzania and neighbouring Uganda. The epidemic lasted for *six months*.

Grammar focus

Unit 1

Auxiliary verbs

We use the auxiliary verb *have* with perfect tenses (present perfect, past perfect).
I **have** lived in the country all my life.
I **had** always wanted to live in the city.

We use the auxiliary verb *is* with continuous tenses (present and past continuous) and to make the passive voice.
We **are** looking for a new place to live. We **were** thinking of a flat by the sea.
The flat that we liked **was** sold immediately.

We use the auxiliary verb *do / did* with questions and negatives in the simple tenses (simple past and simple present).
Where **do** you live? I **don't** know.
Did they move? They **didn't** tell me.

We sometimes use the auxiliary *do / did* in emphatic affirmative sentences in the simple past and simple present. In this case, the auxiliary is always stressed in spoken language.
I **do** like living in the country. I just love the peace and quiet.

Present tenses

We use the present continuous to talk about things that are happening now or about now and about temporary and changing situations.
I**'m researching** my family tree.
Right now I**'m working** part-time, so I have some free time.

We don't usually use the present continuous with state verbs. Some common state verbs are: *agree, appear, be, believe, belong, contain, like, feel, fit, forget, have, hate, last, love, matter, mean, need, own, prefer, realise, remember, seem, understand, want.*

However, some state verbs are used as action verbs in informal contexts, for example *like* and *love*.
I**'m loving** it.

We use the present simple to talk about habits and routines and about facts or things that are always true.
My parents **travel** to Russia every year.   My parents **come** from Russia.

We use the present perfect to talk about something that started in the past but continues now.
My parents **have lived** in the US for a long time.
They**'ve** never **forgotten** their home country.

Future forms

We use the present simple to talk about schedules or timetables.
I **start** my new job on Monday.

We use the present continuous to talk about fixed arrangements in the future (arrangements with other people or travel arrangements).
We **are flying** to France on Monday. We **are meeting** our son there.

We use *be going to* to talk about plans and intentions.
I**'m going to start** my own business.

We also use verbs such as *intend, plan, expect* and *hope* to talk about future arrangements and intentions.
We **expect to get** financial backing for our project.
We **hope to fill** a niche in the market.

We use *will* to talk about decisions and plans which are made spontaneously, at the time of speaking.
That sounds good. I**'ll think** about it.

We use *will* to talk about future predictions. We usually use *be going to* when a prediction is based on strong evidence, for example when we can see that something will happen.
I think I **will find** retirement difficult.
The current government is in trouble. It **is definitely going to lose** the election.

We can also use modal verbs such as *may, might* and *could* to talk about predictions.
The government **could get** a majority. They **might just win**.

Future continuous and future perfect

We use the future continuous to talk about an action in progress at a certain time in the future.

We form the future continuous with *will* + *be* + verb + *-ing*.

We often use the future continuous with phrases such as *In 2020, this time next year, in two years' time.*
This time next year I**'ll be doing** something completely different.
In five years' time they**'ll be enjoying** their retirement.

We use the future perfect to talk about an action completed by a certain time in the future.

We form the future perfect with *will* + *have* + past participle.

We often use the future perfect with phrases such as *by 2020, by this time next year, in two years' time.*
By 2020 measles **will have disappeared**.
In ten years' time many global health goals **will have been achieved**.

Units 1 Exercises

Auxiliary verbs

1 Choose the correct auxiliary.

1 The city of Mumbai *has / was* known as Bombay until 1996. Some residents still *don't / didn't* use the city's new official name.

2 At the beginning of the 21st century the population *did / was* recorded as nearly twelve million. According to recent estimates it *has / had* risen to about 14 million and *is / was* still growing.

3 Mumbai *is / has* been home to the Hindi film industry since the early twentieth century. Major financial institutions *were / are* concentrated in Mumbai.

2 Complete the text with the correct auxiliaries.

I (1) _____ usually have time for a holiday but right now I (2) _____ renting a summer house on the coast. I (3) _____ always loved the sea and I (4) _____ love spending time at the beach. Yesterday evening the sun (5) _____ gone down and the waves (6) _____ crashing on the beach. The air (7) _____ filled with salt. It made me feel totally alive.

Present tenses

3 Put the verbs in the box in the correct space.

include	are starting	provide	has become
are researching	has led		

The availability of online resources (1) _____ to widespread interest in genealogy. Indeed, genealogy (2) _____ one of the most popular topics on the internet. For people who (3) _____ their family history, census records often (4) _____ useful information. Records (5) _____ age and occupation, place of birth and address. Now some companies (6) _____ to offer these records online.

4 Write sentences using present tenses.

1 My family / live / in different parts of the globe
2 My brother / currently / work in Peru
3 My parents / live / in Florida in the US / since they retired
4 My sister / stay / in our hometown in the UK
5 I'm in Dubai but / I / think / of moving back home
6 We / not get / together as a family / very often

Future forms

5 Match the two parts of the dialogues.

1 I've missed the bus again.
2 Any plans for this evening?
3 They never stop arguing.
4 Can you help me with this?
5 They've played really well so far.
6 What time do we leave?

a Yes, I think they'll win this year.
b Not now. I'm going to start cooking.
c The train goes at 12.52.
d I'll drive you to work.
e I'm meeting the guys after work.
f It looks like they're going to split up.

6 Rewrite the sentences using a future form, so they have a similar meaning.

1 We intend to backpack around India next year.
   We _____ next year.
2 They might join us.
   Perhaps they _____ us.
3 She's absolutely certain to get the job.
   She _____ the job.
4 Let me help you with that.
   I _____ you with that.
5 We've arranged to meet them at 3 o'clock.
   We _____ them at three o'clock.

Future continuous and future perfect

7 Complete the sentences with the future continuous or the future perfect.

By the year 2031, we (1) _____ (*know*) about AIDS for fifty years. Over the next twenty years, an international task group called AIDS2031 (2) _____ (*look*) at new ideas for AIDS prevention and treatment. During this time the number of people needing treatment (3) _____ (*increase*). So the group (4) _____ (*also / try*) to raise awareness of the issue – and money to support programmes of treatment. The group hopes that by 2031 somebody (5) _____ (*finally / find*) a vaccine for AIDS, and that, in particular, people in developing countries (6) _____ (*benefit*) from new scientific advances.

8 Complete the sentences with a suitable verb.

In three years' time …
Fifteen-year-old: I'll have _____ school.
Eighteen-year-old: I'll be _____ my twenty-first birthday.
Young couple: We'll have _____ married.
Fifty-year old: I'll be _____ the same boring job.
Sixty-year old: I'll be _____ forward to my retirement.
Ninety-year-old: I'll have _____ longer than I expected.

Unit 2

Questions

When a question word is the object of a present simple or past simple question, we use *do*, *does* or *did*.

<small>object</small> <small>subject</small>
What *vitamin in the body* <u>*does*</u> *the sun* activate?

When a question word is the subject of a present simple or past simple question, we don't use *do*, *does* or *did*.

<small>subject</small> <small>object</small>
Which country *has* **the international car registration letters TR?**

In questions with prepositions, we usually put the preposition at the end of the question.
What *does the Roman numeral C* **stand for?**
Who *did the Terracotta Army* **belong to?**

In formal language the preposition can be used first before the question word.
For what *does the Roman numeral C* **stand?**
To whom *did the Terracotta Army* **belong?**

The definite article

We use the definite article *the* …
- when the person or thing has been referred to before.
  She always makes a particular mistake. **The** *mistake is very common.*
- in superlative phrases.
  It's one of **the most common mistakes.**
- when we define which one we are referring to.
  The mistake that she makes *is very common.*
- when a person or thing is unique: there is only one.
  The president *made a hilarious mistake.*
- with singular nouns which stand for a general type.
  The apostrophe *is often misused.*
- with adjectives used as plural nouns.
  The illiterate *in society are at a severe disadvantage.*

In addition, we use the definite article with …
- musical instruments.
  He plays **the guitar.**
- dates and decades.
  I grew up in **the eighties.**
- seas and rivers, deserts and groups of mountains.
  They went trekking in **the Himalayas.** *We went to a hotel by* **the Red Sea.**

We don't use articles …
- with plural or uncountable nouns when we are talking about things in general.
  They have lots of **drinks,** *but not much* **food.**
- abstract nouns.
  Friendship *is built on* **trust.**
- with streets, towns and most countries and continents.
  I live in **Elmtree Avenue** *in* **Cardiff** *– that's in* **Wales.**
- with meals.
  I'm making **lunch.**
- with seasons.
  Winter *is my favourite season.*

Language note: We don't use articles with some institutions where the focus is on the general purpose of the building (for example, *hospital, school, university, prison*). Compare:
He is in hospital. (= he is in a hospital because he is ill, it isn't important which one)
He works at the hospital. (= a particular hospital)

Narrative tenses

We use narrative tenses to tell a story.

We use the past continuous to talk about actions in progress in the past or temporary situations in the past. We often use the past continuous to describe background events. We also often use the past continuous for activities that are interrupted by a completed action.
I **was reading** *a book. It* **was raining.**
I **was making** *dinner when my friend arrived.*

We use the past simple to talk about actions in the past which are complete or happened at a specific time. We usually use the past simple to tell the most important events in a story.
The doorbell **rang.** *I* **opened** *the door.*

We use the past perfect to talk about events in the past that happened before the main events in the story.
I **hadn't expected** *it to be him. We* **hadn't seen** *each other for years.*

	he had finished his homework		he went to the cinema	
Past ←	↓		↓	→ Present

Unit 2 Exercises

Questions

1 Write the questions for the answers. The words in bold can help you with question words.

1 _____?
  Elephants have **four** teeth (but new ones grow when they wear out).

2 _____?
  Tigers have stripes on their fur and skin.

3 _____
  More than half of the world's animals and plants live **in tropical rain forests**.

4 _____?
  The Sahara desert covers about one-third of Africa.

5 _____?
  The snake smells with its tongue.

6 _____?
  It takes an oyster **five years** to make a pearl.

3 Rewrite the sentences in exercise 2 in a more formal style.

2 Complete the sentences with a preposition from the box.

for	with	without	from	to	of

1 Which plant do Pandas get 99% of their diet _____? (bamboo)
2 What is about 75% of a human brain made up _____? (water)
3 How many bones are babies born _____? (300)
4 Which animals are fingerprints unique _____? (primates and koala bears)
5 Which of these two things can humans last longest _____: food or sleep? (food)
6 How long can a tarantula spider live without food _____? (over 2 years)

The definite article

4 Complete the text with the definite article or no article.

A typo is (1) _____ name for a mistake in (2) _____ typing process. This might mean that a letter is missing, that two letters in (3) _____ word are mixed up or that a different letter has been used in place of (4) _____ correct letter. (5) _____ typos are very common in (6) _____ messages on (7) _____ internet or in (8) _____ instant messaging where (9) _____ users have typed things quickly. (10) _____ internet users often make (11) _____ typos when they type (12) _____ addresses into (13) _____ web browsers. (14) _____ people who register (15) _____ typos of (16) _____ well-known internet addresses can make lots of (17) _____ money.

5 Decide if the sentences are correct. Cross out definite articles that are incorrect.

1 Where did you learn to play the violin like that?
2 The winter is my favourite season.
3 They used to live in the US but at the moment they're in the South America.
4 Last year we went trekking in the Himalayan Mountains.
5 I think the mobile phone was a fantastic invention.
6 I always eat the cornflakes for the breakfast and a sandwich for the lunch.
7 The Danube river starts in the Black Forest in the Germany and flows into the Black Sea.
8 We met in the nineties – on the first of January 1992.

Narrative tenses

6 Complete the story with the correct tense.

The witness (1) _____ (*stand*) in the witness box. While she (2) _____ (*answer*) questions from her lawyer, a man in the courtroom (3) _____ (*stand up*). He (4) _____ (*pull*) out a knife and (5) _____ (*attack*) the witness. There was chaos in the courtroom: people (6) _____ (*scream*) and (7) _____ (*ran*) about. Officers quickly (8) _____ (*arrest*) the man who (9) _____ (*already / drop*) the knife. Somebody (10) _____ (*call*) an ambulance for the witness who (11) _____ (*fall*) to the floor and (12) _____ (*bleed*) heavily.

7 Complete the dialogues using the words in brackets.

1 **A** What were you doing when I tried to phone you this afternoon?
  B (work / garden)
2 **A** Why was your partner angry yesterday?
  B (because / forgot / birthday)
3 **A** Did everybody stay much longer last night?
  B (everybody / leave / you / go home)
4 **A** How did you break your leg?
  B (stand / ladder / fall)
5 **A** Did you enjoy your meal yesterday?
  B (Yes, / I / never try / sushi / before)
6 **A** How long have you known her?
  B (we / meet / six months / ago)

Present perfect simple and continuous, past simple

We form the present perfect with *have* + past participle.

We use the present perfect simple to talk about single completed actions and to emphasise the result of the action.
Sea levels **have risen** between 10 and 25cm.
People **have dumped** huge amounts of waste into the oceans.

We form the present perfect continuous with *have* + *been* + present participle.

We use the present perfect continuous to describe an action that started in the past and continues now, and to emphasise how long it has happened.
Sea levels **have been rising** for years.
People **have been dumping** waste into the oceans for centuries.

We usually use the present perfect simple with state verbs.
~~She's always been loving the sea.~~   She's always loved the sea.

The present perfect simple and present perfect continuous can often be used in the same way, with little difference in meaning.
I've **worked** here since 2008.
I've **been working** here since 2008.

We often use these time phrases with the present perfect simple and continuous: *already, never, yet, for* and *since*.

We use the past simple to talk about finished actions in the past and when we specify the time of an action.
The tsunami **occurred** in 1899.

We often use these time phrases with the past simple: *ago, in* + year, *last (year/week), yesterday*.

We can use *for* and *never* with the past simple to refer to completed periods of time.

Adjective order

We use adjectives in this order:

opinion	size	age	colour	origin	other adjectives

An **enormous blue** whale. (size, colour)
An **interesting Scandinavian** legend. (opinion, origin)
An **old rubber** boot. (age, other adjective)

Modals of speculation (present and past)

We use *could, may, might, must* and *can't* to speculate about events or situations.

We use *must* when we are certain something is true.
He **must** be a magician. (= I am certain he is.)

We use *may, might* and *could* when something is possible.
He **may** be cheating. (= It's possible.)

We use *can't* when we are certain something isn't true.
He **can't** have faked that trick. (I am certain he didn't fake it.)

In the present, we use modal verb + infinitive.
He **can't know** that information.

In the past we use modal verb + *have* + past participle.
He **might have guessed** the number.

Impersonal passive

The impersonal passive is formed with *it* + the passive voice. It is used with reporting verbs such as *say, claim, rumour, know, think* and *believe* to report a general opinion.
It is said that you if you touch the statue, you will have good luck.
It is thought that the fountain has magical powers.

We use the impersonal passive to report a general claim or belief, without reference to a particular person or agent.
It is believed that drinking the water will cure illness.
It is rumoured that the statue cries tears or blood.

The impersonal passive is often used in written and academic English.

Past perfect simple and continuous, past simple

We form the past perfect with *had* + past participle.
She **had heard** footsteps.

We use the past perfect when we are talking about the past and want to talk about an earlier time in the past.
He came to the inn because he **had lost** his way.

We form the past perfect continuous with *had* + *been* + present participle.
She **had been waiting** for guests.

We use the past perfect continuous when we are talking about the past and want to talk about actions that were in progress at an earlier time in the past.
He **had been looking** for a place to stay when he saw the inn.

We use the past simple to talk about finished actions in the past.
He **knocked** at the door and **asked** for a room.

Units 3 & 4 Exercises

Present perfect simple and continuous, past simple

1 Complete one sentence in each pair with the present perfect and one with the present perfect continuous.

1 I _____ (*sail*) on a boat three times and each time I got sea sick.
  I _____ (*sail*) for two years now.
2 Environmental organisations _____ (*try*) to protect whales without much success.
  Environmental organisations _____ (*try*) to protect whales for years.
3 Floods _____ (*cause*) chaos for several weeks.
  Floods _____ (*cause*) serious damage to the town.
4 The fishing industry _____ (*decline*) for years in our area.
  The fishing industry _____ (*decline*) because of overfishing.
5 I _____ (*collect*) lots of shells on the beach.
  I _____ (*collect*) shells since I was a small child.

Adjective order

2 Correct the sentences.

1 We travelled on an old wooden beautiful ship.
2 We discovered an amazing uninhabited tiny island.
3 We lay down on the golden sandy wide beach.
4 We looked at the cloudless blue lovely sky.
5 We thought of our North European depressing grey home.

Modals of speculation (present and past)

3 Complete the text with the modals in the box.

could have warmed   must have   might have heard
might have written   can't use   could be   must do
might have hidden

You perhaps (1) _____ of Uri Geller. Some people think he (2) _____ psychic powers. Others think he (3) _____ his mind to control objects: he (4) _____ tricks. There (5) _____ explanations for most of his performances. For example, when he bends a spoon, he (6) _____ it before. When a card disappears, he (7) _____ it in his sleeve. Or when he guesses the number of a car belonging to a member of the audience, he (8) _____ the number down in the car park.

4 Rewrite the dialogues using modals, so that the meaning doesn't change.

1 **A**: I'm sure I've lost my watch, it's gone.
  I _____
  B: Perhaps you just left it at home.
  You _____
2 **A**: This definitely isn't the right address.
  It _____
  B: Perhaps you wrote down the wrong number.
  You _____
3 **A**: My glasses are here somewhere, I'm sure.
  My _____
  B: Well, I'm sure they haven't just disappeared.
  They _____

Impersonal passive

5 Report the sentences using the verb in brackets. Use *It* + passive.

1 The hundreds of stone circles in Senegal and Gambia are from around 750 AD. (*estimate*) _____
2 The circles are built round the burial mounds of kings and chiefs. (*believe*) _____
3 The heavy stones were transported on rollers. (*think*) _____
4 A small stone near a large stone means that somebody was buried with their child. (*claim*) _____
5 V-shaped stones represent two relatives who died on the same day. (*say*) _____
6 Small stones left on the large stones in the circles shine at night. (*report*) _____

Past perfect simple and continuous, past simple

6 Complete the text with the correct tense.

Police (1) _____ (*find*) the mystery man on an English beach. He (2) _____ (*try*) to kill himself and was completely wet. (3) _____ (*not speak*) and he (4) _____ (*cut*) out all the labels in his clothes. The newspapers (5) _____ (*call*) him the piano man because he (6) _____ (*draw*) pictures of a piano. But four months later the man (7) _____ (*speak*): he (8) _____ (*lie*). The man (9) _____ (*work*) with mental health patients in a former job and he (10) _____ (*copy*) their behaviour for four months.

7 Write B's questions. Use the past perfect simple or continuous.

1 **A**: I was completely exhausted.   **B**: what / you / do?
2 **A**: We finally found the dog.   **B**: where / it / go?
3 **A**: I felt very dizzy.   **B**: you / take / your tablets?
4 **A**: He was sick three times.   **B**: what / he / eat?
5 **A**: Our phone bill was enormous.   **B**: who / you / phone?
6 **A**: He was covered in sweat.   **B**: he / run?

Unit 5

will for present habits

We can use *will* to talk about general truths and regular actions and habits in the present.
*Crops **won't grow** without sufficient water.*
*In the week **we'll eat** things like pasta and rice dishes and at the weekend **we'll cook** meals that take more time.*

We often use the adverbs of frequency such as *usually*, *often* and *sometimes* with this meaning of *will*.
*On a Sunday he**'ll always go** to the same cafe. He**'ll usually order** coffee and he**'ll read** his newspaper.*

In spoken language we can also use *will* to criticise or express disapproval of regular habits. When *will* is used like this, it is stressed.
*Those children **will keep** banging the doors.*
*She **will watch** TV late at night and fall asleep on the sofa.*
*He just **won't** listen.*

used to, *would* and past simple

Affirmative	Negative	Question
I **used to** play tennis.	I **didn't use to** play tennis.	**Did** you **use to** play tennis?
I **would** play tennis.	I **wouldn't play** tennis.	–

We use both *used to* and *would* to talk about repeated actions or habits in the past that don't happen now.
*I **used to** drink lots of milk as a child. I **wouldn't drink** juice.*

Would is not very common in questions with this use.

We use *used to* to talk about habitual states in the past. We don't use *would* to talk about states.
*~~I would love ice cream.~~   I **used to** love ice cream.*

We use the past simple to talk about one event at a specific time in the past. We also use the past simple to talk about something that happened a fixed number of times or for a fixed length of time.
*He **bought** me an ice cream.* (= one time)
*He **bought** me an ice cream three times.* (= several times)
*He **bought** me ice creams all summer.* (= for a fixed length of time)
*He **would buy** me an ice cream every weekend.* (= regular action)

be used to / *get used to*

We use *be used to* + verb + *ing* / *noun* to talk about a situation which you are comfortable or not comfortable with.
*I**'m used to** working on my own.* (= I've done it for a while and I'm fine with it.)
*I**'m not used to** the noise.* (= It's a new situation and I'm not happy with it yet.)

We use *get used to* + verb + *-ing* / *noun* to talk about a new situation you are becoming or have become comfortable with or haven't become comfortable with yet.
*I**'m getting used to** sending text messages.* (= it's becoming easier.)
*I **haven't got used to** instant messaging.* (= I haven't become comfortable with this yet.)

Don't confuse *be used to doing* and *used to do* (past habits).
*I**'m used to getting up** early.* (= It's something I do now.)
*I **used to get up** early.* (= It was a habit in the past.)

Unit 5 Exercises

will for present habits

1 Write sentences using the prompts and *will*.

1 get up / late
On a typical Sunday they _____

2 go / gym
Then _____

3 meet friends / for lunch
_____

4 go for a walk / in the afternoon
_____

5 in the evening / watch / a film or do / some work
_____

6 go to bed / about midnight
_____

2 Rewrite the paragraph by replacing present simple verbs with *will + infinitive* where possible.

The Yoruba people in Nigeria name their children in a ceremony eight days after the birth. Sometimes a child gets a name which reflects how or when he or she was born. For example, parents give twins special names which mean the first born and the last born. At the naming ceremony other family members give their own names to the child and each family member calls the child by this name – so one child has many different names.

_____
_____
_____
_____
_____
_____
_____

used to, *would* and past simple

3 Complete these sentences about childhood eating habits. Use *used to / would* or the past simple. Sometimes there is more than one possibility.

When I was a child …

1 We _____ (*eat*) the same things every week: Friday _____ (*always / be*) fish day.

2 I _____ (*love*) milk but I _____ (*stop*) drinking it when I _____ (*get*) older.

3 I _____ (*help*) my parents to make food. That's why I _____ (*decide*) to become a cook when I _____ (*leave*) school.

4 My mother _____ (*make*) wonderful strawberry cakes. We _____ (*pick*) the strawberries in a field near our house.

5 I _____ (*not be*) a fussy eater. I _____ (*like*) most foods.

4 Which verbs in bold can be replaced by *used to* or *would*? Write alternative forms where possible. If there are no alternatives, write –.

To preserve food in the past, people (1) **knew** several different techniques. Early hunters (2) **dried** meat and fish using fire. People in northern areas (3) **freeze-dried** fish and vegetables. But cooling foods (4) **didn't work** in southern areas. In the Mediterranean, people (5) **salted** food to preserve it. The Chinese (6) **started** to use spices to preserve food around 2700 BC. The year 1810 (7) **saw** the invention of the tin can and this (8) **led** to widespread use of canning.

1 _____
2 _____
3 _____
4 _____
5 _____
6 _____
7 _____
8 _____

be used to / get used to

5 Match the parts of the sentences.

1 They've just bought a computer so they are still
2 He's from Norway - he isn't
3 We've just moved so we haven't
4 This is my first job so I'm
5 They've just had a baby so they are
6 I've always lived in a city so I've got

a got used to living here yet.
b getting used to sleeping less.
c used to the noise.
d getting used to email.
e used to living in a hot country.
f not used to working in an office.

6 Complete the text with the correct form of *be used to* or *get used to*.

It's hard to (1) _____ (*get used to / grow*) older. I (2) _____ (*be used to / see*) my face look older every year in the mirror. But I (3) _____ (*not get used / think*) of myself as 'middle-aged'. I (4) _____ (*not be used / buy*) clothes for 'the older person'. And I (5) _____ (*never / get used / be call*) 'old' by young children.

Unit 6

Passive voice

We form the passive with *be* and a past participle.

present simple	*Important speeches* **are given** *every day.*
past simple	*An important speech* **was given** *yesterday.*
present perfect	*An important speech* **has been given** *this afternoon.*
past perfect	*A speech* **had been given** *the day before.*
present continuous	*An important speech* **is being given** *right now.*
past continuous	*An important speech* **was being given** *on stage.*
future	*An important speech* **will be given** *tomorrow.*

In spoken language we can use *get* instead of *be* to form the passive.
A copy of his speech **got leaked** *to the press beforehand.*

We use the passive when …
* it isn't important who did the action.
The speech is being broadcast all over the world.
* we don't know who is responsible for the action.
The speech was printed in many newspapers.
* the action is more important that the person or thing that did it (the agent).
His most famous speech was given before the election.

If we want to say who did the action we can use *by* + agent.
The speech was downloaded by thousands of people.

We can use the passive to avoid responsibility by not saying the name of the person responsible for the action.
Mistakes have been made in key areas. The decision has been taken to review all working procedures.

The passive is very common in scientific, technical and academic language. It is generally more common in written English.

Causative *have* / *get* something done

We use *have* / *get* + noun + past participle to talk about when somebody else does something for us or to us. The action is something we want somebody else to do.
We're having our house painted.
I get my nails done *once a month.*

Get is more formal than *have*.

Compare:
Our house was painted. (= Somebody painted our house. We don't know why.)
We had our home painted. (= Somebody painted our house because we wanted them to paint it.)

quite

Quite can have different meanings depending on what type of word it is used with.

It means *fairly* when used in front of gradable adjectives or adverbs.
Talking about money can be **quite embarassing.**

In American English, quite means *very*.
He is **quite rich.** (= He is very rich.)

Depending on the context, it can mean *to some degree* or it can mean *totally* in front of verbs such as *like, enjoy, understand* and *agree*.
I **quite like** *them* (= I like them to some degree.)
I **quite agree** *with you.* (= I totally agree with you.)

In front of ungradable adjectives and adverbs, it means *completely*.
He's **quite crazy** *when it comes to money.*

Quite can be used in front of quantifiers such as *a lot, a bit, some* to emphasise the amount.
She has **quite a bit of money**, *you know.* (= She has more than a bit.)

Unit 6 Exercises

Passive voice

1 Complete the sentences with the correct form of the passive.

1 One of the most famous speeches ever made _____ (give) on August 28, 1963.
2 It _____ (deliver) by Martin Luther King.
3 200,000 listeners _____ (move) to tears by the speech.
4 Since that day thousands of people _____ (inspire) by its message.
5 The speech _____ (describe) as a masterpiece of rhetoric.
6 The phrase 'I have a dream' _____ (repeat) eight times and the speech _____ (often / know) by this name.
7 The speech and its message _____ (remember) for a long time.

2 Decide if the verb in the sentences is active or passive. Then complete the sentences with the active or passive form of the past simple.

1 He _____ (rewrite) his speech several times.
2 I _____ (give) a watch for my birthday.
3 They _____ (followed) without their knowledge.
4 We were lost and _____ (ask) the way at a petrol station.
5 The book _____ (find) in an unexpected place.
6 She _____ (speak) in a very loud voice.

Causative *have* / *get* something done

3 Complete each sentence with the past participle form of the correct verb in the box.

cook	do	organise	polish	wash	write

1 She has her letters _____.
2 She has her appointments _____.
3 She has her clothes _____.
4 She has her shoes _____.
5 She has her shopping _____.
6 She has her meals _____.

4 Rewrite the sentences with *have* or *get* something done.

1 Somebody cuts my hair every two months. _____
2 Somebody checks and cleans my teeth twice a year. _____
3 Somebody has done my nails a couple of times. _____
4 Somebody painted our house last year. _____
5 I'd like somebody to clean my house. _____
6 I'd love somebody to iron my clothes. _____

quite

5 Choose the correct meaning (a or b) for the phrases in bold.

1 They spend **quite a bit of money** on food.
  a a small amount
  b a large amount
2 It is **quite impossible** to live on so little money.
  a nearly impossible
  b completely impossible
3 I **don't quite understand** the calculations.
  a I have a few problems understanding
  b I don't understand at all
4 He's **quite mean** with money.
  a He's very mean.
  b He's fairly mean.
5 It took him **quite some time** to save up.
  a a long time
  b a short time

6 Put the sentences in the correct order.

1 quite / a billionaire / achievement / It's / some / to become
_____
2 understand / your money / quite / your reluctance / I / to risk
_____
3 in / quite / to invest / It's / a new company / risky
_____
4 win / sure / going to / He's / the lottery / quite / he's
_____
5 our savings / watching / enjoy / quite / grow / We
_____

Unit 7

so and such

So and *such* have a similar meaning to *very*.

We use *so* before an adjective or adverb.
*That slogan is just **so clever**!*

We use *such* before a noun phrase.
*It was **such a good advert**.*

We also use *so* with quantifiers such as *much / many* and *little / few*.
*They decided to increase their advertising budget because they had **so few** customers.*

After the adjective, quantifier or noun phrase we can use a *that* clause to talk about a result or consequence. *That* can sometimes be omitted.
*They make **such good products that** they have little competition.*
*The advert was **so popular that** it had over a million hits on Youtube.*

In informal spoken language, *so not* is often used before an adjective instead of an adjective with a negative prefix.
*That's **so not cool**. (= That's really uncool.)*
*That advert is **so not realistic**. (= That's totally unrealistic.)*

Reported statements and questions

We use reported speech to say what someone said. In reported speech the verb usually goes one tense 'back'.

Direct statements	Reported statements
present simple *'I **like** their website.'*	**past simple** *She said (that) she **liked** their website.*
present continuous *'I'm **looking** for something.'*	**past continuous** *He said (that) he **was looking** for something.*
present perfect *'We've **found** the answer.'*	**past perfect** *She said (that) they **had found** the answer.*
past simple *'I **thought of** an interesting question.'*	**past perfect** *He said (that) he **had thought of** an interesting question.*
will, can *'I'll **explain** it to you.'*	**would, could** *She said (that) she **would** explain it to me.*
am / is / are going to *'I'm **going to** do some research.'*	**was / were going to** *She said (that) she **was going to** do some research.*

Language note: if something is reported which is always true, the tense usually stays the same. Verbs in the past perfect and other modal verbs (would, could, should, etc.) also stay the same in reported speech.
*'Arsenic **is** poisonous'* → *He said arsenic **is poisonous**.*
*'It **could** kill you'* → *He said it **could** kill you.*

To report statements we usually use *say* and *tell*. We say something (to somebody) and we tell somebody (about something). These verbs are often followed by *that*, however *that* can be omitted.
*He **told me** that he'd read an interesting book.*
*I **said** I'd like to read it.*

To report questions we usually use *ask* with a question word. For *yes / no* questions we use *if* or *whether*. The word order is the same as in statements.
'Does anything eat wasps?' → *A colleague **asked if** anything ate wasps.*
'Why does my skin squeak on glass?' → *He **asked why** his skin squeaked on glass.*

In reported statements other words can also change.
- pronouns: *'My son asked **me** a question.'* → ***She** said that **her son** had asked **her** a question.*
- places: *'I found the answer right **here**.'* → *She said she had found the answer right **there**.*
- this / that: *'It's in **this** book.'* → *She said it was in **a** book.*
- times: *'I looked at the website **last week**.'* → *She said she had looked at the website **the week before**.*
*'I'll find out **tomorrow**.'* → *'She said she would find out **the next day**.'*

Reporting verbs

We report requests with *ask* + object + *to* infinitive.
'Come with us please.' → *The police **asked the man to go** with them.*

We report commands with *tell* + object + *to* infinitive
'Sit down.' → *They **told him to sit down**.*

We can also use other reporting verbs to report what somebody said or did. Different verbs take different structures. Some verbs can take more than one structure.

verb	structure
admit, confirm, complain, mention	(*that*) + clause
assure	object + (*that*) + clause
deny	+ -*ing*
insist	prep + -*ing*
accuse	object + prep + -*ing*
refuse, promise, claim, agree	*to* + infinitive
beg, remind	object + *to* + infinitive

Unit 7 Exercises

so and such

1 Complete the sentences with *so* or *such*.

1 Advertising is _____ a huge industry.
2 There are _____ few places where there is no advertising.
3 Their advertising campaign was _____ successful that it increased profits by 20%.
4 It was _____ a terrible product that it was hard to make it sound good.
5 He's _____ creative, he always has _____ good ideas.
6 They spend _____ much money on advertising.

2 Join the sentences. Use *so / such* and *that* …

1 She has great ideas. The campaign will be a big success.
_____
2 He is very tall. He can't buy clothes in a normal shop.
_____
3 They are nice people. I'm sure you'll get on with them.
_____
4 We are late. We won't make the flight.
_____
5 It's a fantastic restaurant. It's always full.
_____
6 They have few staff. There are always queues.
_____

Reported statements and questions

3 Complete the reported interview with a scientist. Use a question word from the box and a suitable form of the word in brackets. There may be more than one answer.

whether	what	if	why	how long	when

1 We asked _____ it _____ (take) him to get results from his latest research.
2 We asked _____ he _____ (continue) with the research for so long.
3 We asked _____ it _____ (be) a team project.
4 We asked him _____ a commercial product _____ (be) available on the market.
5 We asked _____ the product _____ (be) affordable for all.
6 We asked him _____ his next research project _____ (focus) on.

4 Report the scientist's answers. Change tenses and pronouns where necessary.

1 It has taken me twelve years.
_____
2 I was always convinced that I would find a solution.
_____
3 A large team always works on projects of this kind. I just had the overall responsibility.
_____
4 A pharmaceutical company is already developing something. It will be available early next year.
_____
5 The price of the product will be very reasonable.
_____
6 I'm afraid I can't say anything right now. It's top secret.
_____

Reporting verbs

5 Choose the best reporting verb in the box for each situation.

deny	remind	beg	agree	accuse	insist

1 OK, I'll come to the police station. _____
2 Remember that anything you say can be used in evidence against you. _____
3 I want to see my lawyer now. Right now. _____
4 Please, please don't tell my wife. _____
5 I don't know what you are talking about. _____
6 You took that lady's bag. _____

6 Rewrite the sentences in exercise 5 using the verbs and the correct structure. Remember to change pronouns where necessary.

1 _____
2 _____
3 _____
4 _____
5 _____
6 _____

Units 8 & 9

Conditional structures

We can use *if*, *providing*, *as long as*, *unless* and *even if* to introduce conditional structures.

- *Providing (that)* or *as long as* mean 'only if a certain thing happens or is done'.
  Providing / As long as you work hard, you will be successful.

- *Even if* is an emphatic way of saying *if*.
  It's a good idea to try something, **even if** *you don't succeed.*

- *Unless* means the same as *if not*.
  Unless *you ask him, he won't help you.* (= If you don't ask him, he won't help you.)

Unreal conditionals

We use unreal conditionals to talk about unreal situations.

- we use the **second conditional** to talk about an unreal **future** situation. It is unlikely or almost impossible that the situation will happen.
  If + past simple, I / you, etc. *would / might / could* (*not*) + infinitive
  If I **didn't have** *children, I'd* **move** *abroad.*

  Language note: we can say *If I were* or *If I was*. *If I was* is more informal.

- we use the **third conditional** to talk about unreal situations in the **past**.
  If + past perfect (*had* + past participle), I / you, etc. *would / may / might / could* (*not*) *have* + past participle
  If I **had become** *a pilot, I* **would have flown** *all over the world.*

- we use a **mixed conditional** to talk about an unreal situation **in the past** that has a consequence or result **in the present**.
  If + past perfect (*had* + past participle), I / you, etc. *would / might / could* (*not*) + infinitive
  If I'd **chosen** *another career, I* **might be** *happier now.*

Wishes and regrets

To talk about wishes in the **present**, we use:
- *wish / if only* + past simple / past continuous
  I **wish I had** *a better job.* (= I'd like a better job now.)
  If only *I were sitting on a beach now.*
To talk about wishes and regrets in the **past**, we use:
- *wish / if only* + past perfect
  I wish I **had got** *a proper education.*
  If only I **hadn't said** *no.*

- *should have* + past participle
  I **should have divorced** *him.*
- *It's a pity* + past simple
  It's a pity *I never learned to play a musical instrument.*
- *regret* + verb + *-ing*
  I **regret not helping** *my parents more when they were older.*
- *my biggest regret is that* + clause in the past tense
  My biggest regret is that *I didn't live life to the full.*

Phrasal verbs

A phrasal verb is a two-word verb consisting of a verb and a particle, for example *set off* and *think over*.

Some phrasal verbs take direct objects and some do not (they are 'intransitive'). Some common intransitive verbs are *set off*, *die down* and *look down*.

Most phrasal verbs which take objects are **separable**. This means the verb and the particle can be separated by an object.

If the object is a **noun**, it can go after the verb and particle, or between the verb and particle.
Please **pick up** *that litter.* OR *Please* **pick** *that litter* **up**.

If the object is a **pronoun** it goes between the verb and particle.
Please **pick** *it* **up**.

Some phrasal verbs are **non-separable**. This means the verb and the particle always come before the object.

Verbs followed by *-ing* and infinitive with *to*

Some verbs are followed by an *-ing* form. These include *carry on, enjoy, fancy, finish, give up, imagine, keep (on), mind* and *suggest*.
~~They enjoy to go to weddings.~~   *They* **enjoy going** *to weddings.*

Some verbs are followed by the infinitive with *to*. These include *afford, agree, arrange, expect, manage, promise, refuse* and *seem*.
~~The bride promised loving him.~~   *The bride* **promised to love** *him.*

Some verbs can be followed by the infinitive with *to* or the *-ing* form of the verb and there is little or no difference in meaning. These include *begin, continue, hate, like, love, prefer* and *start*.
I **don't like dancing**.
I **don't like to dance**.

However, some verbs are followed either by the infinitive with *to* or by the *-ing* form of the verb with a difference in meaning.
I **stopped** *to ask the way.* (= I stopped moving.)
I **stopped smoking** *last year.* (= I no longer smoke.)
I **tried to tell** *her what he was like* (= I attempted to tell her.)
I felt dizzy and **tried taking** *an aspirin* (= I experimented.)
I **forgot to take** *photos*
I'll never **forget going** *to that wedding* (= I'll always have a clear memory of the wedding.)
I **remembered to buy** *the present.*
I **remember** *falling over* (= I have an image in my mind of it.)

Units 8 & 9 Exercises

Conditional structures

1 Tick (✔) the two sentences in each group with the same meaning.

1 a Even if you work hard, it doesn't mean you'll get rich. ✔
  b If you work hard, it doesn't always mean you'll get rich. ✔
  c Unless you work hard, it doesn't mean you'll get rich.

2 a If you don't tell me what's wrong, I can't help you. ✔
  b Unless you tell me what's wrong, I can't help you. ✔
  c Providing you tell me what's wrong, I can't help you.

3 a We'll get there on time if we don't hurry up.
  b We'll get there on time as long as we hurry up. ✔
  c We'll get there on time providing we hurry up. ✔

Unreal conditionals

2 Complete the text with the correct forms of the words in brackets.

I was adopted as a child and I often wondered: What (1) _____ (*my life / be like*) if I lived with my birth mother? When I was older, I knew if I (2) _____ (*not find*) my birth mother, I would always wonder about her. So I found her. But if I (3) _____ (*not know*) she was my mother, I (4) _____ (*not get on*) with her at all. She made it clear that if I (5) _____ (*not contact*) her, she would never have tried to find me. I was disappointed but I knew if I hadn't met her, I (6) _____ (*still / wonder*) about her today.

3 Complete the second sentence so that it means the same as the first.

1 He is alive thanks to a vital operation.
  If he hadn't _____ alive.

2 I found out the truth because a friend told me.
  I wouldn't _____ told me.

3 Her biggest dream is to write a famous novel.
  If she _____ would come true.

4 We're unemployed because we criticised the boss.
  We wouldn't _____ the boss.

Wishes and regrets

4 Rewrite the same regret using different structures.

'Why did I leave? I really regret it.'

1 If only I _____.
2 It's a pity I _____.
3 My biggest regret is _____.
4 I wish I _____.
5 I should _____.

5 Complete the regrets.

1 Bad cook: I wish (*learn / cook*) _____.
2 Failed student: I should (*work / hard*) _____.
3 Unfit person: I regret (*be / so lazy*) _____
4 Only child: My biggest regret (*not / have / a brother or sister*) _____
5 Unhappy single: If only (*be / so fussy*) _____.

Phrasal verbs

6 Complete the sentences with the correct option.

1 He forgot to give me my _____ back.
  a prosperity   b life   c pen
2 We set off for the _____.
  a door   b desert   c architecture
3 I picked the _____ up from the floor.
  a coin   b inspiration   c problem
4 We came across the most wonderful _____.
  a experience   b place   c ridicule
5 He looks after his _____ during the day.
  a money   b job   c daughter

7 Complete the dialogues.

1 A: I think they're your keys on the floor.
  B: I'll (*them / pick / up*) _____.
2 A: That's my final offer.
  B: I'll (*it / think / over*) _____.
3 A: She has an unusual name.
  B: Yes, I've never (*that / come / across*) _____.
4 A: Can I use the car?
  B: Yes, but (*it / look / after*) _____.
5 A: I'm just borrowing your sunglasses.
  B: Please (*them / give / back*) _____.

Verbs followed by -ing and infinitive with to

8 Complete the text with the infinitive with *to* or the *-ing* form.

Last winter my friends suggest (1) _____ (*go*) on a skiing trip. I'd never fancied (2) _____ (*ski*), so at first I refused (3) _____ (*take part*). But my friends kept on (4) _____ (*ask*): they thought I would enjoy (5) _____ (*try*) something new. Finally I agreed (6) _____ (*join*) them. We had arranged (7) _____ (*have*) lessons and I actually managed (8) _____ (*learn*) quite quickly. I even started (9) _____ (*have*) fun.

9 Rewrite the sentences using the verb in brackets.

1 She has no memory of falling.
  (*not remember*) _____
2 They didn't lock the door.
  (*forget*) _____
3 Using a dictionary might help you.
  (*try*) _____
4 We had a break and ate our sandwiches.
  (*stop*) _____

Unit 10

Defining and non-defining relative clauses

Relative clauses are formed with a relative pronoun and a clause:

- *who* (for people)
- *which* (for things)
- *that* (for people or things)
- *where* (places)
- *whose* (belonging to a person or thing)
- *when* (times)

> **Language note:** *whom* is the object form of *who* and is sometimes used in formal, written language. It is rarely used in spoken language.

We use **defining relative clauses** to identify a thing, person, place or time. Without this information the sentence isn't complete or doesn't make sense.

In defining relative clauses where the pronoun is the object, the pronoun can be left out.
*Tears help people to establish a bond with **people (that) they care for**.*
*He used an experiment **(that) he carried out at Vassar College**.*

We use **non-defining relative clauses** to add extra information about a person or thing, or add a comment on the whole sentence. Without this information the sentence still makes sense.

We use commas to separate the clause from the rest of the sentence.
*Cold air and wind, **which dry out the eyes**, cause reflex tears.*
*People with tears were clearly identified as being sad, **which in itself isn't surprising**.*

In non-defining clauses we don't use *that* and we can't leave out the pronoun.
~~*Emotional tears, that result from emotional experiences, are unique to humans.*~~ *Emotional tears, **which** result from emotional experiences, are unique to humans.*
~~*The experiment, was repeated several times, produced clear results.*~~ *The experiment, **which** was repeated several times, produced clear results.*

> **Language note:** non-defining relative clauses are mostly used in formal or written speech.

Present participle clauses

In present participle clauses, a present participle (verb +-*ing*) is used in one clause instead of a subject and a main verb.
***Feeling** disappointed, she refused to speak to him.* (= Because she felt disappointed, she refused to speak to him.)

Present participle clauses are used to link information so that more information is given in shorter sentences. Participle clauses are usually used in written language. In spoken language we usually use main verbs.
*He sits in front of the TV every day, **watching** endless sitcoms and **thinking** about life.* (= He sits in front of the TV every day. He watches endless sitcoms and he thinks about life.)

The subject of the verb in the participle clause and in the main clause must be the same.
***I was wondering** what to do, so **I phoned** a friend. Wondering what to do, I phoned a friend.*
***I was wondering** what to do, when **my phone rang**.* ~~*Wondering what to do, my phone rang.*~~

When the participle clause is negative, *not* is used before the participle.
***Not realising** what had happened, I went to bed.*
***Not knowing** what to do, I went for a walk.*

> **Language note:** the present participle can express actions in the past as well as the present.
> ***Switching off** the alarm clock, I usually sleep for another half an hour.* (= I switch off the alarm clock.)
> ***Switching off** the alarm clock, I slept for another half an hour.* (= I switched off the alarm clock.)

The present participle is often used after conjunctions and prepositions such as *before, after, when, while, on, by* and *without*.
***After getting** the email, I deleted it.* (= After I got the email …)
***On hearing** the news, I drove over there straight away.* (= When I heard …)
***Without listening** to his explanation, I finished the phone call.* (= I didn't listen to his explanation and …)

Emphasising (cleft sentences)

We can emphasise part of a sentence using these structures:

- *It is / was* + person / thing + relative clause
  ***It was an American engineer who** invented the 'laff box'.*
  ***It's the canned laughter that** really gets on my nerves.*
- *What / the thing that* + clause + *is / was*
  ***What I noticed about him is** that he's always laughing.*
  ***The thing that I like about her is** her great sense of humour.*

Compare the following sentences. Notice the different parts of the sentence that are emphasised.

World Laughter Day was first celebrated in Mumbai in 1998 and organised by Dr Madan Kataria.
- ***It was in 1998** that World Laughter Day was first celebrated.*
- ***It was in Mumbai** that World Laughter Day was first celebrated.*
- ***It was World Laughter Day** that was first celebrated in 1998.*
- ***It was Dr Madan Kataria** who organised World Laughter Day.*

In speech, the important parts of the sentence in a cleft sentence are additionally emphasised through stress and intonation.

Unit 10 Exercises

Defining and non-defining relative clauses

1 Put in relative pronouns and add commas where necessary. If the pronoun can be left out, write the pronoun in brackets.

1 Sadness is an emotion _____ everybody feels.
2 It is the emotion _____ people feel when they have lost something or someone important.
3 Sadness is a temporary mood _____ usually lasts only a few hours or days.
4 People _____ sadness results from the death of a relative or friend will never completely lose that feeling.
5 People _____ suffer from permanent or very deep sadness are said to be depressed.
6 Sadness _____ is often seen as a negative emotion is necessary in order to appreciate happiness.
7 Research has shown that sadness is contagious _____ biophysicists have suspected for years.
8 Research has also shown that the time _____ teenagers go to bed greatly affects their risk of feeling sad.

2 Rewrite the two sentences using relative clauses to make one sentence.

1 I met an amazing woman. Her attitude to life greatly inspired me.
_____
2 He told me a joke. I'd heard it lots of times before.
_____
3 He looked rather depressed. That was unusual as he tends to be very cheerful.
_____
4 The article was about what determines the mood of a country. I read it yesterday.
_____
5 Barcelona was a pleasant place to work. I worked there in the nineties.
_____
6 I'm following the work of a team of scientists. They are researching happiness.
_____

Present participle clauses

3 Rewrite the text replacing the participle clauses with main verbs.

On retiring from work, I didn't know what to do with my life. After getting up late, I had breakfast in my pyjamas every day. Then I usually read the newspaper, not knowing what else to do. Later I often went for a walk around the village, doing some shopping along the way. In the afternoon, I did little jobs at home, waiting until it was time for dinner. In the evening I watched TV before going to bed.

_____
_____
_____
_____
_____

4 Join the two sentences using a participle clause.

1 I talked to a friend. I found out some upsetting news.
_____
2 He shouted at her to be quiet. He left the room.
_____
3 They thanked her for her help. They went home.
_____
4 She saw his email was open. She decided to read his messages.
_____
5 We waited for the bus. We started to feel better.
_____
6 I met my friends. I told them what had happened.
_____

Emphasising (cleft sentences)

5 Match the two parts of the dialogue.

1 Why are you laughing?
2 What's special about her comedy routine?
3 Why didn't you like him?
4 I thought you enjoyed romantic comedies.
5 How can we cheer him up?
6 You don't look very happy.

a It was his laugh that I just couldn't stand.
b The thing that always makes him smile is watching cartoons.
c It's the way he tells jokes that cracks me up.
d It's this miserable weather that always gets me down.
e The thing that she does best is mimic other people.
f What I don't like about them is the silly dialogue.

6 Complete the sentences to add emphasis.

1 My English teacher makes me laugh the most.
It _____ makes me laugh the most.
2 People who laugh really loudly drive me crazy.
What _____ people who laugh really loudly.
3 I really enjoy watching political satire.
The thing _____ is political satire.
4 I first saw a live comedy performance in 2008.
It _____ saw a live comedy performance.
5 I love her infectious laugh most of all.
The thing _____ her infectious laugh.
6 I find it difficult to deal with people who have no sense of humour.
It _____ I find difficult to deal with.

Audioscript

Unit 1

1.05

Part one: these days we live very busy lives, and in the rush to keep up with the present it's easy to lose sight of the past. We tend to live and work further away from our families, and therefore become disconnected from where we've come from and who we are related to. But a sense of who we are - our roots – is very important to us.

Researching your family's history is therefore a great way to discover your roots and keep that information alive.

1.06

Part two: it may sound obvious, but the best place to start your research is with members of your own family, particularly older relatives, who can tell you about names, dates and places relating to people you may never have met. Some of the stories they tell though can be a bit painful, so don't push them too hard; but they'll give you enough information to get you started in the archives.

Another place to look is on the internet. More and more countries are putting information online and allowing people the opportunity to search it. In Britain and the United States, for example, it's now possible to find detailed information about births, and deaths from the past two hundred years. There are also records of marriages and divorces online too now, that go back more than a hundred years. This information is held at their national archive sites, but perhaps even more interestingly it's now possible to find records of people who arrived in these countries by boat in the 19th and 20th centuries.

1.07

1 I'm optimistic about growing older. Progress in medicine and changes in lifestyle mean that your retirement years can now be the best years of your lives. I turned 65 last year and since I retired I've learnt how to sail and spend much of my time out on the water. And through voluntary work with young offenders, I've met people who I would never have met in my old job, people who have given me a totally new perspective on life. I'm certainly going to make the most of this time.

1.08

2 What am I optimistic about? Well, I'll give you an honest answer. Right now, the only thing that I'm optimistic about is that things will get better before long because they certainly can't get any worse. I've just lost my job and with the state of the economy, it's going to be difficult to find a new one in the near future. I'm going for a job interview tomorrow but I doubt that I'll get the job.

1.09

3 I'm optimistic about blogging. The fact that everyone, anyone can publish what he or she thinks and share it with a huge community of readers, without editing or censorship, well, it's just mind-blowing, real democracy in action. I'm interested in the way blogs shape political decisions – and that's not just wishful thinking, it's happening already. I firmly believe that the days when blogs will determine elections are just around the corner.

1.10

4 Erm, well, I'm optimistic about climate change. It seems that every day we read dire predictions about the unstoppable advance of global warming

but at the same time companies and governments are starting to invest heavily in green technology. Attitudes are changing fast so I'm confident that we're going to see a green future. But er … having said that, I must admit that I have serious doubts that this will be in my lifetime. The days of unlimited renewable energy, for example, are light years away.

1.11

5 I'm optimistic about my career. I've just been promoted and my new job starts next month. I'm going to be working in a different branch of the company so I'm moving house as well in a couple of weeks. I'm a bit apprehensive about starting again in a new place but I'm positive it will benefit my career with the company.

1.12

1 In general, I think modern life is more stressful than it was in the past. Mobile phones, for example, force us to live life at a faster pace. We're constantly answering the phone or reading text messages and you have to make instant decisions all the time. There's just no time for thinking and, you know, reflecting on what you want to say and what you think about something. Especially at work. And at home, … household appliances and gadgets are getting more and more complicated all the time – I find just working out how to use them is really stressful. So as a rule I find it easier to live without too much technology at home – apart from certain basic things like my TV and washing machine which I couldn't do without.

1.13

2 I'd say modern life is much better than it was in the past. Well, what I mean is, the quality of life is much better now than in the past. My parents lived through the war, they were hungrier and people died younger. Everybody had less money and a harder life. And it typically took longer to get to places. My parents never even dreamed of travelling to visit family in America or Asia. So in many ways I think things are much better now. An exception to this is the quality of the products you buy. In my parents' time products were mostly better quality – made to last. Shoes, clothes, things for the home. Now things just don't last, you have to throw them away and buy new ones. But by and large, things have just become a lot easier and better. That's what I think, anyway.

1.14

3 Modern life is, generally, healthier than in the past. I mean, I know that there is still a lot of pollution and so on but really we are living much healthier lives. In this country you can't smoke anywhere in public places, and that has had an enormous effect on public health. Food is also better, more varied, fresher and, in most cases, healthier. OK, not counting junk food which, personally, I think is a terrible aspect of modern life. But people, ordinarily, are living longer – and better than two or three generations ago.

Unit 2

1.16

1 So, errr … yes that's about it for the future perfect. Does anyone have any more questions? Right! Let's take a look at this poem I've brought in, you were asking about this yesterday and …

1.17

2 Right! Stop talking now and listen! Good … good … now, as I was saying the homework for tomorrow's class is …

1.18

The right answer quiz

1 The driest place on earth is Antarctica. Parts of that continent have seen no rain for two million years. A desert is technically defined as a place that receives less than 254 mm of rain a year. The Sahara gets 25 mm of rain a year. Antarctica's average annual rainfall is about the same, but 2 per cent of it, known as the Dry Valleys, is free of ice and snow and it never rains there at all.

2 No human objects at all can be seen from the moon with the naked eye. It's true that you can see several objects from space, but space is quite close. It starts about 100 km from the Earth's surface. At a few thousand km into space, you cannot see any human constructions. The moon is over 400,000 km away from the Earth. On the moon, you can hardly even see the continents.

3 The word for *centipede* comes from the Latin for 'a hundred feet' and though centipedes have been studied for over a hundred years, nobody has found one with exactly a hundred legs. Some centipedes have more, some have fewer.

4 The Canary Islands are named after dogs. Canary birds are named after the island, not the other way around. The islands get their name from the Latin name for the largest of the islands, which the Romans named 'Isle of Dogs' (*Insula Canaria*) after the large numbers of dogs there, both wild and domesticated.

5 The ant's brain is largest in proportion to its size. An ant's brain is about 6 per cent of its total body weight, while a human brain is a little over 2 per cent of body weight. Ants have been around for 130 million years and there are about 10,000 trillion of them at large while we speak. The total mass of ants on the planet is slightly heavier than the total mass of human beings.

6 The correct answer is a grapefruit. The whale's throat is very narrow, making it impossible to swallow a car, or even a human being. Apart from the throat though, everything else about a blue whale is big. At 32 metres in length it is one of the largest creatures that has ever lived. Its tongue weighs more than an elephant, its heart is the size of a family car, its stomach can hold more than a ton of food.

1.19–1.24

1 You've written the *e* and *i* the wrong way round. Remember the rule: '*i* before *e*, except after *c*'.

2 What?! What did you just say? … Oh, sorry, I thought you said something else.

3 You are talking about your birthday party, aren't you? No? Oh, we seem to have got our wires crossed.

4 **A:** As Alexander Pope wrote, 'A little knowledge is a dangerous thing'.
  B: Er, that's not quite what he said … He actually said 'A little learning is a dangerous thing'.

5 **A:** Do you want an expresso?
  B: Espresso! Esss! Why do you always say expresso, it drives me crazy!

6 **A:** … so after the earthquake they had to evaporate the city and everybody left.
  B: … Erm, I don't think you meant 'evaporate', that's when you know … a liquid becomes a gas. I think you mean 'evacuate'.

1.26

The wrong word

Everybody makes language mistakes, whether it's in their own language or a foreign language. Sometimes instead of the word that they wanted to say, a speaker uses a similar-sounding word. This is called a malapropism, from the French phrase *mal à propos*, which means 'inappropriate'. Malapropisms occur in everyday conversations, on the radio, in speeches and presentations. In some cases the word just sounds strange, for example *I'll do it to the best of my mobility* instead of *to the best of my ability*. However, mistakes like *he's a civil serpent* instead of *civil servant* can be very funny, particularly when they are said by a well-known person in a particular context. Sports commentators and politicians seem to produce the funniest malapropisms. Former US president George W. Bush, for example, made so many malapropisms and other linguistic errors that these mistakes became known as 'Bushisms'. His classic slips of the tongue included 'weapons of mass production' instead of 'weapons of mass destruction', and 'nuclear power pants' instead of 'power plants'.

Speakers don't only use the wrong word, they often mispronounce words too. This can be because somebody doesn't know the pronunciation of an unusual word – for example words that are more common in written language. However, a speaker can also mispronounce a word by mixing up the sounds in words. This is called a spoonerism. Mixing up sounds often creates nonsense words – for example *wook out the lindow* instead of *look out the window*, but it can also create a funny change in meaning, such as *a lack of pies* instead of *a pack of lies*. Many people use spoonerisms accidentally when they are nervous or speak too quickly, but comedians also use them deliberately as a comic play on words.

1.27

1 We're late, have you taken a shower yet?
2 He can't hear you. He's deaf.
3 I walked through the metal detector at the airport.
4 I'll have a muffin and a cup of coffee.
5 Can you give me a specific example.
6 The car won't start, it must be a flat battery again.

1.31

Ben was in Los Angeles on business. When his meetings were over he went to the train station. He needed to catch the next train to be in time to catch the wedding rings at his best friend's wedding in San Francisco. However, Ben's wallet was stolen in the train station. He lost all his money, his credit cards and ID as well as his ticket to San Francisco. As he was a stranger and had no ID, nobody at the station wanted to lend him money for a ticket. While Ben was trying to decide what to do next, a well-dressed man sitting next to him on a bench left his coat unattended for a couple of minutes. Sticking out of the man's pocket was a train ticket to San Francisco. Ben could see that the man had more than enough money to buy a new ticket.

1.32

1 **A:** … Well, so you can imagine how surprised everyone was when he said he was a vegetarian.
   B: Ugh, vegetarians.
   A: What do you mean?
   B: Oh, they're such a pain. Think they're better than everyone else, it's so annoying.
   A: Oh. So you think vegetarianism is a bad idea.
   B: Oh no, that's not what I said at all. I mean, it's fine to be a vegetarian. What I meant was that I don't care what people eat. Just don't act superior to us.
   A: My mother's a vegetarian.
   B: Oh. Well, I'm sure she isn't like that.
   A: Mm.

1.33

2 **A:** Two tickets to the airport please.
   B: I'm afraid there aren't any buses leaving from this station. You need to go to the next one.
   A: Excuse me?
   B: No buses from here.
   A: So… I have to take a taxi then?
   B: No. You can take a bus …
   A: So, are you telling me there aren't any buses to the airport?
   B: No, what I said was there aren't any buses from this station. This station is closed for repairs.
   A: So, how do we get to the airport from here?
   B: You need to walk to the next station, and take a bus from there.
   A: Fine. Thank you.

1.34

3 **A:** Mrs President, is it true you're resigning because of your husband's business connections?
   B: Oh you must have misunderstood, I'm not resigning. I'm just saying that I'm taking a short break.
   A: But is this because of your husband's business connections? Why isn't your husband answering questions?
   B: What I've been saying all along is that the time has come for me to step away from politics and concentrate on my family life. It has nothing to do with my husband or any business contacts. Thank you very much.
   B: Thank you. No more questions, thank you thank you.

1.36

Hao, China

Well I think, when I start to speak, at first stage I always mess up with the tense and once I spoke to a friend from Canada, I think I confused him because I used the wrong tense. Um, I was talking about someone … I was talking about someone who is already dead, but I used present tense, like 'he is' but … and make … made him think that he's still alive or something.

1.37

Eldar, Bosnia

So uh … what mistakes do I make uh … when I talk in English? Since this is not my native language, sometimes I … I guess this happens to other non-native speakers … sometimes I … I tend to, you know, construct uh … sentences using the grammar of my native language and then trying to translate this in this … in English. I think this is the … the most … most common thing non-native speakers make.

1.38

Frank, Germany

My… hm … most common mistakes in English probably are um … yeah … mixing up words which are very similar in German than English words, for example I used to say 'sensible' instead of 'sensitive' stuff like this which is sometimes a bit funny. I also mix up um … um … yeah, grammar stuff like 'going to' and 'I will do', future terms – it's called future terms isn't it. Um, it's a quite common mistake um … I used to do and little stuff like make a difference between 'these' and 'those', or 'this' and 'that' just little stuff I think, yeah.

1.39

Antonia, France

Some sounds are quite difficult for me to do. Like with the aitch. We are not supposed to to pronounce the aitch in French so it's something I can of er forget sometimes.

1.40

Patricia, Brazil

I would say that I sometimes make some mistakes and I guess one of the things I found quite difficult about English is, um, the prepositions and the use of prepositions. So I, I guess that, I make some mistakes sometimes using prepositions. Um, but apart from that hopefully I don't make so many mistakes.

1.41

Erica, Italy

The mistake I still make all the time is to forget to spell acronyms. So instead of saying ai, es ai, pee, I forgot and I say asap and then people look at me with like empty glaze and say, 'What you talking about?'

1.42

Maria, Spain

I've been speaking English for years and years and years but I've, I still make the mistake with *his* and *her* because in Spanish we've got just one word with no gender so my husband still corrects me and when I say, talk about a woman and say 'his something' and the other way around always and I think it will always happen.

1.43

Faisal, Saudi Arabia

I'm a little bit confused about the difference between 'do' and 'is', 'does' as well. Um, because um, I mmm I have to, I have to er, read about it er more and more, so I think after that I will be fine.

Unit 3

1.44

The pilot who saved 155 lives by landing his stricken aircraft on the Hudson River in New York has described the moment his windscreen was 'filled with big, brown birds'.

Captain Chesley B Sullenberger III said US Airways Flight 1549 flew into a flock of birds at 1,000 metres moments after taking off from LaGuardia airport. Moments later, he was forced to tell air traffic controllers 'We're gonna be in the Hudson.'

The veteran pilot told crash investigators from the National Transportation Safety Board that he heard a 'thump' followed by 'a smell of burning birds' and then 'silence' as both the Airbus A320's engines cut out.

His first instinct as the birds struck was to duck and then he cried out 'My aircraft!' when he realised what had happened.

Mr Sullenberger, 57, a former fighter pilot, said he then made a split-second decision to bring the aircraft down in the Hudson River because he knew it was 'too low and too slow' to reach a safe landing spot without hitting nearby buildings, which would have caused a 'catastrophic' crash.

Flight controllers asked him if he could make it back to LaGuardia, or nearby Teterboro airport, but he replied 'We can't do it. We're gonna be in the Hudson'. That was his last communication with the ground.

At the moment of impact first officer Jeff Skiles was flying the plane and he described catching sight of a large number of dark brown birds approaching in 'perfect formation'. After they hit, Mr Sullenberger immediately took over the controls.

Two of the plane's flight attendants told investigators there was an eerie quiet in the cabin after the engines stopped and it was 'like being in a library' as smoke and the smell of burning filled the plane.

But Mr Sullenberger set the aircraft down so smoothly on the water that the flight attendants compared it to an ordinary 'hard landing' on a runway.

The pilot – known to colleagues as 'Sully' – then issued a one word command to 'evacuate' and stayed on board himself until everyone else was safe. All 150 passengers and five crew survived after being picked up by nearby boats.

1.45

1 Here, gimmie that pen will you? Thanks.
2 Ugh! Rain. Doncha hate it when it rains?
3 Hey, didja hear the news?
4 Is that the time? I've gotta go.
5 I dunno what you're talking about.
6 Can you please be quiet? It's kinda difficult to study with all this noise.

1.47

The images you see here are reproduced from the Carta Marina, one of the most fantastic ancient maps still in existence. Carta Marina is Latin for map of the sea, but this is actually a map of the Northern countries, the part of the world now known as Scandinavia.

The map was drawn by Olaus Magnus, a Swedish priest living in Italy in the sixteenth century. It was printed in 1539 on nine large wooden blocks. The original map produced a document that was 1.70 metres tall by 1.25 metres wide. The map is remarkable for its small painstaking detail.

Contrary to popular modern belief, mariners of the time did not believe that they would sail right off the edge of the earth. They were, however, quite nervous about what they would find in their travels. The Carta Marina is especially famous for the fantastic colourful sea monsters and the tiny intricate details depicted on it. Let us examine a few.

In the top left corner, next to the small island, you can see the wreckage of many boats and several great floating trees. These show the dangers of sailing there. To the right of Iceland, a boat has hooked onto a huge yellow and green monster. What's more interesting is that on the back of the monster you can see two sailors cooking a meal.

In the seas below Iceland you can see other famous sea monsters of the time. The large green head emerging from the sea is that of a Leviathan, a legendary sea serpent that measured over one hundred metres. Just underneath is a monstrous pig, with eyes on its sides and a small crescent moon on its back. You can also see other giant sea creatures, including what looks like an enormous lobster.

These illustrations of monsters were common on old maps such as the Carta Marina, but eventually the practice died out with modern mapmaking. However, stories about sea monsters have existed in almost all cultures that have contact with the sea, and many still persist to this day.

1.50

These two graphs show the rise in sea levels. On the left we see a steady rise over the past 120 years. In fact, over the past century, and until 10 years ago, the seas were rising at a rate of 1.8 mm a year, but over the past ten years this rate has increased to almost 3mm per year. This can be interpreted as a serious increase, and is most likely because of global warming. Global warming affects sea level rise in two ways: through thermal expansion and through the melting of the continental ice sheets. All the data suggests that these trends will continue, and the sea levels will continue to rise.

The other graph shows a much longer time period since the last ice age in fact. This data indicates that the sea level in fact rose and rose steadily for thousands of years and only stabilised around six thousand years ago, more or less. Now, this could mean that sea level rise is a natural phenomenon over thousands of years, it's been happening all along and it's just a natural thing. Looking at this data one could almost think that the current rise is not that serious. That there is no need to worry. However, I think that the recent data indicates that the pace is accelerating. In effect, it is happening much more quickly, and my feeling is, well I think that it's safe to say that this is a result of increased human activity contributing to global warming.

Unit 4

1.52

Number 12. *The Conjurer*, by the Dutch painter Hieronymus Bosch. This is not one of Bosch's best-known paintings, but it is very interesting nevertheless. This painting in particular shows how people are deceived and tricked by illusion.

The painting shows a magician, the conjurer, at a fair or market of some kind. The fair could have been in any town in Europe in the 1500s, there were many of them. The main character is the conjurer. He is holding up a small object, perhaps a pearl. It may be a fake pearl, but he has the audience's attention. The spectator is very interested and is leaning forward. Misled by the magician, he does not realise that a person, who must be the magician's assistant, is reaching into his purse to take his money.

Bosch shows the magician as an intelligent person through the owl, which you can see peeping out of his bag.

There is a woman next to the magician's assistant. She is showing with her hand that true miracles are a matter of the heart, not a cheap trick. At the back of the group of people stands a man dressed in black. He may understand what is really happening, but he is happy to remain an observer.

The figure of the conjurer reappears in other paintings by Bosch, and is representative of the tension between magic and the real world.

1.53

1	a labourer	6	a civil servant
2	a flight attendant	7	a director
3	a translator	8	a baker
4	a politician	9	a mathematician
5	a supervisor		

1.56

Mysteries of the silver screen: Plot Devices

A plot device is an object or character whose sole purpose is to drive forward the plot of a story. There are many kinds of plot devices that are used in mystery stories, especially films, and in this talk we shall examine four of them: the 'locked room', the 'MacGuffin', the 'plot voucher' and *'deus ex machina'*.

The locked room plot device means that the crime in the mystery, usually murder, is committed in a closed community - such as in a country mansion, train or on an aeroplane. There is a carefully restricted number of people who are all suspects. This device allows the viewer to play detective for themselves – the murderer is one of the people present, but who is it?

A 'MacGuffin' is the name given to an object or device that helps move the plot of a film forward – but that isn't necessarily the most important thing. It could be a mysterious object that the heroes and villains of the film are interested in, or a secret weapon that they want to have or that they need to destroy. Hitchcock himself explained the term in 1939 '... we have a name in the studio, and we call it the "MacGuffin". It is the mechanical element that usually crops up in any story. In crook stories it is almost always the necklace and in spy stories it is almost always the papers. We just try to be a little more original.'

A third common plot device, especially in film, is what the writer Nick Lowe calls the 'plot voucher'. The plot voucher is also an object. It is typically given to the hero or protagonist in the film and allows him or her to escape from a situation that would be otherwise impossible. This could be a small object that allows the hero to open a locked door, or something that stops a fatal bullet.

The final plot device I'm going to talk about are those that are used to bring a film to a conclusion. One of these is the *deus ex machina*, which translates literally as 'god from the machine'. This occurs when a seemingly impossible problem is suddenly and quickly solved with the introduction of a new character or object. For example, all seems lost for the hero but at the very last minute a new detective arrives on the scene and saves the day.

A variation on this, especially in mystery films, is 'the big reveal'. This is the final part of the story, where the whole truth is explained, often by the lead detective. There may have been other moments where the audience thought they knew the answer to the mystery, but the truth is only confirmed in the big reveal at the end.

1.57

A: What did you think of the film?
B: Mm. I though it was **kind of** predictable.
A: Predictable?
B: Yeah. **All that stuff** at the end … Anyway, I don't like those old mystery movies.
A: Oh, I do. I love those films. I love suspense **and that sort of thing**.
B: I don't hate them but they don't surprise me. If I see a suspense movie I **kind of** want to feel tense. I want to feel nervous **and stuff**.
A: You're being **a bit … kind of …** difficult.

1.58

1 A: It says here that if you drink the waters of the Fountain of Youth, you'll stay forever young.
   B: Really? I wonder who thought up that money-spinner.
   A: What do you mean?
   B: Oh, come on, it's nonsense. Do you really think water can make you look younger? Sorry, but I find that a bit hard to believe.
   A: Well, no, I don't think … obviously I don't think it can make you look younger or stay young forever, … no of course it can't … But there might be something in the water, you know minerals or something, that can have some sort of beneficial effect on your health.

B: Hmm, maybe. But let's face it, you could say that about any spring or fountain.

A: I suppose so.

🔘 1.59

2 **A:** This is the Statue of *Daikokuten*. Apparently, if you rub the statue's head and shoulders, it'll bring you fortune and wealth.

B: I doubt it, somehow.

A: Oh, don't be such a misery. It can't do any harm.

B: Hmm, it's unlikely to do any good either.

A: I don't know, power of positive thinking and all that. Besides, it's a gesture of respect more than anything.

B: Oh, go on then.

🔘 1.62

Gülgün, Turkey

It was a small thing but it was real strange event. I used to er, travel from my countryside to er, my city for my education er and when er in my one trip the bus stopped suddenly. Yeah. And the driver said, 'I saw a girl in the middle of the street.' In the middle of the night, it was a night trip. Yeah, and it takes 10 hours from my countryside to my city and everyone er got off the bus and we didn't see anything, any girl or something because it was dark and um, not crowded road, y'know. Um, we didn't see anything everybody got on again er and we just and the driver said that, just said that, yeah.

🔘 1.63

Kang Sik, South Korea

When I, when I sleep, I usually, I think, er, twice a month I see, um, I see my body when I sleep. It's er, it's like a dream. And then I see my body and then it's er. When I see my body it's so, it's amazing and sometimes it's terrible. Y'know I can't, I can't explain how, er how it happen to me but sometimes I enjoy it.

🔘 1.64

Charlotte, England

Uhm... a mysterious or magical experience. I, when I was about 15, which is far too old to have such an experience, I was with my older sister, I have to say, um, and we saw a cat in a field disappear 'cos it was dusk and it did disappear. It didn't run away anyway, it disappeared and we were convinced it was some sort of spooky thing. Um, which I'm sure it's not but at the age of 14, 15 it's a bit odd to think that.

🔘 1.65

Matthew, United States

I was er ... younger, I can't remember exactly when it was but I had an out-of-body experience. And, uhm, I was lying in bed one night and I wasn't asleep but I guess I was about to fall asleep and, and at that moment, I, I felt like my whole body coming out of my body and um, it like started at my feet and started coming up and up and up and through my, you know my chest and then right out the top of my head and then, then this body of mine, you know with this presence or my consciousness or whatever was up in the corner of the room and it was looking down at my other body, my physical body which was lying there in bed.

Unit 5

🔘 1.66

1 My name? Well, my full name is Elvis Roberto Gomez Jimenez, yes, you heard correctly, Elvis, but I always use my second name, my Venezuelan name – Roberto. My parents named me after their favourite American singer and I've ... I've never forgiven them. I was always teased in school, especially as I can't sing ... can't sing at all. Some parents <u>will</u> insist on giving their children strange names ... they don't think about ... you know, that a name is for life.

🔘 1.67

2 This is Zhang Ping. Zhang, is our family name. Western names usually put the family name last but we say the family name first. The other name, Ping ... we thought a long time about our daughter's given name and its meaning. We wanted our daughter to have a peaceful life, so we chose the name Ping, it means peaceful. In China it can be the name for both a girl and a boy.

🔘 1.68

3 My name is Katrin Evadottir. In Iceland we've kept the traditional naming system, a parent will usually pass on their first name to their children as a family name. It's a way of showing who the child belongs to, who you are descended from. It's more usual to take your family name from your father – my cousin's surname is Benediktsdottir which means 'daughter of Benedikt'. But my mother was a single mother and so she gave me her name. My surname 'Evadottir' means 'daughter of Eva'.

🔘 1.69

4 If you want my full name, it's William Stanford III, but I just call myself Will Stanford. I was named after my father, who was named after his ... his father. I'm kinda proud of having a traditional family name. However, when I was little my mom always called me 'junior' and I hated that. She'll sometimes call me junior even now. She won't accept that I'm all grown up.

🔘 1.70

5 My name is Rozamond van Rijn. I'm Dutch but because I live here in Germany, ... my name, you know ... people will often ask me about my name. When I got married I kept my own name because, well, ... that's what we do in the Netherlands. Here in Germany women will keep their own names or they'll use a double name from both names. Sometimes men change their last names and take their wife's name too.

🔘 1.72

Every child, every generation is a product of their times. And this is certainly true for the net generation, often referred to as 'Generation Y'. These children were born from the late 1970s to the late 1990s. Growing up in relative affluence in many parts of the world, with abundant attention from family and friends, this generation is strong-minded, self-confident – and sometimes rather self-centred.
Many Generation Y children in more affluent societies have fewer brothers and sisters than in previous generations or are only children, and they are often quite spoilt and protected by their parents. In China, for example, these children are known as 'Little Emperors'. In general, Generation Y is better dressed, better fed and better looked after than previous generations. The downside is that many of this generation are not used to standing on their own two feet.
Largely due of course to being the first generation to grow up with computers and the internet, this generation is well-informed and technologically savvy. While older generations are still getting used to sending emails, members of Generation Y are competent and constant users of mobile phones, instant messaging, music downloads and social networking sites – and are used to multitasking – using different technologies at the same time and switching between tasks. They are creative, publishing their own blogs, websites, videos and music. And they are part of a global online community with access to information and other young people from all over the world.
Consumer culture is another defining characteristic of Generation Y. Its members are financially more secure than previous generations who have had to get used to consumerism. In India, for example, where half of the population is under 25, young people no longer see a good education and a permanent job as their main aim in life. As the service industry booms, so young people are learning to adapt to a more flexible, easy-going job culture where jobs are changed on a regular basis and where money is the prime motivation – money that can be used to buy consumer products such as cars and electronic equipment.

🔘 1.75

1 **A:** ... so there I was, stuck at the airport, with no money, no passport and nothing.

B: No. It must have been terrible.

A: Mmm. It was ...

B: What did you do?

A: Well, I called my parents and they drove all the way to pick me up. Thankfully!

B: Oh that's good then. Good old mum and dad! Speaking of driving, did you know I got my driving licence?

A: Really?

B: Yes, finally! You know I never really thought I would get it. But I am now officially allowed to drive a car!

A: That's great! I could have called you to pick me up ...

🔘 1.76

2 **A:** What are you doing right now, Rob?

B: Me? Nothing much, why?

A: I was wondering if you wanted to go and get a sandwich, from that new place just down the street.

B: Yeah, sure. That new Italian sandwich shop?

A: That's the one.

B: I haven't been there before, but everyone says it's really good.

A: I know, I ate there yesterday. Amazing cheese.

B: Oh, listen, before I forget ... do you have Janet's number?

A: Janet who used to work here? Yes, why?

B: Haven't you heard? She's had a baby. I was going to call to congratulate her.

A: Really! I had no idea. By the way, Silvia is pregnant too.

B: Wow. It's a year for babies then.

Audioscript

1.77

3 **A:** Are you calling about going out this Saturday?

B: Yes, how did you know? Well, can you come? We're all going to the cinema, and …

A: No, I can't. My dad won't let me.

B: Oh, why not? It'll be fun. Can't you, you know, convince him?

A: Umm. Probably not. I've also got loads of homework.

B: Oh that's a pain …

A: I know. Next time, right? Oh, I've just remembered something … did you know we've got our history test this week?

B: I know! I know! I've been revising for that test for ages and I still don't understand what the League of Nations was about …

1.78

4 **A:** Right, remember that your class reports are all due next Tuesday. You can leave them on my desk, or just email them to me …

B: Excuse me, can we talk about the end of term teachers' dinner?

A: I'm sorry, the what?

B: I know this is your first year as head teacher but we usually have a dinner with all the teachers at the end of the first term.

A: Oh. Well, of course. Who wants to organise it?

B: I will, if nobody objects.

A: That reminds me though, we need to talk about the school cafeteria, there have been some complaints from students and from staff.

C: Oh gosh, yes the cafeteria. Think we need to change our catering company, it's been pretty bad recently.

D: Bad? It's been awful! The other day I …

A: Yes, yes, we all know this. Shall we schedule another meeting to discuss other options?

Unit 6

2.09

Rhetoric is the art or study of using language to persuade or please people. In ancient Greece people in formal education were taught rhetoric and little else. It was considered of great importance to be able to speak in public, argue a case and most importantly persuade others to agree with what they were saying. People were thought to be more powerful if they were able to employ good rhetoric.

Nowadays, rhetoric is no longer widely taught, and is often considered a rather negative term. However, speechwriter and communications expert Max Atkinson believes that rhetorical techniques are still very much alive and well today. They are an important and essential factor of the way a good speaker can move an audience. Sometimes these techniques are called claptraps. The word 'claptrap', which usually means nonsense, is used by Atkinson to refer to the techniques employed by speech makers to get applause, ie clapping, or another positive reaction. It is sometimes thought that these are very difficult techniques – that they are obscure, complex or incomprehensible. Nothing could be further from the truth. As we shall see, the techniques are not only very simple, but are also strangely familiar to us. In fact, most people already use them both in conversation and in speeches, without realising that this is what they are doing.

2.10

Here then, briefly, are three of the main techniques you can use to make your words more powerful.

Contrast: this can take the form of contrasts, such as 'Not this, but that'. One famous example is Kennedy's phrase '*Ask not what your country can do for you, ask what you can do for your country*'. A contrast can also be formed as a comparison: 'more this than that' or finally, as opposites 'black or white'.

Puzzles and questions: this means using a puzzle and solution format. The speaker sets up a puzzle or problem, then asks a question which he or she will answer. For example 'So much for the past. What about the future?' or 'These are our problems, what are our solutions?'

Lists of three: the list of three things is by far the most popular technique. It can be a list of three different words, like Julius Caesar's *Veni, vidi, vici*; three identical words: *no, no, no* or three phrases: *Government of the people, by the people, for the people.*

If using one single technique to package a message has a good impact on an audience, it makes sense to think that combining more than one at the same time is likely to have a greater impact.

2.11

1 **A:** Oh, morning.

B: Morning. I hope I'm not disturbing you. Listen, do you think I could borrow your drill? Mine isn't working for some reason.

A: Sure, no problem. Come in, I'll just get it. Would you like a cup of coffee …?

2.12

2 **A:** Hello?

B: Oh hello, it's Emily, Alex's mother.

A: Oh hi!

B: I was wondering if you could help me with something? I have a meeting tomorrow and I need somebody to pick up Alex from school.

A: Tomorrow? Erm, yes, I can do that. Why don't I just take him home with my boys and you can pick him up when you're ready.

B: That's fantastic, thank you. I should be finished about 5 o'clock.

A: That's fine.

B: OK, thank you. See you tomorrow.

2.13

3 **A:** Come in. Ah, … what can I do for you?

B: Are you busy? I've got a problem with my computer and I can't get hold of the IT department. Do you think you could take a look at it?

A: I'm afraid I can't. I have to be in a meeting in five minutes.

B: Oh, OK. Well thanks anyway.

2.14

4 **A:** Hello!

B: Hi, how are you? … Umm, can you do me a big favour? Our washing machine has broken down and I can't get it fixed until next week. Could I come round this afternoon perhaps and do some washing? I'd be really grateful … and I'll bring some cake.

A: Well, since you put it like that … yes, of course! I'm in all afternoon, just come round.

B: Thanks, you're a star. See you later.

2.15

Ahmet, Turkey

Um … to talk about how my parents they taught me about money. I can't say they directly taught me how to, how I should spend my money. When I was thirteen I, I left my house and I went on a boarding school and I had to learn by myself how to spend my time, how to allocate the, my money to different, to different hobbies that sort of thing.

2.16

Eamon, Ireland

My mum and dad always told me, in actual fact never borrow money off of anyone, in actual fact you should never do or you're going to make enemies if you borrow the money off them and that's what I learnt from them.

2.17

Mieke, Belgium

Um, how did my parents teach me about money, well they gave me pocket money and I had to buy the things I wanted with my pocket money and if I didn't have enough I had to get a holiday job or whatever, so um… I think that's a good way, you know. They were people who were great on saving money so they taught me that.

2.18

Magdi, Sudan

And er my parent and I think they, they taught me a very, very useful wisdom about, about how to save money. Er, we have wisdoms there in our culture I can translate it in English also because it, I think in England there is the same wisdom er… they taught me er… white penny for a black day, white penny for a black day here, if you take care of pennies, pounds, pound will take care of themselves. This is, this is my thought about, about saving money.

2.19

Isidora, Greece

My parents taught me er that er money isn't the important thing in our life. You must use the money er to, to have um a good life but it isn't a goal for a, of life.

2.20

Douglas, Scotland

Money, and learning about money. Yes, well, of course, when I was growing up in the 1950s, there weren't supermarkets er so, what it meant was that you had to do shopping every day and also at that time it was relatively unusual for mothers to work. So my mother didn't work. She was at home and we didn't have a car. So, from a very early age, I mean probably from the age of about four or five, uhm she used to give me money, send me to the local shops and I would buy meat or bread or whatever it happened to be er for that day. And then of course, er travelling to school on the bus, you had to pay the bus fares.

Unit 7

2.22

A slogan should be so memorable that it leaves the key message of a brand in the mind of the target audience.

Ideally the brand name should be included in the slogan. After all, why run an advertisement in which the brand name is not clear? One of the best techniques for bringing in the brand name is to make the slogan rhyme with it. Here are some slogans we've selected from our database – see how well it works if the brand name is the rhyming word. So for the Natwest Bank: *To save and invest, talk to Natwest.* For Quavers crisps: *The flavour of a Quaver is never known to waver.* Or for Thomas Cook travel: *Don't just book it, Thomas Cook it.*

Another possibility is to use a rhyme and mention the brand name without the brand name itself actually rhyming with another word. For example a slogan for a Mars chocolate bar: *A Mars a day helps you work, rest and play*, where Mars is the brand name but *a day* rhymes with *play*. Or an advert for Flanders, Belgium: *Savour the flavour of Belgium*, where Belgium is not part of the rhyme. Note however that when the brand name is not the rhyme, the slogan doesn't evoke such a strong identification with the product. It could easily be *An apple a day helps you work, rest and play*, or some other product rather than just Mars. Instead of *Savour the flavour of Belgium*, *Savour the flavour of a Quaver* would also be possible.

Another important advertising rule is 'sell the sizzle, not the steak'. This means sell the benefits of a product not just the product itself. A good slogan should therefore include a key benefit. For example, for the weight loss company Weight Watchers®, the slogan *Taste. Not waist.* cleverly refers to the effect on your tastebuds and on your waistline.

Lastly, a slogan should refer to a characteristic about the brand that makes it different from its competitors in some way. For the British Mail on Sunday newspaper the slogan *A newspaper, not a snoozepaper* implies that other newspapers are not such exciting reads, and the slogan for Safeway supermarkets *Everything you want from a store, and a little bit more* implies that because Safeway offers so many products and services, other supermarkets are simply not as good.

2.23
A study in scarlet
Dr Watson has just started to share lodgings with Sherlock Holmes. Watson does not know what Holmes does for a living but he is very curious to find out. At the start of this conversation, Watson is reading a magazine article about how much somebody can learn about another person by observing them, for example what job they do. The writer even claims he can read a person's innermost thoughts.
I slapped the magazine down on the table. 'I never read such rubbish in my life!'

'What is it?' asked Sherlock Holmes.

'This article,' I said, pointing at it as I sat down to my breakfast. 'It is not practical. I should like to see the writer put in a carriage on the Underground and asked to say the jobs of all his fellow travellers. I would bet a thousand to one he couldn't do it.'

'You would lose your money,' Holmes remarked calmly. 'As for the article, I wrote it myself.'

'You!'

'Yes. I am skilled in both observation and deduction. The theories which I have expressed there are really extremely practical – so practical that I depend on them for my living.'

'And how?' I asked involuntarily.

'Well, I'm a consulting detective if you can understand what that is. Here in London we have lots of government detectives and lots of private ones. When these fellows have a problem, they come to me and I manage to put them on the right scent. They lay all the evidence before me and I am generally able, by the help of my knowledge of the history of crime to set them straight.'

'But who are these people?'

'They are mostly sent on by private inquiry agencies. They are all people who are in trouble about

something. I listen to their story, they listen to my comments and then I pocket my fee.'

'But do you mean to say,' I said, 'that without leaving your room you can unravel some knot which other men can make nothing of, although they have seen every detail for themselves?'

'Quite so. I have a kind of intuition that way. Now and again a case turns up which is a little more complex. Then I have to see things with my own eyes. You see I have a lot of special knowledge which I apply to the problem. Observation with me is second nature.'

I walked over to the window and stood looking out into the busy street. 'This fellow may be very clever,' I said to myself, 'but he is certainly very conceited.'

'I wonder what that fellow is looking for?' I asked pointing to a plainly dressed individual who was walking slowly down the other side of the street looking anxiously at the numbers. He had a large blue envelope in his hand.

'You mean the retired sergeant of the marines,' said Sherlock Holmes.

'Nonsense,' I thought to myself. 'He knows that I cannot verify his guess.'

The thought had hardly passed through my mind when the man whom we were watching caught sight of the number on our door and ran rapidly across the roadway. We heard a loud knock and heavy steps ascending the stair.

'For Mr Sherlock Holmes,' he said stepping in to the room and handing my friend the letter. Here was an opportunity of taking the conceit out of Holmes.

'May I ask,' I said, 'what your trade may be?'

'Messenger, Sir,' he said. 'My uniform is being repaired.'

'And you were?' I asked with a slightly malicious glance at my companion.

'A sergeant, sir, Royal marines, sir.'

He clicked his heels together, raised his hand in salute and was gone.

2.24
A: You know I'm fed up of seeing all those adverts to get a perfect body or perfect teeth every time I look at a website. I find them really offensive.

B: I know what you mean. Still, they're pretty harmless compared to some adverts.

A: Like what?

B: Well, you know adverts that are blatantly sexist or that make fun of somebody's religion …

A: Right … yes, … but I find these adverts really annoying. Especially those ones about getting a flat stomach. Everyone knows there's no miracle way to get a perfect body even if you really wanted one.

B: Well, the main purpose of advertising is to sell products …

A: But all the same, it's just taking advantage of people's insecurities.

B: People click on them, though! I bet you click on them as well …

A: Well, I did do it out of curiosity once or twice …

B: There you are. If nobody did that, the ads would soon disappear.

A: OK, but even so, it's so hard to ignore them, they're completely in your face …

B: Of course they are! That's the whole point.

A: Yes, but …

Unit 8

2.26
1 The American Dream exists. It is possible to live the American Dream … as long as you have lots of money.

2.27
2 I think the American Dream is a great idea. Erm, basically it says that, providing you work hard and really want something then you will get it. You can be anybody you want to be, you just have to want it enough.

2.28
3 Isn't it a dream that most people in this country have – to live a better life than their parents did? That's what I always heard. I think it's a bit of an illusion – just an idea that people carry in their minds. Many people today would argue that their lives are, in fact, not as good as their parents' lives.

2.29
4 Make more money. Have more expensive things. Buy more cars. Buy bigger houses. Don't think about tomorrow. Don't have any free time because you're always working. That's living the American Dream, in my mind.

2.30
5 My family were immigrants to this country, and they always had this idea fixed in their heads that things would be better for their children because this is America. And they were right. As long as you work hard, and teach your children right, then things can get better for them. It's a good idea for a society.

2.31
6 We need a new American Dream, because unless we stop buying and consuming and polluting so much we're going to destroy the environment that makes the American Dream worth living. I think we need a dream that focuses on a more simple life and less on making money all the time.

2.32
7 I have a suspicion, at the back of my mind, that the American Dream is a myth. It's impossible to achieve but it keeps people busy. Most people cannot achieve the American Dream, even if they work very hard.

2.35
Nature and animal documentary films are universally popular. What is also universal is that scenes in nature films – as in many other documentaries – are often staged. Dramatic moments such as birth, death and combat are vital for the success of a nature documentary. But the capturing of those scenes can be very difficult if not impossible.

In the 1940s and 1950s Disney was famous for its true life nature films. One famous scene from the 1958 Disney film *White Wilderness* showed hundreds of lemmings dramatically jumping off a cliff in the Canadian Arctic into the Arctic Ocean below. The film supposedly illustrated the migration of lemmings. However a few decades later it was revealed that this – and many of the scenes in similar films – were far from true life. Firstly the lemming scene was shot in Calgary – 2,000 kilometres south of the Arctic. Disney had paid local children in the Arctic to catch the lemmings and then shipped them to the film location. The so-called Arctic Ocean shown in the film was in fact a river. Secondly the lemmings didn't jump off the cliff – they were pushed, with the help of a specially-built turntable. And thirdly, the facts portrayed in the scene were simply not true: Canadian lemmings don't actually migrate – and in that area of Canada there are actually no cliffs to jump off at that time of year. One of the cameramen who worked on the film said that the chances of getting particular shots in the wild are nearly impossible. Roy Disney, Walt Disney's nephew responsible for wildlife films, justified the cruelty of the lemmings' death by saying that the lemmings probably would have died anyway.

Today nature documentaries are a growing industry – and documentary makers are still using the same old tricks. Scenes are still staged with captive animals, trained to behave in certain ways. Some scenes are shot in studios with film sets designed to look like a natural habitat. Even Sir David Attenborough, perhaps the most respected presenter of natural history films, has admitted that a scene in his film *Arctic Warrior* showing the birth of a baby polar bear was 'stretching the truth'. The narration of the event referred to the terrible arctic conditions outside – but the scene was actually shot in Frankfurt Zoo. In his defence Attenborough said that the zoo was listed in the credits. The birth of the baby bear was included as part of the story of a polar bear's life. The scene could never have been filmed in the Arctic because the life of the baby and cameraman would have been at risk. Attenborough felt that the stretching of the truth was therefore justified in this case.

2.36

1 **A:** Hello, darling. This is a surprise, I'm just about to go into my meeting.
  B: Oh, I'm so glad I caught you. I suppose I could have waited until later but …
  A: Is something wrong?
  B: No, no. I have some good news and, er, … I just couldn't wait to tell you. Guess what, you'll never believe it …
  A: What? Sorry, but I do have to go into the meeting now.
  B: Well, … I'm pregnant!
  A: Oh wow! That's wonderful news! Hey, I'm gonna be a dad! … When …

2.37

2 **A:** Hello.
  B: Oh hello, I'm calling from Go! TV. I'm very pleased to be able to tell you that your family has been chosen as the family for our 24-hour documentary series.
  A: Erm …what's that?
  B: Yes, I know this might come as rather a surprise but as soon as we read your partner's casting application …
  A: Application?
  B: Yes, as soon as we read about you and saw those lovely photos, we knew you were the right family for our programme.
  A: Oh, … well, I don't know what to say … Erm, I'm sorry but I think I need to talk to my partner about this …

2.39

Dilamar, Brazil

And uh … um … My greatest dream when I was child was um … be a teacher. Yes, but I it …uh … I never uh … I started university, but I always give up everything that I start in my life so … I'm here, in England, work like uh … like … like a cleaner.

2.40

Judy, Australia

Um … My greatest dream was actually to be a professional tennis player but that didn't happen, but I have played tennis all these years and had a lot of fun and made great friends from it.

2.41

José, Spain

Um … My greatest dream as a child was to become a footballer, a professional football player. I think for, for all the boys of my, of my school when I was a child was very popular to become a football player because it's your main interest you know. It's the main thing you, you think about. Um … now, when you are older you think about another things; you think about your studies, your opportunities, eh, politics or other things. Now, my, my dream is to become a, a um professor at the university.

2.42

Karina, Russia

Um, I wanted to save the world. When my grandfather told that the roads were, er, very bad I thought when I grow up, I'll change everything and we'll have the best roads ever. And, all the time like this and then when I, I became older I start thinking uhm, is this possible to change everything so you should be a president or a magician, which is, which is much better.

2.43

Javier, Spain

My big dream as a child … Well, my big … My dream as a child was the same that I have now. Um, I would like to be a professor at the university, I always was that is to be that. So now I work at the university as a researcher and I'd like in the future to go … to go back to Spain and try to find … finish my PhD and try to find a job at the university and teach there. That's my dream, that was my dream as a child.

2.44

Alison, England

What's your greatest dream or ambition as a child? As a child I wanted to be a paramedic, but um … as time has gone on I think from seeing the reality of life and yeah I, I don't think my stomach could handle that sort of thing anymore.

2.45

Mingyu, South Korea

I wanted to go every single countries in the world and try their um, er local food and I'd still like to do it, I love to go new places and try new things, food and their customs and so it's always interesting.

Unit 9

2.46

One day in ancient times, the sun looked down and saw a large bird with bright red and gold feathers. The sun blessed it, 'Glorious Phoenix, you shall be my bird. I shall look after you and you shall live forever!' The phoenix was overjoyed to hear these words but living forever didn't make it happy for long. Children were always chasing it, wanting some of its beautiful, shiny feathers. Tired, the phoenix flew away towards the east and came across a hidden desert. Here, flying freely, it could sing songs of praise to the sun alone.

Five centuries passed. The phoenix was still alive, but age was slowing it down. It couldn't fly as high nor as fast as when it was young. The phoenix asked the sun to give it its strength back. It sang, 'Sun, glorious sun, make me young and strong again!' But the sun didn't answer. The phoenix thought the situation over and decided to return to the place of its origin.

The journey was long, and because the phoenix was old and weak, it had to rest along the way. Each time it landed, it picked up pieces of bark and all kinds of fragrant leaves. When at last the bird returned to its home, it landed on the tallest palm tree on the highest mountain. The phoenix built a nest with the cinnamon bark and lined it with the fragrant leaves.

The phoenix sat down in its nest, and once again, sang, 'Sun, glorious sun, make me young and strong again!' This time the sun heard the song. It shone down on the mountainside with all its strength. The phoenix let the sun's rays beat down upon its beautiful, shiny feathers until, suddenly, there was a flash of light and the nest went up in flames.

After a while the flames died down. The phoenix had disappeared and only a heap of silvery-grey ash remained. Suddenly out of the ashes rose a new phoenix. It flapped its wings, and grew until it was the same size as the old phoenix. Then it set off for the faraway desert again.

Legend says that even today the phoenix lives in that desert. Every five hundred years, when it begins to feel weak and old, it flies west to the same mountain. It rebuilds its nest in the palm tree, the sun burns it to ashes, and from these ashes the phoenix is reborn. And so in modern times the rising phoenix has come to stand for rebirth, change and survival.

2.47

Alarmed, Ted tries to back away but he almost trips over a small bridesmaid under foot (they're like vermin) and in an attempt to avoid crushing her he loses his balance and lurches towards the table bearing the wedding cake. Everything seems to go into slow motion as Ted pitches and reels, his arms flailing like windmills, in a desperate attempt to regain his balance and avoid the irresistible, inevitable accident which we can see hanging before our eyes. The tiny bridal couple on top of the cake sway and totter as if they were sitting on top of a volcano. Ted moans as his feet go under him and in one dreadful slapstick movement he falls, face first, into the wedding cake.

2.48

1 **A:** … and there was 50 per cent off. I couldn't see the price because I didn't have my glasses on, so I asked the assistant what it cost with the 50% off. And he couldn't work it out! I mean, it wasn't something hard like erm …, I don't know, 17% or something. How can you not know what 50% of something is? What do they teach them in schools nowadays?
  B: All right, all right, calm down. Admittedly, some people today don't seem to be able to do maths in their heads … erm, I suppose it's because they're used to using calculators or computers or whatever … but the things we did in maths in school … well, algebra for example, … I've never used half the things we learned.
  A: Hmm, I don't know. It may well be true that some of the things we learnt in school are, a bit … a bit irrelevant nowadays but …

2.49

2 **A:** … you know, it's strange, she gets terrible marks in all her tests, but she got that new mobile phone and had it worked out in ten minutes.
  B: Whereas you couldn't work out how to change your ring tone.

A: Oh, come on … all right, I take your point but …

B: It's skills that count today. You don't have to have it in your head or have learnt … you know, things by heart.

A: Mmm, you may be right. I don't like it, but you may be right.

Unit 10

🔘 2.50

Most people associate tears with people who are crying because they're upset, angry or extremely happy, but there are actually three different kinds of tears.

So what are these three kinds of tears? Well, firstly there are basal tears. These are the ones which are regularly produced by the tear glands which are above your eyes, under the eyelids, and protect the eyes by keeping them clean and wet. Basal tears are spread evenly over the eye by blinking. They are made up of a mixture of water, oil and mucus.

But there are other tears which have no connection with the emotions either. These tears also protect the eyes … so how are they different? The second kind of tears is called reflex tears and their job is to wash out foreign objects that come into contact with the eye – when an eyelash or an insect gets stuck in your eye, for example. Reflex tears can also be caused by the smell of onions or smoke, which contain chemicals and tiny particles. In addition, cold air or wind, which dry out the eyes, cause the tear glands to produce reflex tears. In English we often say our eyes are 'watering' when this happens.

And then there are 'real' tears, emotional tears. These are produced by emotional stress or pain and have been found to contain more hormones than other types of tears. Most mammals produce basal or reflex tears, but only we humans cry emotional tears.

Emotional tears and reflex tears also come from the tear glands. Some of the tears drain away through the tear ducts in the corner of your eyes. But when too many tears are produced, they roll down your face. Your tear ducts are also connected to your nose, which is why tears sometimes run down into it. Both reflex tears and emotional tears are more watery than basal tears.

What's the function of emotional tears? Well, studies indicate that our bodies use them as a way of re-establishing balance of the nervous system. They are a way for us to calm down after a period of stress. Research across cultures also indicates that emotional tears help people to establish a bond with people they care for. Tears express vulnerability and most people react with sympathy to tears.

🔘 2.52

The sound of canned laughter is something our ears have grown used to. But the invention of the laugh track was a sensation in its time.

When shows moved from the theatre to TV, they were still filmed in front of live audiences. Sometimes the audience missed a joke and didn't laugh, sometimes people laughed too long, upsetting the timing of the programme and sometimes they laughed too loudly, drowning out the actors. It was an American sound engineer who came up with an idea to solve the problem. In the 1950s Charles Douglass invented the 'laff box', a machine that could produce laughter. The machine was like a small organ with keys for different types of laughter. Douglass collected recorded laughs from different television shows and isolated them on tape. Touching the different keys could produce male or female laughter of different ages, small giggles, quiet chuckles or roaring belly-laughs. Volume could be adjusted using

a special pedal. The thing that American producers liked most was the fact that the laff box allowed them to simulate an audience or to film outside a studio, as well as solving the problems with a studio audience. Although the machine was an innovation, fake laughter itself was far from a new concept. In the sixteenth century theatre owners used to pay people to join the audience and laugh at comedy performances, and in France in the nineteenth century professional laughers were recruited by agencies to perform this service on an organised scale. Even today paid laughers are still hired to join TV studio audiences and audiences at important film screenings.

Nowadays it is computers with pre-recorded laugh tracks that are used to produce canned laughter. However in many countries canned laughter is now seen as being slightly old-fashioned. One observer attributes this to the fact that how people watch TV has changed. In the fifties and sixties, households only had one television. The whole family would watch TV together – and laugh together. Today many people watch TV alone in their rooms or on their computer using headphones. What has also changed is the way people laugh: laughs have become quieter and less aggressive. Uncontrolled belly laughs and roars of laughter were often responses to over-the-top situations or visual jokes which were popular in the fifties and sixties. As sitcoms today are usually based on witty conversation, people tend to laugh in a more controlled manner. This means that laugh tracks can sound rather contrived to today's ears.

🔘 2.55

Two hunters are out in the woods when one of them collapses. He doesn't seem to be breathing and his eyes are glazed. The other guy takes out his phone and calls the emergency services.

He gasps 'My friend is dead! What can I do?' The operator says 'Calm down, I can help. First, let's make sure he's dead.' There is a silence, then a gunshot is heard. Back on the phone, the guy says: 'OK, now what?'

🔘 2.56

1 A: … so anyway, I was late for work and I was running down the street …

   B: Just a second, don't you usually cycle to work?

   A: Usually, yes, but my bike had a puncture. Anyway, as I was running, I noticed that people were smiling at me all the time, but I didn't think anything of it and I just smiled back. And then I saw two people pointing at my boots and …

   B: Hang on, didn't you think it was a bit odd that so many people were smiling at you …

   A: Well, yes, but I was in a rush so I didn't think too much about it. But then I looked down and noticed I'd got two different boots on, one brown and one black. The stupid thing was …

   B: Wait a minute, how come you didn't notice?

   A: Well, I put them on without putting the light on and because they're similar styles, I hadn't even noticed. The stupid thing was, I didn't have time to go back home and I had to wear different-coloured boots all day. Everyone in the office thought it was hilarious.

🔘 2.57

2 A: OK, I'd like to thank you all for coming. What I'm going to do today is first take a look at the first quarter sales figures and then move on to our marketing strategy for the coming months. Now, if you look at the first slide, you'll see that …

B: May I interrupt for a moment? Could you just draw the curtains because of the sun … thank you.

A: Right, yes, … erm, you'll see that we had a very satisfactory first quarter. Indeed one of our best net quarterly profits in the last few years and …

C: Could I just say something here? Are you sure that …

A: Sorry, if I could just finish … I wanted to say that this was actually our best quarterly performance for the last seven years and …

D: I'd like to say something if I may. I think …

A: One moment, I'd just like to point out that international sales accounted for 64% of the quarter's revenue and, in fact, …

E: Excuse me for interrupting, but what I think the others were trying to say is that you seem to be showing the wrong figures …

🔘 2.58

Giorgio, Italy

Erm … the funniest person I know is probably my brother. My brother um is older than me and uhm always know er when I'm sad how to make me feel happy … um …. he always has a joke suitable for me and … he always try to make me feel good and that's because I love him.

🔘 2.59

Georgios, Greece

Funniest person I know, um … there are a few from movie industry but the funniest I know is, is, is an uncle is my uncle who has this ability to be theatrical and dramatic at the same time and y'know he's, he was always there, the attention, he liked to have people around. He's very special, he's very funny and he always remind me of an actor actually, a Greek actor, um, from the old school um, so I think the funniest person I know is my uncle, Letharios.

🔘 2.60

Luisa, Chile

The funniest person that I know, erm … I think it's my brother because he's a very famous actor in my country, in Chile. He's a comedian, er, actor and he appears in a lot of series and films in my country.

🔘 2.61

Erik, Sweden

And er, the funniest person I know is actually a person I met, Faisal. He's er, very funny because, well first you don't really understand what you, he's saying so first you laugh at him and then when he says it, tells you it's a joke, you laugh with him. Because, well, he's a genuine character.

🔘 2.62

Quirin, Germany

The funniest person I know is actually one of my friends. He is always joking, he's always a funny word to say. Yeah.

🔘 2.63

Raphael, Brazil

Er …. the funniest person yeah, er, well she's my girlfriend, I think she's very funny even when she doesn't want to be. I think this is very good for our relationship. I don't know. Usually when, when she gets mad with me she's, I just don't let her know that's she's being funny.

Irregular verbs

Infinitive	Past simple	Past participle
be	was/were	been
beat	beat	beaten
become	became	become
begin	began	begun
bend	bent	bent
bet	bet	bet
bite	bit	bitten
blow	blew	blown
break	broke	broken
bring	brought /brɔːt/	brought /brɔːt/
build /bɪld/	built /bɪlt/	built /bɪlt/
burn	burnt/burned	burnt/burned
burst	burst	burst
buy /baɪ/	bought /bɔːt/	bought /bɔːt/
can	could /kʊd/	(been able)
catch	caught /kɔːt/	caught /kɔːt/
choose	chose	chosen
come	came	come
cost	cost	cost
cut	cut	cut
deal /diːl/	dealt /delt/	dealt /delt/
dig	dug	dug
do	did	done
draw	drew	drawn
dream	dreamt/dreamed	dreamt/dreamed
drink	drank	drunk
drive	drove	driven
eat	ate	eaten
fall	fell	fallen
feed	fed	fed
feel	felt	felt
fight	fought /fɔːt/	fought /fɔːt/
find	found	found
fly	flew	flown
forget	forgot	forgotten
forgive	forgave	forgiven
freeze	froze	frozen
get	got	got
give	gave	given
go	went	gone/been
grow	grew	grown
hang	hung/hanged	hung/hanged
have	had	had
hear	heard /hɜːd/	heard /hɜːd/
hide	hid	hidden
hit	hit	hit
hold	held	held
hurt /hɜːt/	hurt /hɜːt/	hurt /hɜːt/
keep	kept	kept
kneel	knelt/kneeled	knelt/kneeled
know	knew /njuː/	known
lay	laid	laid
lead	led	led
learn	learnt	learnt
leave	left	left
lend	lent	lent
let	let	let

Infinitive	Past simple	Past participle
lie	lay	lain
light	lit	lit
lose	lost	lost
make	made	made
mean	meant /ment/	meant /ment/
meet	met	met
must	had to	(had to)
pay	paid	paid
put	put	put
read	read /red/	read /red/
ride	rode	ridden
ring	rang	rung
rise	rose	risen
run	ran	run
say	said /sed/	said /sed/
see	saw /sɔː/	seen
sell	sold	sold
send	sent	sent
set	set	set
shake	shook	shaken
shine	shone	shone
shoot	shot	shot
show	showed	shown
shrink	shrank	shrunk
shut	shut	shut
sing	sang	sung
sink	sank	sunk
sit	sat	sat
sleep	slept	slept
slide	slid	slid
smell	smelt/smelled	smelt/smelled
speak	spoke	spoken
spell	spelt/spelled	spelt/spelled
spend	spent	spent
spill	spilt/spilled	spilt/spilled
split	split	split
spoil	spoilt/spoiled	spoilt/spoiled
spread	spread	spread
stand	stood	stood
steal	stole	stolen
stick	stuck	stuck
swear	swore	sworn
swell	swelled	swollen/swelled
swim	swam	swum
take	took /tʊk/	taken
teach	taught /tɔːt/	taught /tɔːt/
tear	tore	torn
tell	told	told
think	thought /θɔːt/	thought /θɔːt/
throw	threw	thrown
understand	understood	understood
wake	woke	woken
wear	wore /wɔː/	worn
win	won /wʌn/	won /wʌn/
write	wrote	written

Macmillan Education
Between Towns Road, Oxford OX4 3PP
A division of Macmillan Publishers Limited
Companies and representatives throughout the world

ISBN 978-0-230-03318-4

Text © Lindsay Clandfield, Rebecca Robb Benne & Amanda Jeffries 2011
Design and illustration © Macmillan Publishers Limited 2011

First published 2011

Original design by Macmillan Publishers Limited
Page layout by eMC Design Ltd
Illustrated by Jonathan Burton, Celia Hart, Piers Sanford, Laszlo Veres
and Barbara Mercer
Cover design by Macmillan Publishers Limited
Cover photograph used by permission of the Museum of the History of
Science, University of Oxford/Keiko Ikeuchi.

Authors' acknowledgements

Lindsay Clandfield: I would like to thank all the co-authors on this project
who have worked tirelessly alongside me through the brainstorming,
researching, writing and rewriting stages that a project like this invariably
goes through. We made it there in the end! I would also like to thank
everyone at Macmillan for their help and support. Finally, once again this
book is for my wonderful sons Lucas and Marcos and my wife Sofia. My
apologies for my many absences during this project.

Rebecca Robb Benne: Thanks to the many students I have taught and
observed in lessons for their endless inspiration to try something new.
Thanks to the team at Macmillan who have done a wonderful job on this
particular level of the course. And thanks to Christian, Laura and Gabriel
for sharing me during the writing of this book.

Amanda would like to thank staff and students at The Isis Oxford school
of English; Staff and students (Jiwon and Marta) at The Oxford English
Centre; Noriko Sekido; Yilong Huang; Paulina Chang; Aleixandre
Leoneti; Gemma Celestino; Miriam Sanchez.

The authors and publishers would like to thank all the teachers and
consultants who have piloted and reviewed the material. Particular
thanks go to the following people: Andrea Córdova, Susana Flores
(Anglo Multimedia School of English, Haedo, Buenos Aires, Argentina);
Ma. Cristina Maggi, Ma. Cristina Buero de Chinton (Friends' School
of English, Adrogué, Buenos Aires, Argentina); Mirta Zampini, Aldana
Anchorena, Elizabeth Rainieri, Ma. Soledad D. Mangiarotti, Pamela
Sabrina Pecorelli (IECI, Haedo, Buenos Aires, Argentina); Alejandro Jorge
Listrani (Cultural Inglesa de Palermo, Ciudad Autónoma de Buenos Aires,
Argentina); Lilian Itzicovitch Leventhal (Potential/Colegio I.L.Peretz,
São Paulo, Brazil); Ana Maria Miranda (Cultura Inglesa Ribeirão Preto,
Ribeirão Preto, Brazil); Magali de Moraes Menti (FACCAT - Escola
Municipal Lauro Rodrigues, Porto Alegre, Brazil); Simone Sarmento
(PUCRS, Porto Alegre, Brazil); Laura Lee Lehto (Cultura Inglesa,
Fortaleza, Brazil); Viviane Cristine Silva Grossklauss, Analice Sandovetti
(Cultura Inglesa Jundiaí, Jundiaí, Brazil); Celia Aguiar de Almeida
Costa (Cultura Inglesa de Juiz de Fora, Brazil); Corina Celia Machado
Correa (Associação Alumni - São Paulo, Brazil); Jane Godwin, (The
Four, São Carlos, Brazil); Caroline Toubia (The Holy Family School,
Jesuite, Egypt); Amany Shawkey, Heidi Omara (Macmillan Publishers
Ltd, Egypt) Caroline Franz , Dana Jelinkova (MVHS Muenchner
Volkshochschule, Munich, Germany); Irene Rodriguez, Haydee Gutierrez
Palafox, Antonio Morales de la Barrera, Javier Ramos de Hoyos (The

Anglo Mexican Foundation, Mexico City, Mexico); Viviana Caruso
de Curtius (freelance author and consultant, Mexico City, Mexico);
Emma Dominguez (Academic Studies Manager, The Anglo Mexican
Foundation, Mexico City, Mexico); Katarzyna Rogalińska-Gajewska
(Archibald, Warsaw, Poland); Małgorzata Woźniak, Dorota Pachwicewicz,
Agnieszka Kilanowska (Centrum Językowe 'Euroclub', Gdańsk, Poland);
Fabiola Georgiana Hosu (Little London School and Nursery School,
Dimitrie Cantemir University, Bucharest, Romania); Lydia B. Korzheva
(Diplomatic Academy, Moscow, Russia); Ludmila A. Pokrovskaya (Russian
Academy of Foreign Trade, Moscow, Russia); Olga S. Petrischeva
(Moscow State University of International Relations, Moscow,
Russia); Albina Valieva (The international Language School 'Denis
School', Moscow, Russia); Karen Dyer, Cathy Harris, Frank Hodgkins
(International House, Madrid, Spain); Carlos Trueba (E.O.I. Villaverde,
Madrid, Spain); Patricia Plaza Arregui, (E.O.I. Malaga, Spain); Maria
Esther Álvarez Rico (E.O.I. Sagunto, Valencia, Spain); Burcu Tezcan Ünal
(Bilgi University, Istanbul, Turkey); Dr. F. Ilke Buyukduman (Ozyegin
University, Istanbul, Turkey); Sarah Shaw (The British Council, Chiang
Mai, Thailand); Aomboon Burutphakdee (Payap University, Chiang Mai,
Thailand); Claudia Edwards (London School of English, London, UK);
Sally Jones (Regent Oxford, Oxford, UK); Katherine Griggs (Community
English School Oxfordshire Adult Learning, Oxford, UK).

A special thank you to Jackie Halsall, Sarah Paterson and all the staff and
students at Eckersley, Oxford and Regent, Oxford for all their help with
Global voices.

The authors and publishers would like to thank the following for
permission to reproduce their photographs:
Alamy p69(tl), Alamy/M.Beddall p120(l), Alamy/DbImages p126(br),
Alamy/Foodfolio p129(cml), Alamy/A.Hampton Picture Library p74(tml),
Alamy/Imagebroker p130(cl), Alamy/Ikon Images p121(l), Alamy/J.
Leighton p74(tl), Alamy/Mediablitzimages(uk)Ltd p60(cl), Alamy/A.
Paterson p70(cl), Alamy/A.Segre p129(tm), Shoosmith Railway Collection
p26(tl); Aurora p96(bl); Bananastock pp88, 100(bl), 124(bl); Bettman
Archive p55(br), 78(cl); Brand X pp31(bl), 64(bl), 79(tm); The Bridgeman
Art Library/The Conjuror (oil on panel) (pre-restoration), Bosch,
Hieronymus (c.1450-1516) / Musee d'Art et d'Histoire, Saint-Germain-
en-Laye, France / Giraudon p42(b), The Bridgeman Art Library/
Aristotle and Plato: detail from the School of Athens in the Stanza della
Segnatura, 1510-11 (fresco) (detail of 472), Raphael (Raffaello Sanzio
of Urbino) (1483-1520) / Vatican Museums and Galleries, Vatican City,
Italy p67(tl), The Bridgeman Art Library/ Two Figures,, Tapies, Antoni
(b.1923) / Private Collection / © DACS / Index p115(tl), The Bridgeman
Art Library/Jane Austen (1775-1817) illustration from 'Little Journeys
to the Homes of Famous Women', published 1897 (engraving) (later
colouration), English School, (19th century) / Private Collection / Ken
Welsh p117(b); Damon Coulter p50(tr); Corbis pp 16(bl), 36(br), 112(bl),
Corbis/JamArt p104(bl), Corbis/S.Bassouls p69(cr), Corbis/S.Bonini
p48(b), Corbis/Z.Macaulay/Cultura p35(tl), Corbis/H.Diltz p22(cl),
Corbis/K.Eriksen p110(cml), Corbis/R.Farris p10(cl), Corbis/P.M.Fisher
p71(t), Corbis/A.Gea/Reuters p70(b), Corbis/E.Hoppe p37(tr), Corbis/J.
Hrusa pp105, 3(tr), Corbis/B.Kraft p82(cl), Corbis/H.King p74(tmr),
Corbis/J.Lund p43(cr), Corbis/F.May/EPA p25(br), Corbis/M.Meyer
p98(tl), Corbis/M.Segar/Reuters p43(br), Corbis/H.Armstrong Roberts
p84(bl), Corbis/T.Spiegel p36(cl), Corbis/Tetra Images p130(tr),
Corbis/Underwood & Underwood p84(bml), Corbis/A.Wiegmann
p94(bl), Corbis/U.Wiesmeier p97(cr); Contour p79(cr); H.Crystal,
pp3,15,39,63,87,111; Fotolibra/Archive Images p30(b), Fotolibra/P.Bolton
p121(r); Mary Evans Picture Library pp19(tl), 19(cm); Getty pp28(br),
44, 62(cr), 129(cm), 129(br), Getty/AFP pp66(b), 85(c), Getty/Barcroft
Media p102(b), Getty/S.Barr p83(bl), Getty/G.Breton p32(b), Getty/M.
Daly p91(tr), Getty/D.Evans pp 3(c), 73(cr), 118(cl), Getty/FPG p9(tr),
Getty Images for Burda Media p10(bm), Getty/M.Fond p59(tr), Getty/T.
Hill p59(br), Getty/P.Grand Image p48(cl), C.Peterson p23(tr), Getty/J.
Sullivan p79(tl); GoodShoot p133(tr); Judith Rich Harris p128; Yilong
Huang p40(b); Hulton Archive pp33(tr), 43(tr), 66(cm), 81(tr), 93(tr),